# A Guide to the Reading Workshop

GRADES 3–5

LUCY CALKINS

*first*hand

HEINEMANN

DEDICATED TO TEACHERS™

*This book is dedicated to my mother, Virginia Calkins. She is—and has always been—my hero. She is the person I most admire and the audience I most value. I've grown in the sunlight of her appreciation. At the end of the day, my eight brothers and sisters and I still, after all these years, know that 3799 Windover Drive is where we are most at home. My dad joins me and all my siblings as Mum's fan club; it's amazing to me that although Dad will be 90 this summer, he doesn't allow any of us to worry about him. Instead he works with zeal at his practice as a physician, at his writing, at his projects, and at his efforts to support us all. I salute him.*

*firsthand*
An imprint of Heinemann
361 Hanover Street, Portsmouth, NH 03801
www.heinemann.com

*Offices and agents throughout the world*

"Dedicated to Teachers" is a trademark of Greenwood Publishing Group, Inc.

The asterisked trade book titles in this text have been officially leveled by Irene Fountas, Gay Su Pinnell, and their trained levelers. Other systems that use level designations are not equivalent to theirs.

Post-its ® is a registered trademark of the 3M company.

The authors and publisher wish to thank those who have generously given permission to reprint borrowed material:

Excerpts from *Charlotte's Web* Copyright © 1952 by E. B. White. Text copyright renewed 1980 by E. B. White. Used by permission of HarperCollins Publishers.

Duke, N., & Pearson, P. D. (2002). "Effective practices for developing reading comprehension." In A. E. Farstrup & S. Jay Samuels (Eds.) *What Research Has to Say About Reading Instruction* (3rd ed; pp. 205–206). Copyright © 2002 by the International Reading Association. www.reading.org.

Cover photo: Peter Cunningham
Interior photos: Peter Cunningham
Additional classroom photography: Melanie Brown
Cover and interior design: Jenny Jensen Greenleaf
Composition: Publishers' Design and Production Services, Inc.

**Library of Congress Cataloging-in-Publication Data**

CIP data on file with the Library of Congress

ISBN-10: 0-325-02826-5
ISBN-13: 978-0-325-02826-2

Printed in the United States of America on acid-free paper
16    15    14    13         ML    2    3    4    5    6

# Contents

## UNITS OF STUDY FOR TEACHING READING
### A GUIDE TO THE READING WORKSHOP

# Acknowledgments

I thank my editor, Kate Montgomery, who has been my closest writing partner, my coach and guide and critic and champion. Kate edited the writing units of study as well as these units. I rely on her judgment; she has made many of the decisions that define the Units of Study series. I am especially grateful to her for caring every bit as much as I do, for always taking the high road, and for her never wavering in her commitment to making the series worthy of its mission. And I thank her for her unerringly right-on critique. As a writer, there is no greater pleasure than to pass a draft to Kate and then to have it come back to me. "You ask if I like this—I don't," she'll write, from time to time. Then, too, there will be notes like "You hit it out of the park." "How are you getting all this done?" and "Finally we've got the book we need, one that…." If only every writer had an editor such as this.

I thank my husband and best friend, John Skorpen, for companionship, love, and support and for joining me in the project of raising our wonderful sons, Miles and Evan, who make us proud every day. John is not convinced that the series will ever be over, and I can't wait to show him otherwise!

I thank those who lead the Teachers College Reading and Writing Project with me—Laurie Pessah and Kathleen Tolan, Senior Deputy Directors; Mary Ehrenworth, Deputy Director for Middle Schools; and Amanda Hartman, Lead Coach. I thank Chris Adams for providing steady, trustworthy leadership. I thank Beth Neville, Associate Director, for working above and beyond to analyze our data (as well as for so much else). Joe Yukish has lent us his wisdom and let us stand on his shoulders. I thank my assistant, Mary Ann Mustac, who knows what I need even before I do. This team has shouldered much of my work over the last 18 months, and I'm grateful.

In the Acknowledgment sections in other volumes, I thank the giant network of people who worked to make this series what it is. For now, there are just a few people you need to know from the start. First on that list is Kathleen Tolan, who has been an enduring and constant partner from before the beginning until after the end of this effort. You will come to know Kathleen in the upcoming books she coauthored, and you will come to understand why she is regarded, at the Project, as the master teacher of us all. Mary Ehrenworth joined this effort toward the end of it, and she and I spent a flurry of three intense months totally consumed with the final two books in the series. You'll learn more about Mary's enormous contributions in the Acknowledgments to those volumes, but know she's been a gift. Then, too, you need to know from the start of my gratitude to Julia Mooney, writer-in-residence and a coauthor of *Constructing Curriculum*. Julia understands this project in all its detail as no one else does and has lavished thoughtful, attentive care on it.

Jean Lawler brought this work through production at Heinemann—and did so for the two other *Units of Study* series as well. The first unit in this series is dedicated to her, and that doesn't begin to capture the depth of our gratitude. I also thank Jean's editorial colleague, Heather Anderson, for her thorough, insightful collaboration and efficient management. Jean and Heather could not have done all they have done without the contributions of David Stirling and Stephanie Levy. As production manager, David has always kept the big picture in mind while Stephanie excels in handling zillions of details. Charlie McQuillen, like Kate, Jean, and David, has been a lead member of the Heinemann team for all three series. Charlie's job is to stay in touch with readers and to coach me to make something readers want. If I have done so, a big part of this is due to Charlie. His wit and warmth have meanwhile helped bring the Heinemann team together. Peter Cunningham, one of the world's great photographers, captured the heart and soul of the children with whom these units of study were piloted. Thanks to all.

The ideas in this series were first developed more than two decades ago when Randy Bomer, author of *Time for Meaning*, was Deputy Director of the TCRWP. All of the thinking in these books is grounded in that early work, so it carries his intellectual DNA—and I'm forever grateful for that. Scores of reading experts have also contributed to the think tank at the TCRWP, but none have contributed more than Marie Clay, founder of Reading Recovery, and Dick Allington, author of *What Really Matters for Struggling Readers*.

Finally, I am grateful to you, my readers. I know that you will bring your experiences, insights, wisdom, skepticism, ideals, and passions to these books, adding all that you know and feel and want between the lines of these books. And I know that you'll take these words with you into your classroom, where they'll reach children, who are the reason why all of this matters.

# A Letter to School Leaders

**D**ear Colleague,
If you have just brought Units of Study into your school, you'll have some predictable questions. I want to take a minute to answer those questions.

## "How can I get a quick sense of this curriculum?"

You'll need to get a quick sense of this whole curriculum. You can't, after all, read all of these books, in all their detail—at least not just yet! My suggestion is this:

- Read this *Guide to the Reading Workshop,* ideally in its entirety, but certainly chapters 1-4 and the beginnings of chapters 6 , 7, and 10.

- Then I suggest you read the front matter to each of the Units of Study books. It will give you a fairly detailed sense of the trail each unit takes.

- If you can, watch a few of the scenes on the DVD—each is about five minutes long. In the How to Use the DVD guide on the Resources CD-ROM, I've marked which segments I recommend you turn to if you only have 30–45 minutes.

## "How does it work if I give the same set of units to teachers at different grade levels?"

You will consider how to disperse these units so that they can actually support a 3–5 curriculum in reading. You'll see four units, with two volumes for three of them, and wonder how to divide these up among your teachers. "After all," you may think, "the kids can't cycle through the same units year after year, can they?"

I need to reassure you about that. These units are new—and not new. They're being written at this level of (I hope) excellence and of detail for the first time, yes. But the units themselves have been the mainstay in thousands of classrooms for many, many years. Briefer versions of these were written and distributed by the thousands a decade ago. These units have also been an important part of the summer institutes that we teach every year at Teachers College. And yes, teachers have taught these units repeatedly to third graders, fourth graders, fifth graders, and even to kids throughout the middle grades.

This doesn't mean the units have been taught in exactly the same way each year. Every year, always, every teacher needs to be encouraged to deviate from "the script," if you want to call it that, from the teaching story we tell in the units. You will need to encourage teachers, from the start, to bring in their own anecdotes in place of mine, the stories of their own kids in place of mine. And you will want to encourage teachers to weed these minilessons. When I give two anecdotes and a quote to make a point, teachers will choose one of those anecdotes, and perhaps only have the quote, to make the point. They'll see that one of my mid-workshop teaching points addresses a really big topic for their kids and they'll pump that bit of teaching up and turn it into a minilesson. They'll see that their kids need a whole bunch of teaching that isn't here, and they'll write in those entirely new minilessons. They'll see that something I teach is reminiscent of some teaching teachers have been doing with the help of Steph Harvey or Ellin Keene or Harvey Daniels or Linda Dorn or Gay Su Pinnell or a host of others, and they'll loop in that teaching.

But more than this, the content of reading minilessons, like the content of writing minilessons, is rarely something that any of us ever outgrows. For example, you could be reading *Freckle Juice* or you could be reading *Three Cups of Tea,* and the question—"What really, really motivates this character?" continues to be endlessly interesting and important to consider. What motivates a boy to use black marker to make freckles all over his body? What motivates a man to leave his wife and kids behind, to head to the most desolate sections of Pakistan and Afghanistan, to work for ten years to help a remote village build a one-room schoolhouse? What lessons do these characters learn, and what can we learn alongside them? Those questions are enduring ones, and if a teacher reminds readers who are eight of these questions, and then reminds readers who are ten (or twenty, or fifty) it is still excellent teaching. The real learning comes as the readers mull over these questions, using them to read more powerfully. This work will always, by its nature, be done at the reader's own developmental level.

I suggest that when you have first brought the series into your school, you ask everyone to teach the first three units. These are foundational units, units that provide kids with the essentials. More than this, the units are written as a form of professional development. Every minilesson is situated within a little keynote address—in the preludes, I look teachers in the eyes and try to talk about the big goals of that day's teaching, trying to fill them with a belief that this teaching matters tremendously. Within each day's conferring and small-group section, I anticipate the support that kids will need, and show teachers how they can marshal their time to get around, to use a combination of small-group work and conferring to reach their kids. In the early units, I teach the broad overviews of conferring; in later units, I teach this in much more detail.

So yes, I would ask all teachers to start by teaching those units. Frankly, I'd even suggest that the teachers read aloud the books we've read aloud—just for this first year. That's because it is a lot of work to find the places in a book to teach whatever it is that a teacher hopes to teach. Of course, if you have a grade level of teachers that are tremendously knowledgeable about teaching reading and ready to work to put their own stamp on this by altering the read-aloud from the start—fine. Even better! But, in general, in the first year, it will be challenging enough for teachers to work with these units of study as they are written.

### "Do you expect I should ask teachers to follow these units exactly?"

Under no circumstances will you want to require that teachers teach "by the book." From the start, you'll want to encourage teachers to tailor this curriculum to suit their own personalities, their beliefs, their kids.

I do encourage you, however, to ask teachers to stay largely in sync with their grade-level colleagues (unless there is tremendous strife at a grade, in which case I'd still want to be sure that teachers were not working as Lone Rangers).

I'd want to encourage teachers to add a minilesson or two, but to do this in such a way that the unit still lasts approximately the same length of time as other units.

I'd hold teachers accountable to collaborating with other colleagues, to being transparent and planful in their teaching—if they want to write minilessons, that is terrific, but hopefully those are gathered and combined into a notebook that becomes a resource for others to adopt and adapt.

Then, after the first year, teachers will have a stronger foundation from which to make decisions, authoring and altering curriculum. Probably the fifth-grade teachers, that second year with the curriculum, will either decide to lean on Mary Ehrenworth's unit for launching the reading workshop in *Constructing Curriculum* (if the readers they teach are advanced) or they'll bring in a new read-aloud book and make some larger-scale adaptations of *Building a Reading Life.* Those teachers can pilfer ideas from *Constructing Curriculum* and from the minilesson extensions on the *Resources for Teaching Reading* CD-ROM, but mostly they'll probably be eager to develop some new minilessons in response to what they are seeing that kids need.

In a second year with this curriculum, the third-grade teachers may feel ready to lean on Hareem Khan's unit in *Constructing Curriculum* that offers a simpler launch to the reading workshop than does *Building a Reading Life.* The fourth-grade teachers may become the grade that uses *Building a Reading Life,* as it is written, with *Stone Fox* as the read-aloud—but for the second year they'll need to bring in a new read-aloud to it since the third graders will, just for now, know that book.

In such a fashion, your teachers will, during year two, make adaptations on the three foundational units.

After your teachers have taught the three foundational units, the pathway that different grade levels take will probably separate. The final two volumes, encompassing Unit 4, *Tackling Complex Texts,* aims above the heads of many third graders in January. Most third-grade classrooms could profit from this unit at the end of third grade—and it has been a terrific hit with them. But if the entire school is adopting these Units of Study, you might suggest that *Tackling Complex Texts* and the unit in *Constructing Curriculum* on fantasy reading, "Learning from the Elves," be reserved for the older grades. In that case, you'd want to channel third-grade teachers toward units on mystery, humor, series books, biography, on using story structure to help us read fiction, or even a whole unit on envisionment and prediction or on reading with fluency. Teachers can all consult *Constructing Curriculum,* which contains many of those units and also lots of units for the rest of the year in upper-grade classrooms, including the full fantasy unit.

## "How long does each unit take to teach?"

I've written these units with the idea that the first one is a month long, and the others are each a week or two longer. I imagine the three foundational units will last until the December holiday. (Providing a teacher has enough relevant books, reading units can go longer than units in the *Units of Study for Teaching Writing 3–5* series. The writing units should only be one month in length, since nine-year-old children shouldn't be expected to work productively over one single piece of writing for more than a month.)

### "Do I need to buy particular children's literature for the classroom libraries?"

You are probably also wondering about the books that you will need to provide for your classroom. You are right to think about this, and it may be that you'll need to unroll this curriculum over time, with only some grade levels getting started for now so that you can be sure those classes have the libraries they need. In New York City, schools did not have that luxury. Every school was asked to adopt the reading workshop, and asked to do that right away. Many schools initially thought there would be no way that they could provision the classrooms, but when people actually turned schools upside down in search of books, it was astonishing how many books were behind lock and key, or hidden in recesses of closets and basements.

You will need to decide whether class-sets of books can be broken apart and distributed across the school, and whether kits containing expository texts need to be kept intact or can be separated into parts—with their expository texts moving into classroom libraries. You'll also want to think about levels of books that are in your classrooms. Often libraries look, from a distance, as if they contain plenty of books, but careful scrutiny reveals that half the books are probably out of range for the actual readers in that classroom. Your leadership will be required to wrest books that don't belong at one grade level from that classroom, moving them to the grade levels that contain students who can read those books. Meanwhile, our experience suggests that most of you will probably need to order more lower-level books. Remember, a fourth grader who is reading Level M texts needs to read ten of these a week, while a fourth grader who is reading level U texts will be apt to read one of those in that same amount of time. That means that the quantities of books at each level of difficulty should not be the same!

### "How will I provide teachers with professional development?"

Finally, you are probably wondering how you will provide your teachers with professional development. Research is clear that nothing matters more than your teachers' skills, so you are wise to think about this. The series itself is designed as a form of professional development, so you will want to think about how to provide your teachers with release time so they can read and talk about the content of the books, and with opportunities to visit the classrooms of peers who might have gotten off to a strong start with this work. Schools themselves need to be sites for professional development. You may also be interested in bringing one of my colleagues to your school or in sending key teachers to participate in the institutes and conference days we lead. Check the Teachers College Reading and Writing Project (http://rwproject.tc.columbia.edu) or the Heinemann Units of Study (http://unitsofstudy.com) websites for more information.

I know you'll find the series has the capacity to bring you and your staff together as a community of practice. Seize the moment!

Best wishes,
*Lucy Calkins*

# CHAPTER ONE

# Essentials of Reading Instruction

When children come to us at the start of the school year, they don't necessarily come cherishing written language. We see this in the books strewn under the coat rack, grimy with footprints, and in those snarled in the darkest recesses of children's backpacks. We see this in the child who tells us, "I read sixty-two pages last night." Impressed, we ask, "What happened in the story?" and he scrunches up his face and looks up at the ceiling, saying "Uhhhh...." as he wracks his mind for some recollection of what he has read. Nothing surfaces, but he hastens to reassure us: "I read the whole thing—honest. I just can't remember any of it, that's all." He's not our only Teflon reader. We watch one child reach the final page of *Number the Stars*, and we're ready for her to look up, eyes brimming; we know the passage by heart and know how impossibly hard it is to take in. We watch her eyes move down the page to the last paragraph, then the last line. Our eyes well with tears, just thinking about what she will find there. She reads. For a second, she pauses. Then she snaps the book shut, slings it toward us, and says, "I'm done. What should I do now?"

How do we say to her, "You should live differently for the rest of your life because you've read that book?"

How do we teach reading—the heartbreaking, soul-searching kind of reading, the reading that makes you feel as if you are breathing some new kind of air? How do we teach the kind of reading that makes you walk through the world differently because a light bulb is no longer just a light bulb; it's filaments and electricity and the industrial revolution and all that tumbled forth from that? How do we teach the power of reading—the way it allows us to see under the words, between the words, beyond words? How do we teach the intimacy of reading—of belonging to a community that has a shared vocabulary, shared stories, and shared petitions and projects?

The irony is that often when it comes to teaching reading, we convince ourselves that the subject is *So Important* that we outsource it to large for-profit companies that don't know us, don't know our kids, and don't necessarily even know how to teach well. Because we're sure that teaching children to read is the single most important thing we do, we want someone else to make the decisions about how our teaching will go. "Tell me what to do, and I'll do it," we say. And then, when the core reading program channels 19,000 little things toward us, we don't stop long enough to think, "Does this match what I know from my own experiences learning to read?" "Does this reflect what the research shows kids need?" "Does this draw upon what I've learned from all my years of teaching?" We're too intent on racing through those 19,000 steps, on doling out, checking off, drilling, monitoring, and on and on.

We need to catch our breath and to pause long enough to think, to remember, to research, and to make informed choices. Racing faster and covering more is not the answer. Years ago, when I wrote the first chapter of *The Art of Teaching Writing*, I wrote some words that then became foundational not only to that book but also to *The Art of Teaching Reading*. The words are still true today. "If our teaching is going to be an art, we need to remember that artistry does not come from the sheer quantity of red and yellow paint or from the amount of clay or marble, but from the organizing vision that shapes the use of those materials. It's not the number of good ideas that will turn our teaching into something significant and beautiful, but the selection, balance, coherence, and design of those ideas" (Calkins 1994, 2001).

Perhaps the place to start is by thinking about our own lives as readers. (Don't worry—it will take just a minute.) Think for just a minute about the times in your life when reading was the pits, and then think about times when reading was the best thing in the world. What were the conditions that made reading so bad; what made it so good?

I'm pretty sure that you are saying that reading worked for you when you could choose books that mattered to you, when you had lots of time to actually eyes-on-print read, and when you could finish one chapter, and, instead of answering twenty questions, read the next chapter. If you've had the exquisite pleasure of sharing reading—in a book club, a Bible study group, a woman's group, a writing group, or in a friendship that includes books—then the social fabric of reading will be part of what made reading work for you. And I'm pretty sure that when reading was the pits for you, someone else told you what to read,

what to think about, and what to do when you finished reading. You probably felt as if your every move was monitored and judged, making reading a performance for someone else.

How can it be that thousands and thousands of teachers and principals are clear about the conditions that have made reading be the pits, the worst thing in the world, for us—and yet we allow a Big Publishing Company to establish a gigantic system around the teaching of reading that results in us teaching in ways that exactly replicate the worst of what has been done to us? How can it be that half the teachers in America have been convinced to teach in ways that directly counter what we know kids need? Above all, how can this system perpetuate itself when it clearly hasn't worked? The average college graduate in this country reads one book a year. The longer kids stay in school, the less they like to read.

These are important times in the teaching of reading, though. There's been a gigantic crack in the system. Judgment is no longer pending. The verdict is in. Not one of those core reading programs, mandated under No Child Left Behind, has been shown to reliably work.

Meanwhile, there is an increasing sense of urgency in the air. Today's information age requires that young people develop literacy skills that are significantly higher than those that have ever been required of them—and this education needs to be for all students, not just for the elite. Study after study is showing that globalization and new information technologies have made it especially urgent for schools to chart a new mission. In their important book, *Breakthrough*, Michael Fullan, Peter Hill, and Carmel Crévola point out that the old mission for schools used to be to provide universal access to basic education and then to provide a small elite with access to university education. The world has changed, however; whereas twenty years ago 95% of jobs were low-skilled, today those jobs constitute only 10% of our entire economy (Darling-Hammond et al., 2008). Children who leave the school system without strong literacy skills will no longer find a job waiting for them. "The new mission is to get all students to meet high standards of education and to provide them with a lifelong education that does not have built-in obsolescence of so much old-style curriculum but that equips them to be lifelong learners." Those words form the prelude of the book *Breakthrough*, and they could be the prelude to this series as well.

As this nation wakes up to the fact that the education that millions of Americans received in the past simply isn't adequate for today, more and more school systems are taking a good look at the expensive core reading programs of the past and they're thinking, "Could it be that the emperor has no clothes on?" If your superintendent looks to the right and to the left, he or she will see districts where kids soar on every imaginable test—and where funds have been invested not in programs but in teachers, in professional education, in time for collaborative study, and in books. Those places deserve our attention. There's been a crack in the system, and light is shining through.

Clearly, over the next few years, the status quo in reading education won't be enough. This is time for ambitious reform. Consider this statistic—and it is but one of many that can take a person's breath away. During the four years between 1997 and 2002, the amount of new information produced in the world was equal to the amount produced over the entire previous history of the world (Darling-Hammond et al., 2008). The amount of new technical information is being produced at such a rapidly increasing rate that it is predicted soon to double every seventy-two hours (Jukes and McCain, 2002).

The problem and the opportunity coalesce. Now is the time for a new vision for reading instruction. Although the increased urgency caused by globalization and the pressures of the Information Age have led us to spend billions of dollars over the past ten years on the teaching of reading, the emphasis has thus far been mostly on reading programs, and the results have not been compelling. After reviewing the lack of actual evidence that supports even programs that regularly proclaim themselves to be "research based" (including Success for All, Direct Instruction, Waterford Early Reading Program, and Accelerated Reader), Allington wrote, "There is a long-standing federal enthusiasm for packaged reading reform. Unfortunately, we have forty years of research showing that packaged reading reforms simply do not seem reliable to improve student achievement" (Allington, 2006, p. 14). He continues, saying, "None of the proven programs that generated so much excitement a decade ago has withstood the independent research review. None of the commercial reading series has either" (Allington, 2006, p. 14). Over the eight years between 2001 and 2009, despite extraordinary pressures to achieve, reading essentially flatlined. America has yet to find a way to deliver on the promise of a high-quality universal education. With 32% of students dropping out or failing to complete high school on

time, education has become the great civil rights issue of our generation. Only one in ten low-income kindergartners becomes a college graduate in the United States today. With dropouts costing the nation at least $200 billion a year in lost wages and taxes, costs for social services, and crime, education is also becoming the great economic issue of our time (Darling-Hammond, 2010, p. 25).

Research is clear on the reason why commercial reading series and packaged reform programs haven't yielded results. Any reform effort that seeks to improve education by bypassing teachers, by trusting programs rather than professionals, will always fail. The U.S. Department of Education recently released a study showing that the single most important thing that can be done to lift the level of student achievement in our classrooms is to support the development and retention of good teachers. In fact, access to good teachers is more important to the likelihood that students will do well than anything else. It is more important than a student's background, than small class size, and than the fact that a school as a whole is a good one. A mountain of research confirms what all of us already know: the single most important resource a school can provide to its students is an effective teacher. In a recent address at Teachers College, U.S. Secretary of Education Arne Duncan said, "Teaching has never been more difficult, it has never been more important, and the desperate need for student success has never been so urgent…. It's no surprise that studies repeatedly document that the single biggest influence on student academic growth is the quality of the teacher standing in front of the classroom—not socioeconomic status, not family background, but the quality of the teacher at the head of the class" (Duncan, 2009). And yet most of the money that has been spent over the past decade to improve the teaching of reading has been spent on large commercial reading programs that aim to teacher-proof reading instruction. What's needed is exactly the opposite.

In his book, *Time for Meaning*, my colleague Randy Bomer, associate professor at the University of Texas in Austin, writes about what it was like for him to go from another career to becoming a teacher. On his first day of orientation, the district lined the new teachers up like children, and Randy and the others marched single file onto a yellow school bus to be taken on a tour of the district. Randy and the other teachers didn't know each other, so each sat, as children are apt to do, one per seat, each in a separate box, with the seat ahead and behind walling each off in a fashion that Randy would later see as emblematic of his experience in that district. The new teachers were brought to the high school and led into the music room—an amphitheater of chairs on risers—where they sat as if in a chorus, although no one opened his or her mouth. The superintendent took his place on a swivel chair at the front of the room, sitting as if he was a conductor, and offered the new teachers some advice. "When anyone talks back to you, when a kid steps out of line, just write the person's name like so." To illustrate he called on Randy, elicited his name, and then wrote R-A-N-D-Y in large letters across the board. "Each time the kid talks back, just erase one letter," he said, and he proceeded to turn R-A-N-D-Y into R-A-N-D, R-A-N, R-A, R, and eventually, into nothing. "They identify with their names. They don't like to see themselves disappearing" (Bomer, 1995).

Within a few years, it became clear to Randy that this was the district's way of working *with teachers* as well as with students. When he protested what he regarded as excessive test prep or tracking, he sensed that he was being erased. He was dropped from committees and no longer referred to in decisions. "The longer I stayed in the classroom, the more my voice, my judgment, my creativity were erased" (Bomer, 1995). What happened to Randy is what has happened to too many teachers. Too many teachers have felt their creativity, their talent, their beliefs, and their dedication have all been erased—often by decisions that others have made to outsource reading, the heart of our teaching, to corporations. It hasn't worked.

The reading workshop offers an alternative, one where the emphasis is on providing students with the conditions that are supported by *reading* research (not by *market* research). The irony is that there are mountains of scientific studies that confirm what most of us knew just by thinking about the times in our own life when reading has worked and the times when reading has been the pits. The research confirms what most of us knew all along. Kids get better as readers when they have time—lots of time—to read (to actually read, not to answer questions, fill in crossword puzzles, and circle the right answers). It is critical that kids read with engagement, and nothing supports engagement more than kids reading books they can actually read and that are high interest, and the best are books they choose to read. Learning to read isn't magic. For most kids, good instruction makes the difference. Good instruction involves demonstration and supported practice, and it is tailored to the learner based on the teacher's ongoing assessment.

# What Are the Essentials of Reading Instruction?

Over the past ten years, I've twice been part of a group of literacy leaders from across the nation that each time met repeatedly for the purpose of constructing proposed K–5 or 4–5 literacy standards that would be applicable not just to a state but to the nation. The members of these think tanks are always a disparate group of literacy leaders, each representing and leading a different thought collaborative, a different perspective, and yet each time I've participated in this work I am reminded again of the consensus that has emerged around the bottom-line essentials that all children need to thrive as readers. Increasingly, people are coming together around the recognition that youngsters need the following to thrive as readers.

## Learners need teachers who demonstrate what it means to live richly literate lives, wearing a love of reading on our sleeves.

In the end, it's teachers that make the difference in kids' lives. Again and again, the research shows what most of us already knew to be true: good teaching makes a world of difference (Rebell and Wolff, 2008, p. 90; Hanushek et al., 2005; Darling-Hammond and Sykes, 2003; Pressley et al., 2003; Guthrie et al., 2004). Good teachers provide children with the other opportunities to learn that I'll describe in this chapter, but good teachers of reading also wear a love of reading on our sleeves.

Shirley Brice Heath has gone so far as to suggest that the single most important condition for literacy learning is that a person needs mentors who are joyfully literate people, who demonstrate what it means to live joyfully literate lives. Some lucky children grow up in households where families demonstrate the richness of a life of books, but many of our children rely on school to provide them with that image of possibility. And so it is not just nice—it is essential that teachers talk about the books we read, share excitement over hearing an author speak, revel over finding a new book in a favorite series, share the thrill of discovering a website built around a favorite genre. We rejoice in the prospect of a rainy Saturday, telling our students that there is nothing better than curling up with a book while the rain patters against the windows.

When my colleagues and I began the research that has culminated in the publication of this series, we decided that just as teachers across the world had benefited from working on our own writing process so we could then teach writing as insiders in that process, so too we needed opportunities to invest in our own reading so we could bring that insider's perspective into our reading classrooms. In schools across New York City and the surrounding suburbs, we soon formed almost a hundred adult reading clubs. Our schools were filled with conversations about Eudora Welty, Toni Morrison, and Wallace Stegner. For several years, the teacher-leaders of those groups met to study the conditions that we, as adults, need to grow as readers and the qualities of good reading that especially transformed our own reading. Those groups are not all still in place, but the commitment to our own adult reading remains as an enduring feature of all the work we have done over the past three decades, and every page of this series is steeped in a first-hand immersion in literacy.

As the leader of your classroom organization, you are called upon to be the kind of leader who rallies kids on an important mission, who raises the flag—the standard—and calls, "Right this way." If you are going to rally your children to love reading and to compose richly literate lives for themselves, then it is terribly important that you are invested in reading right alongside your kids. The important part is not that you come with degrees in English literature. The important part is that you are public about your own efforts to outgrow yourself as a reader. If working on your reading is somehow "kids' stuff" and beneath you, if every time you say to the children, "One thing I try to do as a reader is…. Watch me as I…. Now you try the same thing." You're thinking it is really a sham because frankly you learned everything you need to know about reading decades ago, the kids will learn that getting better at reading is kids' stuff, that in real life, readers don't think about how we read or work on outgrowing ourselves as readers. How important it is that instead we teach our children that learning to read is a lifelong process and something that all of us can be engaged in alongside each other.

> *If you are going to rally your children to love reading and to compose richly literate lives for themselves, then it is terribly important that you are invested in reading right alongside your kids.*

## Learners need long stretches of time to read.

When we teach reading, we are teaching a skill—like playing the oboe or swimming. And when we teach skills, the learner needs to be doing the thing. That is, there is very little I can do from the front of the room that will make you good at playing the oboe or swimming. The learner needs to be playing the oboe or swimming. And in the same way, our students need to be reading.

Although it is common sense that students need to read a lot to learn to read well, this is also the one single conclusion that is most supported by research. Krashen, for example, shows that 93% of the tests on reading comprehension that collect data on volume of reading show that kids who are given more time to read do better (2004). Guthrie and his colleagues found that reading volume predicted reading comprehension and that dramatic increases in reading volume are important for thoughtful literacy proficiencies (2004). The NAEP Reading Report Card for the Nation (U.S. Department of Education 1999) shows that at every level, reading more pages at home and at school was associated with higher reading scores. Foertsch (1992) examined the factors most closely related to performance on the NAEP and found that the amount of reading that students do in and out of school was positively related to their reading achievement and that despite extensive research suggesting that effective instruction requires moving from an emphasis on workbook pages to an emphasis on extensive reading and writing, children still spend an inordinate amount of time on workbook activities. Allington's entire Chapter 2 of *What Really Matters for Struggling Readers* is a synthesis of the extensive research that spotlights the importance of students reading for long chunks of time. In a study he and others conducted of effective classrooms, the sheer volume of reading time was a distinguishing feature of more effective classrooms. Students in the classrooms of more effective teachers read ten times as much as students in classrooms of less effective teachers (Allington and Johnston, 2002).

After reviewing the overwhelming research on this important topic, Allington concludes, "So how much daily in-school reading might we plan for? I would suggest one and one half hours of daily in-school reading would seem to be a minimum goal given the data provided by these studies…. However my ninety-minute recommendation is for time actually reading" (Allington, 2006, p. 47), and he has gone on to show what that estimated amount of time means in terms of progress through books. A child reading *Stone Fox*, a book containing approx-imately 12,000 words, will finish that book in two or, at the very most, four hours, or two days of reading (perhaps three days if one imagines a lot of concurrent reading in the content areas). A child reading a book in *The Magic Tree House* series will finish it the day it is started, reading seven of those books in a week. Each of these books contains approximately 6,000 words, and for this to be a just-right book for the reader, he or she would need to be reading the book at 100–200 words per minute—hence the calculation that these books should take no more than thirty to sixty minutes. A level W novel such as *Missing May*, by Cynthia Rylant, contains 24,500 words. Most readers for whom this is a just-right book will be reading at least at 150 words per minute, but even if a reader was only reading 100 words per minute, that book would require at most four hours, suggesting readers would read several such books in a week.

The single most important thing we can do to turn schools around, making them into places where youngsters thrive as readers, is to clear out the time and space so that children can learn to read by reading. There is no question but that making more time for reading is a challenge. One of the biggest problems in schools is inflation of curriculum, with people adding and multiplying the things we are to cover. The one thing that most of us long for is more time. But in the end, more time is the one thing that none of us will ever get. The real challenge, then, is to use the time we have in ways that match our priorities.

How important it is for those of us who aspire to teach reading well to be willing to step back for a moment. Howard Gardner says we need to "go to the mountains" from time to time to remind ourselves of what we are really after when we teach. Too often, though, teachers feel pulled to cover this, to get through that. Published programs are filled with reams of busy work. As a result, too often in lieu of real reading, kids spend their time doing what Allington recently summarized as "crap." Speaking at Teachers College, he said, with a twinkle in his eye, "Crap is the technical term reserved for all the non-reading and non-writing activities that fill kids' days—the dittos, dioramas, papier-mâché maps… all that chases real reading and real writing out of the school day." Of course, sometimes kids spend their evenings doing more of the same. Just as it is crucial for kids to read for long chunks of time during the school day, it is equally crucial for kids to read for similar chunks of time in the evening. Remember—exemplary teachers' students read and write as much as ten times as much as kids in other classes. I can't stress enough the importance of kids "just reading."

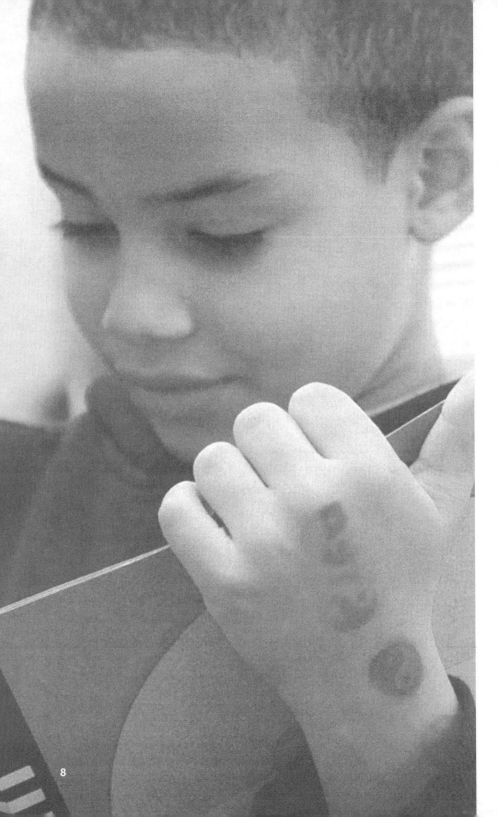

## Learners need opportunities to read high-interest, accessible books of their own choosing.

Readers need time to actually read, and that means eyes-on-print, mental-movie-making reading. Yes, this means they are not filling in dittos or making dioramas, but it also means they are working with texts they can read with that orchestration of cueing systems that allows the magic to happen and meaning to be made. If a child holds a giant tome and stumbles along through it, making swipes at some of the words, that's not reading. Novelist John Gardner describes reading this way:

> It creates for us a kind of dream, a rich and vivid play in the mind. We read a few words at the beginning of the book or the particular story and suddenly we find ourselves seeing not words on a page but a train moving through Russia, an old Italian crying, or a farmhouse battered by rain. We read on—dream on—not passively but actively, worrying about the choices the characters have to make, listening in panic for some sound behind the fictional door, exalting in characters' successes, bemoaning their failures. In great fiction, the dream engages us heart and soul; we not only respond to imaginary things—sights, sounds, smells—as though they were real, we respond to fictional problems as though they were real: we sympathize, think, and judge.

It's not surprising, really, that children need opportunities to engage in high-success reading. I do not know anyone who brings giant pharmaceutical books on a long airplane flight, or to the beach on a summer day. You and I, as adults, rarely read a text that we can't read with 99.5% accuracy. We wouldn't read if we were constantly derailed by complexities that we couldn't assimilate, and kids aren't any different. They, too, want to read books that make sense. The good news is that the sort of reading people want to do is also the reading that helps us achieve.

Over sixty years ago, Betts (1946) studied fourth graders and found that low error rates led to improved learning. For him, independent reading levels were texts that readers could read with 98% accuracy or better, and instructional level texts were those readers could read with 95%–97% accuracy. Swanson et al.'s (1999) meta-analysis of 180 intervention studies showed that for learning-disabled students, one of the three conditions that allow for achievement is that the difficulty level of the task must be controlled enough that the learner can be successful. For readers to flourish, they need to be reading texts with which they can be successful, which means texts they can read with something like 96% or more accuracy, fluency, and comprehension.

This is nowhere more important than for children who struggle. One of the things we know about schools is that they are marked by what educators have come to call the "Matthew effect," for the Biblical reference to the rich getting richer and the poor getting poorer. Too often, kids who can read well are given lots of opportunities in school for just-right reading, and as a result they flourish. Kids who can't read well come to school, ready for the promise of an education, and they're given impenetrable texts. They might as well be given sawdust, really. And the longer they stay in school, the farther behind they fall. When successful readers are given texts that they can read and strugglers are given texts that are impenetrable to them, presumably the logic is that these strugglers will need to read this level of text on the high-stakes standardized test. But just because the reader will starve 120 days from now does not mean that the best way to prepare him or her for that time is to starve him for the duration! In too many classes, even when students are in pull-out situations geared to support their reading, they still are not given materials with which they can have successful reading experiences, and they still are not given the long blocks of time for reading that are so critical.

The other important thing to understand is that children need to read books they can read not only during the reading workshop but across the day. This means rethinking the reading children are doing in social studies and science. Chall and Conard (1991) found that only one of eighteen social studies and science textbooks they examined had a readability level that matched the intended grade in which the textbook would be used. Four of the textbooks were written for students who could read at a level three or four grades higher than the grade for which the book was written, and almost all were written for students two grades beyond the intended level. This doesn't address the fact that even if the text was geared for that grade level, the term refers to what the *average* child at that grade level can do. An average class will typically contain a spread of children, including many who are not able to read at the level that is determined to be average.

What does all this mean? It means that classrooms need to have libraries that match the real children that we actually have in the school, not just the children we wish we had. Publishers may market and sell books for a specific grade, as in advertising a set of books as appropriate for average fifth-grade readers, but many classrooms only have three or four kids who read like average fifth-grade readers! Chances are that many of our kids will need easier books, and many will need more challenging books. Schools need a close alignment between reading assessment and the effort to provision classrooms with books. And of course it is a wonderful thing when schools have book rooms so that teachers can return books that have become a bit easy for their kids and check out new books in their stead.

This also means that schools need a system for estimating text complexity in books, for assessing the level of text difficulty that a particular reader can handle, and for matching each reader to books that are just right for that reader. I discuss this in more detail in the assessment chapter of this book.

It takes just a moment of reflection on our own reading lives to be reminded that it's important not only that young people have access to books they can read, but that they also have access to books they want to read. Choice matters, not a little but a lot. The goal, after all, is not only to teach kids to read, but to help youngsters grow up to be people who value reading. Luring kids to be invested in reading is not a small goal. After all, a 2007 National Endowment for the Arts study, *To Read or Not to Read*, found that Americans are reading less, with people aged fifteen to twenty-four spending two hours a day watching television and less than seven minutes a day reading. If we hope to bring up a nation of readers, it is crucial to allow them to choose among high-interest books that they can read. In fact, Guthrie and Humenick (2004) did a meta-analysis of twenty-two experimental or quasi-experimental studies of reading motivation and achievement and found four factors that were strongly related to student success. Ensuring students had easy access to interesting texts was the single most influential factor, and providing children choice over what they read and whom they read with was the second most influential factor.

## Learners need explicit instruction in the process and skills of proficient reading.

When I was in elementary school, reading comprehension was "taught" through an SRA kit full of cards, each containing a passage followed by a dozen little questions. There were main idea questions, vocabulary in context questions, and inference questions. I'd read the passage, bubble in the answers to the questions, count up my score, and sometimes I would climb from orange to blue or blue to green.

Now, decades later, there is an emerging consensus that my comprehension was being tested rather than taught and that children deserve more than this.

Just as it is not enough to turn down the lights, turn on the music, and say, "Reeeaad, children, reeeeaaaad," so too, it is not enough to barrage young people with paragraphs followed by questions, questions, questions.

Good teaching matters. It is, in fact, the one thing that matters most. Kids absolutely profit from explicit strategy instruction. Bembry (Bembry et al., 1998) has found that students who were, for three years, in classrooms that provide high-quality instruction achieved scores on standardized reading tests that were 40% higher than the scores earned by students receiving lower-quality instruction. That is a staggering statistic, and it is important because many people believe that reading comprehension boils down to intelligence and that some kids will be predisposed to understand complex texts and others won't. Some people think that really, reading is in the DNA. What's a teacher to do?

The answer is that a teacher's job is to teach. More specifically, a teacher needs to explicitly teach the strategies that proficient readers use, that students can do—on paper, in their minds, with partners—to comprehend better. Lots of researchers have detailed what strategy instruction entails; among them are Duke and Pearson (2002), who point out that strategy instruction involves:

- Naming and describing the strategy: why, when, and how it could be used

- Modeling the strategy in action

- Using the strategy collaboratively

- Guiding practice of the strategy, gradually releasing responsibility to the student

- Providing opportunity for using the strategy independently

Researchers also agree, within a certain domain, about the skills and strategies reading entails. Allington suggests that six comprehension studies have been shown, through multiple research studies, to be especially effective on traditional school comprehension tasks. These include activating prior knowledge, summarizing, story grammar lessons, imagery (also referred to as envisionment), question generating, and thinking aloud.

I write more about the topic of the skills and strategies of the reading process in a later chapter. The larger point, however, is that in the end, reading well involves using skills and strategies with increasing finesse on texts of increasing complexity and that readers need explicit instruction in these skills and strategies.

## Learners need opportunities to talk in response to texts.

Talking and writing both provide concrete visible ways for learners to do the thinking work that later becomes internalized and invisible. Think about it. If you want to gain insights on your teaching, your family, your life—what do you do? You meet with someone to "talk things over." If you want to become better at doing something, you bring in a coach, a tutor, or an advisor. Whomever the person is, what you will do is talk. In think tanks, study groups, inquiry projects, graduate courses, seminars—what do you do? You talk. Talk is the medium in which we all outgrow ourselves, over and over. It was Vygotsky, more than anyone, who staked out the theory that accounts for the crucial role of social interactions in supporting learning. The key element in his theory of learning is that "all the higher functions originate as actual relationships between individuals" (1978, p. 957). The words that we say in conversation, the kinds of thinking we do in collaboration, become internalized. If you and I had a conversation about the ending of a book, mulling over why the author may have chosen to end it that way and weighing how the book might have been different had it ended differently, then another time, reading alone, I can reach the ending of a book and think to myself, "Hmm. I wonder why the author decided to end this book this way?" The thinking that I'd be doing would be an internalized conversation.

Because teaching reading is teaching thinking, it is not surprising that social relationships are critical to a reading workshop. Conversations are especially crucial because data suggests that few American students are growing up to be thoughtfully literate. The related finding is this. If one looks at what students spend their time doing in school, it is very easy to project the skills that they will master. If students spend their time answering low-level literal questions, filling in blanks, and recalling facts, then that will be the kind of thinking they can do well. And all too often, that is exactly what is being asked for and what is being learned in American classrooms. In study after study, researchers report that in the typical classroom the assigned tasks overwhelmingly emphasize copying, remembering, and reciting, with few tasks assigned that engage students in discussions about what they've read. Is it any wonder that many students do not seem adept at comparing and contrasting, analyzing, making connections, and thinking interpretively and critically? And yet this is exactly the sort of literacy that is required in the world of today—and of tomorrow. The New Commission on the Skills of the American Workforce describes the candidates that the best employers in the world will be looking for this way: "Candidates will have to be comfortable with ideas and abstractions, good at both analysis and synthesis, creative and innovative, self-disciplined and well-organized, able to learn quickly and work well as a member of a team and have the flexibility to adapt quickly to frequent changes" (2007).

One of the most powerful ways to teach children to think is to teach them to engage in thoughtful discussions, and especially discussions that incorporate thinking under, between, and around texts. Talking well, like writing well, does not emerge *ex nihilo,* and it is helpful to explicitly teach students to make claims that are grounded in the text, to supply evidence for those claims, to talk between the example and the claim, to uncover assumptions, and to explore ramifications. It is also helpful to teach students to develop a line of thinking through sustained talk about one subtopic, and as part of this to elaborate using transitional phrases such as "The important thing about this is…" or "What is worth noticing about this example is…." Then, too, it is important to teach readers to be able to entertain ideas different than their own, to hold more than one idea in mind at a time, and to build upon the ideas of others, following an idea to its conclusion. Teaching youngsters to talk has a great deal to do with teaching them the skills of writing to think—and both are essential.

For this reason, reading workshops not only support talk, but also teach talk. Readers are generally matched to a long-term partner—someone who is able to read and interested in reading similar books. Partners tend to read independently for most of the reading workshop, but in the last few minutes of time, they compare notes, raise and pursue questions, and learn to see the text through each other's perspectives. For something like half the year, readers work in small groups—inquiry groups or book clubs—so their talk can encompass not only a partner, but also other voices and other perspectives. The classroom community as a whole engages in extended conversations around texts that are read aloud.

*We must invent ways to study kids' work, to research and reflect and discuss and imagine what good work entails; we must wrestle with what the pathways toward good work can look like, and we must help kids progress along those pathways.*

**Learners need assessment-based instruction, including feedback that is tailored specifically to them. Strugglers especially need instruction that is tailored to their specific strengths and needs, as well as extra time and extra help.**

Learners are not all the same, nor do they need the same things to progress. Teaching, then, must always be responsive, and our ideas about what works, and what doesn't work must always be under construction.

Certainly when a teacher decides to angle her teaching in such a way as to support a cluster of reading skills (in expository reading, say, the ability to ascertain the main idea, to think between generalizations and particulars, and to synthesize within and across texts), then teaching begins with observing, listening, and small, informal assessments. Those assessments help us analyze what our learners can do, can almost do, and can't yet do.

By taking the time to look at students' work and to theorize about their place along a pathway of development in a cluster of skills, we provide ourselves with the knowledge that enables us to provide explicit, optimistic, concrete, doable guidance so that each learner is able to progress toward goals that are clear. This requires a stance toward teaching that means that always, teachers behave in classrooms as researchers. We must invent ways to study kids' work, to research and reflect and discuss and imagine what good work entails; we must wrestle with what the pathways toward good work can look like, and we must help kids progress along those pathways. Assessment, then, like teaching, can't be outsourced. And assessment can't be something that occurs once or twice or three times a year. Instead, assessment is sewn into the fabric of our teaching. In this series, you'll see that units of study are bookended with discussions of some of the formative assessments that inform these units.

Of course, assessment is nowhere more critical than when it allows us to take our cues from strugglers. If a child enters our classroom already encumbered with labels, then we need to be clear from the start: it is our job to turn that child around so that he or she begins immediately to see that, in fact, learning and progress are within reach. Strugglers cannot wait a week, even, before we begin to show them that indeed, reading can make sense for them, and yes, they can in fact get better as readers in a palpable, observable fashion, making multiple years of growth in just a single year. The first step is for the most knowledgeable person around to assess these readers to find what the reading work is that they can do with success. If this is a fifth-grade child and he needs to be reading books at the level of *Frog and Toad*, then absolutely nothing is gained by taking him instead to *Captain Underpants*. Halfway measures are good for naught, because with texts he can't read well, the child still won't feel everything clicking together into reading and still won't have the chance to read in ways that allow him to learn from reading. If the various stakeholders who are invested in this child—the people who care about him—disagree, then these adults need to come together and talk longer and think harder so that a single, coherent plan is made that will allow this child to be a successful reader (with the texts that are within reach) and then to move forward in giant steps.

There are a few obvious things to be said.

### Strugglers cannot be taken from the language arts classroom—from reading, writing, word study, or reading aloud—for extra help in language arts.

It is especially devastating if a struggler who is already apt to feel disoriented, confused, and behind his or her peers is *sometimes* taken from the regular classroom and other times left to flounder in it, all the more confused and disoriented because it's in fact the truth that the struggler missed half the instruction! Then, too, strugglers can't be outsourced to various and sundry peripheral people in such a way that the child's primary teacher ends up feeling that he or she isn't or even can't be accountable to this child. The classroom teacher must be absolutely clear that this child is hers or his. It can't be that the strugglers who most need people to stand by them end up belonging to everyone and yet, in a real way, to no one.

### Strugglers need to spend 100% of their time reading books they can read with ease.

For strugglers, 90% of their reading time should be spent on books that are easy for them, books they can read with 99% accuracy, and, perhaps as much as 10% of the time, they can be reading books that they read with 96% accuracy, fluency, and comprehension. This means that guided reading can't be about propping a child up to struggle valiantly along through a text that is too hard. Anyone who uses guided reading in such a fashion should reread Gay Su Pinnell

and Irene Fountas's important books on the topic! It is critical that strugglers are reading books within their zone of proximal development not just during reading time, but across the day.

### If strugglers are pulled out of the classroom for extra help on reading, this must be provided by an extra knowledgeable person.

These are children for whom teaching has for too long been confusing, inappropriate, and disheartening. To turn the tide, to get these learners on a trajectory that is positive and self-sustaining, it is important that they work with the most knowledgeable professionals around, not with para-professionals.

### During extra-help time, strugglers need help that is assessment-based, tailored to each particular child, and in sync with what is happening in the classroom.

It cannot be that all strugglers receive the same help during this intervention, because what we know about strugglers is that they are more different, one from another, than most readers are. Strugglers need something, but every struggler does not need the same thing! For starters, some children in grades 3–5 who struggle need help in comprehension and fluency; others need help in phonics and word work. The instruction these readers need will be utterly different.

Above all, children who struggle need access to good teachers, and that means that teachers need high-quality professional development. This subject is such an important one that I devote an entire chapter to it.

## Learners need teachers to read aloud.

Reading aloud is so essential to reading that I have often suggested Teachers College not place a single student teacher in the classroom of a teacher who does not read aloud several times a day. We read aloud to open the day, using stories and poems to convene the community and to celebrate what it means to be awake and alive and together. We read aloud to embark on shared adventures, to explore new worlds, and to place provocative topics at the center of the community.

For children, an adult's proficient read-aloud is a sneak preview of what reading can be. The fact is, as we read, we transmit more than just the story. We model a mood, a stance, an engagement, and a fluency that bring out not just the meaning, but the feeling of many texts and how they go—features that, once children *internalize* them, make their independent engagement with their own texts far more effective.

Of course, it benefits children to hear a variety of texts. Expository nonfiction texts, when read aloud, sound different from stories, just as a poem, when read aloud, sounds different from a letter or a newspaper editorial. Apart from choosing a variety of genres to read aloud, teachers will want to match texts to the interests and proficiency levels of their children and also to plan their read-aloud in ways that optimize its rich instructional potential. I detail ways to do this in the chapter on reading aloud.

### Learners need a balanced approach to language arts, one that includes a responsible approach to the teaching of writing as well as to reading.

Reading is critical, but it is not everything. In a democracy and a world that requires people to speak up, writing needs to take its place alongside reading as one of the basics. I often ask leaders of a school system to tell me what the promise is that they make to youngsters who enroll in their school. Presumably, the school says to all children, "In this school, you will all learn math. Whether the teacher loves math or not, you'll be taught math every day, and in a way that is planned and sequential, where one year builds on another." How is it, then, that so often the school system says to youngsters, "Writing? Maybe you'll luck out and get a teacher who likes to write and teaches writing. Otherwise, you'll do Halloween writing, Mother's Day writing, and spring haikus. But don't worry—you'll be tested in writing. In fact, you won't be able to do well in half the subjects you encounter later on if you don't write well." How is it that some teachers are allowed to describe their curriculum for writing, saying, "I don't really teach writing as a self-contained subject, per se. I do writing across the curriculum. You know, when we finish the movie, I tell the kids to write about it." I tell administrators that when teachers say, "I don't really teach writing as a self-contained subject; instead I integrate writing into other subjects," that is code for, "I don't teach writing." What if a teacher said, "I don't really teach math per se, but we do math throughout the whole day. You know—we add how many pages we read yesterday and today. That's math! We count how many minutes until the end of the day. That's math."

Writing, like reading and like math, is a skill that is developed through time, through practice, and there is no way that a child can be test-prepped into being a skilled writer. Writers grow like oak trees, in the fullness of time. If our schools are going to assume responsibility for the basics, then we need to make sure that reading instruction is one portion of a balanced literacy curriculum, but that alongside reading instruction, there is instruction also in writing.

These tenets, then, have led to the reading workshop structure for teaching reading:

- Learners need teachers who demonstrate what it means to live richly literate lives, wearing a love of reading on our sleeves.
- Learners need long stretches of time to read.
- Learners need opportunities to read high-interest, accessible books of their own choosing.
- Learners need explicit instruction in the skills of proficient reading.
- Learners need opportunities to talk and sometimes to write in response to texts.
- Learners need assessment-based instruction, including feedback that is tailored specifically to them. Strugglers especially need instruction that is tailored to their specific strengths and needs, as well as extra time and extra help.
- Learners need teachers to read aloud.
- Learners need a balanced approach to language arts, one that includes a responsible approach to the teaching of writing as well as of reading.

You will read more about the reading workshop in the next chapter.

# CHAPTER TWO

# The Big Picture of a Reading Workshop

The reading workshop provides a structure to the teaching of reading, one that has been especially designed to make sure that children are given the essentials they need to flourish as readers. This *Guide to the Reading Workshop* and the series as a whole will show you how all the pieces of a reading workshop combine to provide children with the opportunities they need to learn in leaps and bounds.

In this chapter, let's walk through the basic structure of the reading workshop, and then let's consider the values of a reading workshop and the environment and materials of a reading workshop. Finally, it will be important to think about a reading workshop as a schoolwide structure.

## What Are the Structures of a Reading Workshop?

The reading workshop, like the writing workshop, has a characteristic structure. Workshops are deliberately kept simple and predictable, like an art studio or a researcher's laboratory or a scholar's library, because it is the work itself that is ever-changing and complex. Students can approach any day's reading workshop as artists approach a studio or researchers approach a laboratory, planning to continue with their important ongoing work. Each day's teaching in a workshop does not set up a new hoop for the students to all jump through, in sync on that day. Instead, for the bulk of time during each day, students carry on with their work. As they do so, they draw upon a growing repertoire of skills, tools, strategies, and habits. But the bulk of students' time during the reading workshop is spent reading, in the fullest sense of the word: reading, imagining, thinking, recalling, questioning, talking, writing, reviewing, comparing, researching, and reading some more. If you have taught within a writing workshop structure, the reading workshop structure will be very familiar to you.

As I describe it, you'll see how the structure upholds the tenets we all know are necessary to teach children to read. You'll find separate chapters in this book on each of the major components of a reading workshop.

## Minilesson

The workshop tends to go like this: people assemble and expect to work for about an hour, every day. To open the hour-long session, the teacher teaches everyone a short lesson, called a minilesson. This minilesson is usually a quick demonstration of a powerful reading skill or strategy—a way for readers to handle a challenge or, in general, to lift the level of their reading work. The lesson is meant to be helpful to people in their ongoing work, today and in the future, not just an activity to do for the day.

Then, after the ten-minute minilesson, students turn to their ongoing reading work. In the reading workshop, that means readers get their self-chosen, just-right books out of their backpacks, and they settle down to read. Imagine this is a unit of study on characters, and the children are reading fiction. Some have been working on fluency since the start of the year and are continuing to maintain that work, while also thinking about allowing characters in their books to emerge as distinct personalities. Others have been challenged to consider secondary as well as primary characters as they read, letting this work enlarge their understandings also of the protagonist. Some readers have been coached to pause often to retell the current chapter in such a way that when retelling what the main character does now, they also reach back for explanatory information and in that way synthesize what the character already did with what is happening now. Some children might be conscious that as they read, they need to grow ideas, jotting those ideas down in preparation for a conversation about their book. That is, every reader has work to do, and that work grows in part out of assessments and out of one-to-one and small-group teaching and in part out of the cumulative impact of minilessons.

## Children Engage in Ongoing Reading Work; Teacher Engages in Conferring and Small-Group Work

The minilesson ends with a teacher saying, "Off you go," and then children bring bins or baggies containing their books to their reading spots, and they begin reading. They often jot on Post-its or in a reading notebook as they read, but the written responses are usually kept brief because the real goal is for children to have forty minutes in this period for actual reading (and more time during the rest of the day and in the evening). Children are reading books they've selected from their classroom library. Often some of those texts are leveled, to help readers find

accessible books. Later in the year, children will often read books in synchrony with members of a book club, drawing from text sets of multiple copies. These might fall under categories such as historical fiction or social issues or fantasies, and these sets of multiple copies are apt to rotate among classrooms so that perhaps the fifth grades have the historical fiction books in January and early February, and then these text sets of books are brought into the fourth-grade classrooms.

The simplicity and predictability of the workshop is important precisely so that teachers are freed from constant choreographing and are able to observe, to listen, to assess, and to teach into each student's zone of proximal development. Like an artist in a pottery studio or a physicist in a physics lab, the teacher circulates. She pulls close to observe, mulls over what is and is not working, and intervenes to coach, demonstrate, encourage, and celebrate with individuals and small groups. This teaching may reinforce the minilesson, or it might address a child or a group of children's unique needs and goals. The teaching in a conference or a small group, like the teaching that occurs within minilessons, aims to support not just today's work but also that child's reading from that point on.

Conferences and small groups are essential in a workshop, and the small groups often feel like one-to-one conferences, but involving a cluster of children instead of just one child. These forums allow the teacher to tailor her instruction to match the needs and goals of individual learners. Reading conferences are very similar to writing conferences, and both are essential not only for the student but also for us as teachers. It is by conferring that we develop the knowledge, the insight, and the methods to be able to reach learners. A teacher-student reading conference often provides the material for the small-group strategy lessons and the minilessons we later teach. Both conferences and small-group instruction are important enough that I devote an entire chapter to each later in this guide.

In a day, a teacher will move among many readers, helping many to settle and channeling many toward work the teacher believes will be helpful. Then the teacher is apt to lead a four- or five-minute conference with two or three individual readers or partnerships of readers and to coach a small group or two. By this time, the teacher generally needs to address the whole class, usually through a mid-workshop teaching point that sometimes channels kids to work with a partner for a few minutes before they resume reading—and the teacher resumes teaching.

## Mid-Workshop Teaching Point

In different classrooms, kids' endurance for reading will differ. If, after twenty minutes of reading time, children begin to wiggle and squirm, then a mid-workshop teaching point is one way for us to reach all our learners and to try to hold them on course for another twenty minutes of reading. Otherwise, the mid-workshop teaching point can sometimes be a way to peel kids' attention from their books for just a minute while we harvest a bit of teaching from our one-to-one or small-group work that we think has wide implications. There is nothing essential about a mid-workshop teaching point. Sometimes we forego these, and sometimes we'll stop the class and address all of the students more than once. This, of course, is exactly the same situation in a writing workshop.

Then teachers resume teaching, again engaging in some walk-by teaching, more one-to-one (or one-to-two) conferring, and some small-group work.

## Children Resume Ongoing Reading Work; Teachers Resume Conferring and Small-Group Work

One of the powerful ways in which we teach is through leading guided reading groups. The term *guided reading* means remarkably different things to different people, and teachers who teach reading workshops draw on the ideas of whichever expert has been most helpful to them to know how to lead guided reading groups. I generally follow the suggestions of Gay Su Pinnell, who once spent twenty days coaching staff members of my organization and me in her understanding of guided reading, and I also draw on some of the work of Australian educators such as Di Snowball and Brenda Parkes.

Generally, when I lead guided reading groups, I gather four to six children (usually two or three partnerships) and take three minutes to do a book introduction that includes a summary of the book and supports readers in what I anticipate will be tricky aspects of the book. The readers are usually holding the text while I do this, and I might have them point to or find a tricky part, just because their activity serves to highlight that item. Then children read, not in sync with each other, usually silently, and I swing like the big hand on the clock

*The simplicity and predictability of the workshop is important precisely so that teachers are freed from constant choreographing and are able to observe, to listen, to assess, and to teach into each students' zone of proximal development.*

from one reader to the next, tapping each on the arm to signal, "Please read aloud, starting where you are in the text." If a child is in dire need, I say, "Can I take a turn?" and I read to the child, figuring I didn't provide a supportive enough introduction or I put the reader into a too-hard text. After a child or two finishes reading the selection, I signal for that child to reread or to find a favorite page or a tricky part (something like that). When everyone has finished, after no more than ten minutes, I engage the children in the briefest of conversations and then select one skill or strategy to teach, drawing on what I saw as a shared hard part. We practice whatever I teach, sometimes on the white board and sometimes by returning to the passage that contextualized that part in the text. I might give a tiny text introduction for the upcoming section if I want children to continue reading on after the guided reading session is over.

Guided reading is an especially powerful method to use in certain situations. For example, when working with English language learners, this is a way for me to scaffold their comprehension and vocabulary. When bringing readers to a new level of text difficulty, and especially when launching them into a new series at the new level, this is a great way to provide extra training wheels for those readers. When I see children who seem to respond to trouble in knee-jerk, reductive ways, forgetting about meaning and relying only on letters and sounds in isolation, I find that a strong book introduction makes it much more likely that they'll draw on meaning as well as phonics when they encounter difficulty.

Although guided reading is one important way to lead small groups, it is not the only way, and in a strong reading workshop, teachers as well as kids are always developing their repertoire. For teachers, the ideal situation is to have a host of ways in which one can lead small groups, and then to be able to select the method for small-group work that best suits the learners and the moment. I describe this in more detail in the chapter on small-group work.

## Writing About Reading

During any one day's reading workshop, readers typically jot half a dozen Post-its or a few brief entries in a reader's notebook, with most teachers leaving the decision of whether to write in one format or the other up to the readers.

Especially when readers are in book clubs, in which they read texts in synchrony with each other, many teachers ask readers to write a page-and-a-half response to their reading something like once a week.

Either way, the writing that readers do as they read is meant to capture thinking, and that thinking (that Post-it) is typically then put at the center of a partnership or book club conversation that follows independent reading time, during what is often referred to as teaching share time. It is important for children to sometimes devote longer stretches of time learning to draft and revise literary essays. This writing generally occurs during the writing workshop, although the reading and thinking and talking that supports the writing may occur during reading time.

### Teaching Share

The most important word in the phrase "a teaching share" is the word *share*. The workshop ends with a small amount of time for readers to work collaboratively with partners or with a slightly longer time for readers to work with clubs. This time is framed by a teeny bit of teacher-talk, which sometimes takes the form of celebrating what a few readers have done in ways that apply to other readers in other instances, providing the teacher with a chance to balance instruction. If the emphasis had been on writing more thoughtful responses, the teacher can hedge a bit by reminding children that the writing needs to be brief and to not squeeze out time for reading. If the emphasis has been on reading more quickly, pushing oneself to move quickly down the page, the teaching share might qualify that with talk about comprehension. This is a forum for micro-lessons.

Teachers often angle the sharing that children do during this time. They may do this in ways that provide follow-up to the topic addressed in the day's minilesson. For example, if the minilesson demonstrated a few ways in which readers could make their predictions more powerful, during the teaching share the teacher might suggest that readers share their best predictions and then think between those predictions to determine one which represents their best work, using that mentor prediction to help them revise their not-quite-best work.

Then again, often the teaching share time is left more in the hands of children, who choose ways to share work. Partners might decide to read aloud and enact powerful parts of a text or to work on word-solving together. They may decide to discuss the ideas that a reader generated while reading that day. The idea is put at the center of the conversation and talked about for as long as possible. Research has shown that even just five minutes of talk in the midst of reading stirs up provocative thinking, making readers more responsive and critical.

### Read-Aloud Time

Teachers often read aloud a little bit during the minilesson, using the read-aloud text to demonstrate a skill or strategy, but most people think of "the read-aloud" as something that happens outside the reading workshop itself. Often those read-alouds ignite whole-class conversations.

## Qualities of a Reading Workshop

The structures of a reading workshop are important, but it's the tone, the tenor of reading and writing workshops, that particularly characterizes them. Visit a school in which reading and writing workshops are underway, and you'll detect a level of engagement on the part of both teachers and kids that are hallmarks of the workshop approach. You'll have a chance to visit classrooms of teachers who are engaged in teaching reading workshops, because the DVD that accompanies this series captures more than four hours of snippets of classroom life in those classrooms. We didn't carefully control for perfection in those videos. There's a place for that sort of video, where one spends weeks perfecting every detail so that viewers are able to see heaven on earth. That wasn't our goal. Instead, we simply turned the cameras on during three or four different units of study, at three or four intervals during the first half of the school year. The filming occurred in five New York City classrooms, one of which is an inclusion third-grade classroom; in schools in Harlem, the Bronx, Manhattan, and Brooklyn; and in two suburban classrooms, one in Scarsdale, New York, and one in Tenafly, New Jersey. You'll see minilessons, strategy lessons, partnerships, guided reading, conferring, book clubs, inquiry groups, and read-aloud sessions. But more than this, I hope you see a tenor that is characteristic of a good reading workshop, and before I talk about room arrangements and the materials that reading workshop teachers value, before I talk about anything else, really, pertaining to the way the reading workshop takes root in classrooms, I want to try to address three factors that contribute to the tenor of classrooms.

## The Workshop Is Collaborative

### Independent Reading

It may seem ironic to develop the idea that the reading workshop is collaborative by turning first to a discussion of *independent* reading. But the truth is that there is nothing all that independent about independent reading! Think of this even for yourself. It is probably the case that the book you have recently read "independently" has actually been situated in a rich social context. That's certainly the case for me. I'm reading *Stones into Schools*, Greg Mortenson's sequel to *Three Cups of Tea*, the story of how he has established schools across Afghanistan and Pakistan. The book was given to me by a colleague, Amanda Hartman, and she shares my dedication to this cause. I read, thinking of her and of Hareem Khan, one of the coauthors of this series, who lives and teaches on the border of Pakistan and Afghanistan. Most of our students pick up a book because a friend has read it. They may even find some of their friends' Post-its left in strategic places throughout the book. They read, talking back to whatever the friend had to say about the book. "What did Andy mean when he said this is sort of *depressing*?" one child says. "I think it is *deep*—not depressing." And readers read, anticipating the conversations they're about to have, marking pages that deserve to be discussed and starting those discussions in their mind's eye. Then, too, readers who have been sharing their reading with others read differently because we read with others perched on our shoulders, anticipating the responses others will make to the text. If one of our friends is always appreciating the thrilling parts of a story, we come to one of those sections and smile, just knowing that our friend will be glad. If another friend always battles stereotypes, we start to see them as well.

The reading workshop also brims with social connections because most children talk often about friends whom they are emulating and strategies they borrowed from each other. If the classroom teacher is always finding what particular individuals do well and showing the rest of the class the power of that one reader's work, suggesting that others might try the same strategy or aspire to the same quality, then one will often hear a child say, "I'm trying Randalio's idea of noticing startling passages, and then talking about them," or "I'm pushing myself to read faster, using a bookmark as a goalpost, like Grace did 'cause it worked for her." So in all these ways, and other ways as well, even independent reading is imbued with social significance.

### Partnerships

At the end of reading time (if not also during the mid-workshop teaching point), children need a few minutes to talk with another child. Usually readers are in swap-book partnerships (that is, they may both be reading Gary Paulsen books, and one is reading *Hatchet*, the other *The River*, and then they swap). The advantage of swap-book partnerships is that half the time, children are able to talk about books that their partner has recently read and knows well. Meanwhile, swap-book partnerships do not require that classroom libraries be in duplicate. There is no question that reading shared books in synchrony with another person is preferable, however, whenever a teacher can swing this, and most of us make a point to often channel our strugglers into same-book partnerships.

Children do a variety of sorts of sharing within these partnerships. On the DVD, you can watch a partnership between two fourth graders who have just read *Old Yeller* (a same-book partnership). You'll see that the readers decide to go to a startling passage in the book, to read it aloud taking parts (roles), and then they talk about the emotions in the passage before rereading it with more feeling. Finally, the readers close the book and ad lib the passage. In other partnerships, readers might regularly share words that they found challenging and work together to pronounce and understand the words. The mainstay of partnerships, though, is that a partner rereads his or her Post-its, chooses either one that seems especially important or two that go together, puts that Post-it (or those Post-its) on the table between the partners, and then the two children try to talk for as long as they can about the ideas sparked by that one reader's thought. To do this, readers use "thought prompts" such as "I agree because…," "I disagree because…," "That connects with another part of the book because…," "I think that is important because…," "I used to think…, but now I realize…," and so forth. Of course, once these scaffolds are no longer necessary, they fall away, and children simply talk with depth, referencing the text and traveling along a journey of thought.

### Reading Clubs

The partnership conversations that are a mainstay in the fall of the year give way to reading clubs—also called book clubs or literature circles—in the spring of the year. Now the reading workshop still involves a minilesson, time to read, and time to talk, but approximately three times a week the conversations will not be among partners but among club members, and these are readers who are reading multiple copies of the same book in sync with each other. Usually the clubs across a classroom will all be engaged in a genre-based unit of study, as when all the clubs are reading historical fiction books. You will absolutely want to watch the club meetings that are captured in the historical fiction segment on the DVD, and don't wait until that unit to watch these, because your partnerships and read-aloud book conversations at the start of the year all need to work together in ways that enable children to participate in this sort of conversation by the end of the year.

## The Workshop Is a Place that Values Words

It is important to approach a reading workshop keeping in mind that although explicit instruction is incredibly important, we also teach implicitly. Our job is to do nothing less than to induct children into a culture where words matter. Although when teaching reading, part of what we do is name and demonstrate and coach the skills of proficient reading—because we are wanting each of our children to author a life for himself or herself in which words make a difference—it is equally important for us to create a world in the classroom that is saturated with the most beautiful, intense, powerful sort of literacy possible.

As I recounted in another volume, I will not forget my visit to a school in the Bronx, where the fifth-grade class was engaged in an author share. The principal asked me to poke by head into that classroom, and just as I did, a little girl in her Holy Communion finery took her place at the front of the room to read her memoir aloud:

> I'm the kind of girl who has never had a birthday party. I live with my aunt. She cooks macaroni for me and tells me to get going and where have I been? She doesn't think about my birthday. Last summer, I went back to the Dominican Republic and my baby sister—she's big now—they gave her a party. No one could tell I never had one.
>
> Soon I will be ten. I pretend there will be a party and the kids will come, and we'll play "duck, duck, goose" and we'll listen to the radio and there will be a pink cake, "To Marisol." But then my dream ends. I'm the kind of kid who never had a birthday party.

A week later, Marisol turned ten. And all the children, their parents, and their teacher, gave her a big birthday party in the park. There were pink balloons hanging from the trees, and a pile of presents, and those great big fifth graders played "duck, duck, goose" and listened to the radio. And there was a pink

cake—and on it the words, "To Marisol, for all the birthdays that you never had." Later, in the classroom, the children talked about how Marisol is no longer the kind of kid who never had a birthday. They talked about how it had been the words of her memoir that gave them the idea for the birthday party, and about how words can do that. They can give us the ideas for something as big as a birthday or a nation. They talked about how, every July 4, what we celebrate with parades and fireworks is really a time when some people went in a very little room and put words onto the page—a new nation, out of words.

Since then, I've often told this story when I try to convey to teachers the quality of respect for language that infuses reading and writing workshop classrooms. These are listening rooms, where the assumption is that words matter. A poem like Christina Rossetti's "Hurt no living thing…" might be posted as the class constitution. Birthdays might be celebrated with the teacher reading aloud a passage from a book where another character is acting in ways that are characteristic of that child (at his or her best!). Perhaps when a new child enters the school, the entire class gathers in a circle, and the teacher reads aloud a bit of Byrd Baylor's *Everybody Needs a Rock*, and then the newcomer has a chance to choose his or her very own rock from the special plate of rocks collected on a class field trip. Afterwards, that newcomer's rock is passed from child to child, and each member of the class, in turn, says what he or she will do to make the newcomer feel at home. I learned that idea somewhere—perhaps from Ralph Peterson, author of *Life in a Crowded Place*—but I'm sure the ritual has been revised a hundred times over as it becomes part of new classrooms, each with their own culture. The important thing is that inventive teachers dream of ways to make books and poems come to life in the classroom and value not only explicit instruction but implicit teaching as well.

# The Environment and Materials in a Reading Workshop

Let's tour these rooms for just a minute and see what classrooms that support reading workshops have in common. You'll see that usually (not always, of course) the desks have been pushed into clusters so that most children are sitting at tables. Children have long-term reading partners who read the same books as they do. In some classrooms, reading partners sit together during reading time. (Usually reading partners are not also writing partners, and children may not

live at the same desk all day long.) In other classrooms, each reading partnership has a set place in which it meets, but this might be a masking-taped circle on the floor (or even a spot where the masking tape has long since been worn away).

## The Library

In every classroom that supports a reading workshop, there is a classroom library, even if it is not as large as we wish it was! The books are cherished and celebrated. Teachers often talk about visiting bookstores to learn ways that bookstores have invented for promoting books. Special shelves help, titled in enticing ways, and of course those enticing ways will be different, one classroom from another. The best is when the classroom library bears the imprint of the kids in that classroom. Perhaps one shelf will be titled "David's Favorites" and another, "Sad Depressing Books that Make You Cry and Cry," and others will bear titles like these: "Cousins of *Diary of a Wimpy Kid*," "Walter Dean Myers Books," "Light Sports Books," or "Funny Books." That is, although early in the year, when trying to help children find books they can read with ease, some teachers will slot books into leveled bins (level P books, level U books). As the year unfolds, most teachers try to organize the library into shelves and baskets such as those I just described because this helps readers progress from one book to a collection of others like it, and also these collections invite inter-textual connections.

The good news is that no school needs to do the hard work behind this alone; schools can, instead, stand on the shoulders of the countless other schools that have gone through a similar transition. On the *Resources for Teaching Reading* CD-ROM accompanying this series, my colleagues and I include very extensive bibliographies, and we have worked with Booksource, a provider of trade books, to make sure the libraries we recommend are available at the most inexpensive price we could find.

In the bibliographies you will not see libraries organized by grade level. That is, there is no attempt to say that a third-grade class needs books at levels K–Q. I assume that if you are going to invest money, which is scarce and precious, you'll take the time to first assess at least a sampling of your kids to learn the approximate range of book levels that will match the kids you actually have at a specific grade level, and you'll notice the books you already have and those you don't. What we have included in the libraries is a list of our first-choice books (and another of our "we also love these" books) at each level. (Our lists are longer for lower levels because you'll need more books when the books are easier. These should generally take readers a day or two to read, while the books at harder levels generally take closer to a week.) These are recommended books for high-interest independent reading, with the assumption that once readers get linked to a series, an author, or a genre, you'll channel those readers to the school library for more books like the ones they love. Plus, we include very carefully developed text sets for multiple copies of books to support book club work in social issue book clubs, historical fiction book clubs, mystery book clubs, fantasy book clubs, and the like. These collections of books match the units of study that draw on specialized collections. For example, for historical fiction, we include titles we especially recommend related to various eras—books in levels R–U related to the Depression, books in levels Q/R/S related to Westward Expansion, book at levels M–O related to Colonial America, and the list goes on (and on). When possible, we include a few picture books or short stories that also relate to the text set. In a similar way, our bibliography includes recommended books for nonfiction reading, with a list of well-scaffolded expository nonfiction on high-interest topics as well as less-scaffolded expository texts, plus a list of narrative nonfiction. Always, the books are leveled, and there are many at every level.

We have taken seriously the responsibility of developing those book lists and called on scores of our most knowledgeable teachers to help us in their areas of expertise. But there is nothing magical about the lists we compile, and we are eager to learn from your suggestions as well as to provide these to you, as time goes on, on the Teachers College Reading and Writing Project website. We are always especially on the search for high-interest low-level books.

## The Meeting Area

Alongside the bookshelves there will probably be an easel, or something that stands in for the easel that you are still angling to get! The important part is not the actual easel but the pad of chart paper. Most teachers have a couple of charts going at all times, and the teaching point from each day's reading workshop is generally added to one of the charts. So if this is a unit of study on nonfiction reading, there may be a chart about ways readers read expository nonfiction (Readers look over the text and think, "How do I think this whole text will unfold?" Readers read until our minds are full, and then we pause, usually at the end of a chunk, and think, "What's the big thing I've learned so far?" and retell what we just learned). The one main chart that threads through a unit of study might be referred to in half the unit's minilessons, and certainly teachers will refer to this chart in some of their small-group work and their conferences. Meanwhile, however, there will probably be two or three subordinate charts that also thread through the unit. One, for example, might be a chart listing ways partners can share their reading, and another might be a chart about strategies for tackling tricky words. The latter two charts probably were begun in an earlier unit of study and are carried along within and beyond this unit.

If a teacher has access to an overhead projector, a document camera, or a smart board, this can be a helpful resource during minilessons, but they can also alter the tone and intimacy of a minilesson, making the minilesson feel not like a huddle or story time but more like a PowerPoint presentation. I like these tools best if they are kept low down, close to the floor, so the teacher needn't stand and deliver. I do not advise wheeling these machines into the minilesson, and then standing alongside them, teaching with eyes glued to the projected text rather than on the students. I also think that we need to teach listening as well as reading, and that most of the time we should read aloud without displaying the text. Still, these tools can be helpful, depending how and how often they are used.

Whenever possible, teachers put a carpet on the floor of the meeting area. It sets this part of the room apart, making it special, and it makes sitting on the floor more appealing to kids. But whether or not there is a carpet in the meeting area, you'll want your kids to become accustomed to sitting on the floor. Many times a day, you'll want to convene kids to explicitly teach them in an all-eyes-up-here fashion. Classrooms in which reading is taught through a workshop approach induct kids into the ritual of assembling quickly and dispersing quickly. Certainly it would be cumbersome to imagine chairs dragged hither and yon during the reading workshop.

## Materials

### Book Bins/Baggies

In reading workshops, you'll see that readers carry some sort of a container in which they keep their books and other stuff. Sometimes this is a cardboard magazine box that doubles as almost the wall of a carrel, separating the child's reading space from that of the child beside him, and sometimes it is a freezer baggy (cheaper, but risky for stepping on!). Of course, readers keep all their reading materials in their book bins.

### Take-Home Baggies

There is always a take-home baggie in the book bin (or a take-home baggie within the larger baggie). This is the means to support a reader's texts going wherever the reader goes.

### Reading Logs

Each reader in each and every reading workshop keeps a reading log, and I can't stress enough the importance of this tool. Many teachers find that students value their logs most if they are kept in a cumulative fashion, perhaps in a three-holed binder or a folder, with recent logs combined with those from other weeks of the year. This allows readers themselves and others who care about their reading to refer to the log for evidence of growth across time. The log is a record of the book title, the level, the date, the reading place (home or school), the page at which reading began and the page at which reading ended, and the minutes spent reading. At the start of each reading workshop, children pull out their reading logs and record the page number at which they'll start that day's reading, and they record the start time. Then, at the end of reading time, readers record the number of total minutes spent reading and the number of pages read. As a teacher moves about the room, this makes it is easy to notice that in, say, seventeen minutes of reading time, a particular reader may have read fifteen pages (which is what you'd expect) or four pages (which would lead you to want to do some further research). Children, as well as teachers, study data. Children review the data on their reading like runners might study their times or dieters their weight, and there is a lot of emphasis on these data being scientific. If a child records that she only read twelve minutes last night at home, a teacher is apt to congratulate the child on such precise and honest data. If the teacher wants to address the need to make more time for reading (which is likely), that conversation needs to occur far from any discussion of the written record. Because logs are kept out as children read, every day in every class, and because books travel between school and home each day, this makes it more likely that they are accurate records of the reading that is done in home and at school. If children distort the amount of reading they did at home, then each day they'll be forced to read from pages that don't make sense to them.

### Short Stacks of Just-Right Books

Teachers often talk to children about how readers have books at our bedside tables, or books in waiting. This rhetoric, then, paves the way for children to select not a single book at a time from the library, but a "short stack of books." These short stacks function like books that are piled on the bedside table. The short stacks of books are more important than you might realize because they keep children from constantly finishing books and running to the classroom library, where they roam and drift sometimes for long stretches of time. It means that the interval between finishing one book and starting the next is a seamless one.

This also means that when we confer with a child, we can notice the trajectory of that child's reading. If this one book seems too hard, we can see whether that's been the case across many books or whether this is just an exception.

We can also help children to talk and think across books. "In this series, is the character growing any older? Is time seeming to pass? How can she tell?"

Then, too, we can also check on the reading work that kids have been doing even if they are not in class. During gym, for example, we can say to all the children, "Please leave your book bins out at your reading spot so I can look at your short stack of books," and we can quickly look across the books in readers' bins, checking to see whether the levels of text difficulty seem about right, looking at the nature of the readers' Post-its and/or reading notebook entries across time.

### Post-Its

Your children will no doubt keep Post-its in their book bins. I once wrote to the Post-it company suggesting that it supply me with thousands and thousands of free packages of Post-its to share with New York City teachers who have very little because, after all, the reading workshop has no doubt sent sales of Post-its over the moon. The company would have nothing to do with me, alas, and for a week I boycotted them. But I couldn't maintain my freeze. Post-its are too important to me. They're important because kids don't own the books in our classrooms and therefore can't write in them as you and I do—with stars and marginalia and underlined passages. Post-its are the closest thing I know to that sort of earmarking. These and other on-the-run responses to reading, coupled with partnership conversations, can efficiently angle a child's reading without supplanting it with a daily dirge of writing about reading. And so, for example, a reader can have a theory going about a character and can Post-it places where the character acts out of character in ways that are surprising, that suggest the character may be changing. The reader might jot her thought about this briefly on the Post-it and then read on, but later she could elect to come back to this point in the book with a partner.

In the reading bin, readers will also keep temporary scaffolds of various sorts: a list of key questions they can ask themselves, a spectrum of precise words for describing a character, a reminder of the strategies readers use to do whatever that reader has been working toward. One reader might be asked to prop a card of reminders in front of him as he reads. Another might use a bookmark containing some specific reminders. The important thing about these scaffolds is that they are temporary and meant to be removed when readers no longer need the support. It's always helpful to keep in mind that a tool that could provide a scaffold one day can on another day become a box, limiting what a learner does.

# What Does Reading Workshop Across a Whole School Look Like? Creating a Community of Practice

If you were to visit any one of the hundreds of thousands of schools where the reading workshop is the method of choice for teaching reading, you'd find that usually this is a whole-school, and often a whole-district, approach. Sometimes a school system is in transition, allowing the more skilled teachers or the more successful schools to use a reading workshop approach to teaching reading while keeping some of the less experienced teachers tied to a core reading program, a basal textbook. Usually, these districts in transition meanwhile provide teachers the professional development they need to take steps toward the reading workshop. Leaders of these schools will say, "I'm working to be sure all teachers are ready to teach using a reading workshop. For now I think only some faculty members at this school are ready for that." I'll discuss this in more detail later, but for now my point is that usually, although not always, the reading workshop is an approach that a city, a town, a district, or a school adopts.

## Provisioning Classrooms with Books

When a school decides to use the reading workshop as its approach to teaching reading, this means that instead of every child reading selections from reading textbooks in synchrony with each other and then doing a series of activities around those selections, the emphasis in the teaching of reading is on reading real books—trade books. Funds are less apt to be channeled toward mammoth reading programs that come with stopwatches, puzzles, puppets, CDs, books of ditto masters, plaques for the wall, games, and the like, and instead every possible dollar is spent on bringing the best of children's literature into the classroom and on providing teachers with literacy coaches or lead teachers, staff development, and time to study together.

Of course, provisioning classrooms with the best of children's literature is not a small detail. Some people suggest that the minimum number of books that a classroom needs is twenty per child; most schools agree that over time, it will be important to provision children with more books than that. Schools that take the time to develop book rooms are making good use of their energy and resources because this means that text sets containing multiple copies of certain books can be accessed and returned, and this is an important way to support guided reading groups and book clubs. Then, too, in general as a class of children grows across the year, the books they're able to read will change, and book rooms allow teachers to keep our fast-growing kids "in books." I provide more resources, including bibliographies, on the topic of classroom libraries and book rooms on the accompanying CD-ROM.

In a reading workshop, children not only read actual books; they also usually choose the books that they'll read. Those choices, of course, are guided. For example, children are channeled to read books that are at their "just-right" reading levels. They may also be channeled to read a particular genre of books or sent to choose books from a limited collection (perhaps, for a time, books the teacher believes are especially well written).

If a school adopts a reading workshop approach, generally this means that the school will also adopt an assessment system that enables teachers to ascertain the level of text difficulty that each reader can handle, and then classroom libraries will be organized so at last 50% of the books (usually more) are labeled by level of text difficulty. Every school I know relies on a leveling system originally developed by Irene Fountas and Gay Su Pinnell to scaffold their levels, although leveling books by lexile is another possibility. Once books have been leveled, a teacher can suggest that a child will feel strongest reading, say, level T books, and then the child can choose the books he or she will read, choosing from texts that are labeled with level T or are similar in difficulty to those texts, or the child can read texts that are a bit easier than those. Teachers sometimes question whether their school could adopt a reading workshop approach to teaching reading if their school does not have leveled classroom libraries. This is a wise question, because the truth is that whereas teaching a writing workshop requires only that students have pens, paper, and a willing teacher, teaching a reading workshop does require more support. Readers need access to books that they can read—and lots of them.

However, bear in mind that eight years ago, the chancellor of New York City's schools went to one school—PS 172, a stronghold of the reading and the writing workshop—and said, "The approach to language arts in this school is going to be the approach to language arts across the city of New York." Hundreds of New York City schools were caught off-guard by that announcement. They didn't even have classroom libraries (let alone leveled classroom libraries)! Across New York City, people took sets of twenty-five copies of books and dispersed them into classrooms, providing single copies to many rooms and four to six copies for book club reading to other rooms. The layers of materials were excavated from the edges of classrooms, the book rooms, the basements, and in doing so, countless books were uncovered. Schools held leveling pizza parties on a Friday afternoon. Staff rooms became leveling rooms. Instead of knitting while chatting, people leveled a few books. The security guards, para-professionals, student teachers, and parent volunteers were trained in the rudiments of leveling books. After all, it isn't rocket science. You take a book. You look up the level on one of several websites. Perhaps you find the book with its level, in which case you record the level. If you don't find the level, then once you develop a sense for text levels, you make the wisest decision you can, knowing that once the book is in use in the classroom, if it seems harder or easier than others that carry the same level label, then its level can be adjusted.

Most teachers know that any system of assessing the text level a child can read and of assigning books to levels is an approximate one, so when a child especially wants to read a book that is a bit harder, the teacher will work with the child to be sure he or she gets support doing that reading and to be sure a deadline is set for when the reader will finish that book. It's one thing for a child to take three days to read a book his friend loved, promising to have lots of conversations with the friend and getting summaries from the friend, and quite another for a child to lug a giant *Harry Potter* book to and from school for four months as she inches her way through it! I discuss the possible systems for leveling texts and for assessing readers and matching them to texts in the chapter "Assessing Readers: Schoolwide Systems for Tracking Progress."

One way in which children's book choices are guided, then, is that children are channeled to read books that are at their just-right levels (and to progress up levels over time). In addition, the class will always be engaged in a unit of study (more on this later), and the unit will often influence children's choices. That is, it may be that the third graders spend a month in a unit of study on mystery books. Most of the books that third graders read seem to be mysteries, so this doesn't curtail their reading lives to a very big extent, but yes, during a unit of study on mystery reading, what this means is that every child will continue to choose just-right books to read. For example, a child will be reading level T books, but the child will choose from a collection of mysteries that are written at levels he or she can read. During another unit, the emphasis may be on characters (allowing any fiction book to suffice) or on interpretation. Still other units of study might be on expository nonfiction or biography.

In schools that teach a reading workshop approach to reading, this means that instead of purchasing a program that controls the teaching of reading, teachers are decision makers. This means that creating a climate of professional study is crucial. There are a variety of ways in which a school does this.

## Knowledge and the Connection Between Expertise and the Classroom

One challenge, then, is to provision classrooms across the school with books. An even more important challenge is to provision classrooms across the school with expertise. When possible, people with expertise on the teaching of reading will spend some of their time helping teachers as well as helping children. Sometimes the expert's title is literacy coach; sometimes it is reading specialist or director of language arts or lead teacher. The title is less important than the role. The important thing is that schools need to be places where everyone is engaged in professional study, and this is most apt to happen if professional development is built into the fabric of the school.

Usually a school will agree upon a set of methods that are used across the school, in every grade, and in every classroom. This means, then, that the faculty in the school becomes a gigantic community of practice, with people all talking and thinking about methods of teaching that underpin the reading workshop in first grade, third grade, fifth grade, and so on. A cluster of teachers can spend time developing expertise in a particular method. Imagine that three teachers from across widely different grade levels take on a study of the best possible ways to lead guided reading groups. After the small group develops some expertise at whatever they are studying, then other teachers can visit those classrooms to observe what the core group of teachers is doing. With little inexpensive hand-held cameras, informal videos can be made of people using the method under study. In study groups, the school community can read what various experts have said about the method, watch the videos made by experts on the method, and then approximate and emulate, analyze, and question whatever is read and viewed. In this way, the school as a whole can agree upon a rough draft of tentative ideas about that particular method as it lives in that particular school. In this fashion, the school will begin to develop a shared set of methods for teaching reading and shared understandings about those methods.

One of the wonderful things about a reading workshop is that the methods teachers will study and use to teach reading will mostly be methods that they can also use to teach writing. Minilessons, conferring, small-group strategy lessons, teaching shares, work with partnerships, and methods for constructing units of study will be mostly the same, whether one is teaching reading or teaching writing. Of course, some teachers will feel more at home with a method within one venue or the other, and this is one of the ways in which all of us outgrow ourselves all the time.

It's powerful and efficient, then, when a school adopts a shared set of methods for teaching reading and writing, because teachers from divergent grade levels can then work shoulder to shoulder, with one person's knowledge becoming everyone's knowledge. The first-grade teacher may be reading aloud *Mike Mulligan and His Steam Shovel,* and the fifth-grade teacher may be reading aloud *The Giver,* but both teachers will plan for their read-aloud work in ways that can be discussed, and both teachers will shift between demonstrating and scaffolding and removing scaffolds. Schools become beehives of inquiry and collaboration when the entire staff of a school sees itself as co-contributors to an ever-evolving schoolwide repertoire of teaching methods.

There is another reason why shared methods of teaching are incredibly important, and it is this: any method of teaching is also a method of learning. If teachers study conferring and know that it helps to approach a child and ask questions such as "What work are you doing as a reader?" then that method of teaching has powerful implications for kids. *They* need to learn *their* roles in these methods of teaching. They need to know that when the teacher asks, "What work are you doing as a reader?" the teacher is not wanting to know the title and

> *The reason that people choose to teach in reading workshops is not that this form of teaching produces scores. Instead, the reasons to do this are the children, grasping books to their chest, whose lives are forever changed because they are readers.*

page number of the child's current book, and they need to know that if they aren't sure what work they have been doing, it can help to cast their eyes over the anchor chart from the unit of study and to think, "Have I been working on any of those bullet points that my teacher has taught in this unit of study?" Of course, conferring is not the only method that kids need to learn. Every method of teaching is a method also of learning, and the more we can induct kids into the system, the more proactive and powerful they can be in their roles. In schools in which teachers share a set of methods of teaching, kids take over those methods. It is not uncommon for a child to offer to reteach the preceding day's minilesson for the children who were absent, or for children who have developed expertise on a subject to suggest they could lead strategy lessons for others. Older children who buddy with younger children can use those buddy relationships as time for conferring, with the older child functioning very much as she has seen her teacher function. Buddy-reading (a term that I think of as referring to times when older students buddy-up with younger students) can become a forum for cross-grade-level book clubs. Student Council meetings can abide by principles of accountable talk that children experience first within the whole-class read-aloud.

Of course, the job of supervising and supporting teachers also becomes easier when a school becomes a community of practice with all the teachers working within shared methods of teaching. For example, a principal who may not feel confident that he or she necessarily knows how to teach really effective reading workshops can spend time in the classrooms where kids are growing in leaps and bounds. The principal can study what's happening in those rooms and then use the image of good teaching, gleaned from those classrooms, as a resource when supporting and supervising other teachers. Of course, sometimes the principal will want to get out of the role of middleman and spend time enabling one teacher to support the others directly.

Teachers are especially able to learn from each other if the various classrooms are not only all using similar methods of teaching, but are also engaged in a curriculum that makes it likely that, for much of the time, the kids are working in shared units of study. I'll discuss the process of developing curriculum in more detail later, but for now the important thing is that generally, in a school that has adopted a reading workshop approach to teaching reading, the teachers at a specific grade level will meet together toward the end of one school year to map out a (mostly) shared curricular calendar, as I call it, for the upcoming year. This means, for example, that at any one time of the year, the teachers across a grade level will probably all be teaching the same unit of study in reading (and in writing), so teachers can swap minilesson ideas, show each other their students' work, ponder the unit-specific problems that come up, and in general provide each other with professional company.

## Why Reading Workshop?

As you'll see in Chapter 11, the scores that readers who are schooled in reading workshop earn on standardized tests are impressive, but really the reason that people choose to teach in reading workshops is not that this form of teaching produces scores. Instead, the reasons to do this are the children, grasping books to their chest, whose lives are forever changed because they are readers.

I think of Imani. She'd been in a series of foster homes and was, when she entered one of our reading workshop classrooms, living with her mom, who was a single parent and a crack addict. Within a month or two of entering this classroom, Imani became a ravenous reader. Her teacher put a steady stream of books in her hands, books that featured African American girls like herself, books that were not the victim narratives of slavery and prejudice but instead stories of strong sassy girls like Imani. She read *Dancing in the Wings* and *Junebug* and most of Jacqueline Woodson's books. Imani began carrying two or three of these books at a time, reading them constantly, and she became a feminist. She wrote this poem about herself:

> I am
> The chocolate in the twix bar
> The cookie crunch in the oreo cookie
> Not the creamy center
> I am
> B-ball and yoga and
> Books hidden under my bed
> I am
> Not 'ho' or 'yo' or anything else
> The boys in my neighborhood
> Call the girls they think are easy girls
> Who go with them to be somebody
> I am *somebody* already.

When I think of the reasons to teach a reading workshop, I think also of my son Miles. When it came time for Miles to write the essay accompanying his college applications, I felt sure he'd write about one of the service activities that had been so important in his life, or about his relationship with his brother or with his grandfather. But to my surprise, Miles wrote instead about his relationship to characters in books. His essay began:

> When I enter college, I will bring my experiences trekking through the mountains of Vietnam and my memories of a 227-day stint in a lifeboat, accompanied only by a Bengal tiger. When I attend classes as a freshman, my role will bear the imprint of the torturous hours I spent standing along the town square, a scarlet letter emblazoned on my chest. Reading has given me the water I swim in, the heroes I emulate, and the imagination to believe that I can make the world a better place.

I have often said that one of my goals is to give the children of the world what I give to my own children. And so it matters to me that when it came time for Miles to introduce himself to prospective colleges, of all his formative experiences, the one he chose to write about was the moment he experienced vicariously, standing in shame as a woman overlooking the town square, a scarlet letter emblazoned on the chest. Like Miles, your children will let you know that their lives have been changed because of books, and that will be the evidence that kindles your passion for teaching well.

# CHAPTER THREE

# Skills and Strategies of Proficient Readers

It is easy to approach a group of today's kids, worrying from the start over how we're going to combat their resistance to reading. We can enter the school year with elaborate plans in place for how we will check on whether each child actually reads during each day's reading time. After all, some of them could just be sitting there, holding the book, pretending to read. We can plan on using surprise quizzes to catch the kids who sneak out of reading and prizes to combat the resistance we're sure we'll encounter. We can plan on coaxing kids to read for ten minutes a day by allowing them to eat their snacks while they read, or by promising pizzas when they've read three books.

I wouldn't recommend any of this! In fact, I'd suggest you go to the opposite extreme and fill yourself with such a brimming love of reading that you approach your year unable to imagine that a single child won't love reading as you do. Think about the great teachers in your life. Haven't they been people who exuded a passionate commitment to the subject that they taught? We end up caring about those teachers' subjects because their passion rubbed off on us.

For any of us to teach well, don't we need to be filled with a gigantic sense that the content of our teaching matters enormously? How important it is for each of us, as a teacher, to remember that ultimately, human beings want to work hard toward goals that matter, we want to throw ourselves into hard work that is significant, that adds up.

Let me show you what I mean. Right now, think in your mind of one time when your teaching was good. Actually do this. Thumb through your memories of your teaching career, and settle on one time when your teaching felt good.

I'm pretty sure you haven't recalled a time when nothing much was asked of you—no stress, no press. I don't think that when your teaching has been good, this was a time you came in late, left early, put your feet up on the desk, and ate Doritos.

Instead, I'm pretty sure you thought of a time when you poured yourself, heart and soul, into work that was tremendously demanding. The time when your teaching felt good was probably a time in which you worked with zeal and dedication on an endeavor that you believed was important. Your work was hard, but it was important. You probably felt that so much was expected of you that you weren't sure you could pull it off, yet somehow you managed to find the resources in yourself and in others that allowed you to rise to the occasion.

Kids aren't that different from you and me. They also want to work with heart and soul on efforts that matter. A number of years ago, the principal in a nearby high school decided that he would invite a handful of high school students on a five-day sail. The students who signed on as crew members would need to raise money for the trip and to participate in a semester-long grueling extracurricular study of the literature and science of the sea. "If any high school student is interested," the principal, John Chambers, said, "Let's meet at the art gallery in town at 7 pm."

When my friend Mary Winsky arrived with her daughter, the entire street was already lined with cars. They finally squeezed into the room at the museum in time to hear Chambers talking about slides of a previous time he'd taken students on the same trip. "Do you see those reams of papers under that paperweight?" he asked. "Those are statistical calculations of wind and speed. Anyone participating needs to be prepared for sleepless nights spent doing calculations such as these." The next slide showed teenagers on their hands and knees, scrubbing the deck of the ship. "You still interested?" Chambers asked.

From throughout the room came a resounding cry of "Yes." Pam turned to her mother and said, "Oh, Mom, I wish I could get down on my hands and knees and beg for the chance to be part of that sail." Great teachers rally kids to want to work with that sort of zeal. Our goal, when teaching, is to launch ships.

Sometimes, doesn't it seem as if we inadvertently end up teaching reading as if our goal, instead, is to be like the circus man who gets one plate spinning on top of a stick, then gets another plate spinning, and another? We run between the spinning plates, between the kids, trying to keep them cycling round and round, book after book, level after level. What I want to say in this chapter is that spinning plates is not enough. Instead we need to launch ships.

The great teachers in our lives are people who rally us to work harder than we ever dreamt possible, and they do this by helping us know that we are working toward goals that matter. When teaching reading, we need to do nothing less than rally kids to work with heart and soul on journeys that matter to them. To do this, we need to be clear that the content of our teaching is enormously important.

## We Need to Care So Much About the Skills of Proficient Reading that We Can't Stand to Keep that Love to Ourselves

If we are going to rally kids to work with zeal, then we need to care about the content of our teaching so much that we help students care about that content too. Katherine Paterson, author of *Bridge to Terabithia*, describes such teaching, saying, "First we must love music or literature or math or history or science so much that we cannot keep that love to ourselves. Then with energy and enthusiasm and enormous respect for the learner, we share that love."

You may be thinking, "I do that. I love children's books so much that I cannot keep that love to myself. With enormous energy and enthusiasm, I share my love for *Bud, Not Buddy* and *The Secret Garden*." And if that is the case—if you are a teacher who wears your love for books on your sleeve—then this will make an extraordinary difference in your teaching. I cannot say enough about the power of being a person who loves books.

But one of the challenges when teaching reading is this: when every child is reading a different book, then *our content can't just be a particular book*. Our content can't be *Bud, Not Buddy* or *The Secret Garden*. Instead, the content of our teaching needs to be the skills, strategies, and habits that comprise proficient reading.

For some of us, it hasn't been all that easy to get kids fired up about the skills of proficient reading. Teaching kids to locate the main idea can sometimes feel formulaic and uninspiring. It has sometimes been easier to recruit children to work with enormous resolve on their *writing* than on their *reading*, perhaps because when teaching writing, we can show youngsters the work of Sandra Cisneros or Eloise Greenfield and use that work to help youngsters dream that their writing might someday be equally graceful, equally stirring. Then, too, when teaching writing, we share stories of our heartaches and hopes, and we do so in ways that give kids goose bumps. Yet when we try to do the same thing in reading, it doesn't always work the same magic. We pull kids close in a reading minilesson and say, "Watch me as I find the main idea of this passage," and then read a paragraph aloud, pausing to look toward the ceiling and to think aloud, and we aren't always convinced that children say to themselves, "Oh, how I wish I could think aloud like that!"

If we must first love the content of our teaching so much that we can't stand to keep that love to ourselves, does that mean we must first love character traits, prediction, inference, and determining importance so much that we can't stand to keep that love to ourselves?

My answer is yes. Absolutely.

You may be thinking, "*What*? I must love *prediction* so much that I can't keep that love to myself?"

Exactly.

So think for a moment about what prediction means to you. I know that we all hold in our heads terminology for skills like "activating prior knowledge" or "drawing on anticipatory sets," but you need to fill yourself with your own relationship to the content of your teaching. So set aside your grip on other people's words, and think in your own words for a moment. Think about prediction in your reading, your teaching, your life. Try asking yourself questions such as these: "What's it like when readers in my classroom *don't* predict?" That is, what's the big deal about kids who do or don't predict? Then, too, think, "Is prediction a self-contained skill, or is it part of a bigger stance? And if it is the latter, what else is glommed in with prediction, inextricably linked to it?" Or try thinking like this: "What does growth in prediction look like? That is, how is a beginning predictor different than an intermediate predictor, and how are they both different from a proficient predictor?"

When I ask questions such as those, I begin to realize that prediction, for me, is all about drawing on everything one knows to lean forward in life and in reading, to imagine what's apt to happen.

Last spring, when my Rock of Gibraltar, all-strong mother ran into a whole series of medical problems including a stroke that left her unable to drive and not very strong at walking either, I thought about all I knew of her and imagined her future. I used my powers of prediction (and my royalties!) to buy her a used mule as a Mother's Day gift. It wasn't a burro-mule; instead, it was a Kawasaki Mule, a little red land-roving farm truck, with big wheels and a back compartment like a dump truck. She can drive it to the barn, the chicken house, the creek, the neighbors' houses, and does so vigorously, with her three big dogs aboard and with a slew of neighborhood kids hanging on as if attached with Velcro. The vehicle is not all that different than a golf cart, but the ambience is totally different. Instead of conveying an old-lady-with-her-purse aura, the Mule is a

*...if you are a teacher who wears your love for books on your sleeve—then this will make an extraordinary difference in your teaching.*

farmer's work vehicle, rugged and ready for adventure. To choose it, I had to predict how it would intertwine with the unfolding story of my mother's life—and I predicted well. She continues as a powerhouse, despite the unsteady gait.

If you think about it, you and I are constantly using our abilities to read people so we can read the tea leaves and be proactive problem solvers. That is, we read people to predict. I glean all that I can from the unfolding time lines of my kids' lives to channel them toward one summer internship or another. I do similar work when helping teachers find ways to respond to the ever-changing edicts from the Department of Education without losing sight of our North Star.

Of course, I predict all the time as a reader. For me, the predicting that I do as a reader is inseparable from dreaming the dream of a story, from being lost in the story, from making a mental movie as I read. I read, and I am so consumed by the story that I'm on the edge of my seat, almost authoring the story that I have not yet read. If I need to put the book down, my mind keeps imagining the upcoming story. Predicting is a lot like writing the rest of the story in front of the author, and it is the result of engagement. I'm reminded of Joyce Carol Oates, who said, "Reading is the sole means by which we slip, involuntarily, often helplessly, into another's skin, another's voice, another's soul."

When it comes time for me to teach prediction, then, I can most definitely convey to kids that I love prediction so much that I cannot bear to keep this love to myself. The reader who predicts is the reader who synthesizes all she knows about characters, about the places, about how stories go, about the author, and then leans forward into a story enough to imagine the story that has yet to happen. The reader who predicts isn't reading with blinders on, looking only at the words in front of her, but instead knows that reading involves drawing on what has already happened to project what lies ahead. This is the nose-in-the-book reader. This reader is absolutely also empathizing, envisioning, responding personally. Some people believe you can't teach that sort of engagement, that sort of absorption, that some kids simply come to us as nose-in-the-book readers or they don't, almost suggesting that this sort of engagement is in the DNA for some kids and not for others. Talk about passion: how could I *not* react passionately to any hint of a belief that a skill that epitomizes the essence of what it means to be an active, engaged reader is simply something that kids inherit rather than something they learn!

But let me stop. Teachers, here is the thing. I'm not really talking about prediction. I'm *really* talking about what it means to teach any reading skill well, and I just grabbed onto prediction as one example among many. You see, if we accept the research finding that nothing matters more than that kids have access to great teachers—and I do—then it is incumbent on us to be nothing less. And if we are going to be great teachers of reading, then we need to love what we are teaching so much that we can't bear to keep that love to ourselves. Donald Murray, the great Pulitzer Prize–winning writer who founded the field of writing process, has said that to teach anything well, we need to find in that subject some echoing cord of our own being. To teach anything well, we need to be able to come to the classroom all fired up with energy and passion about the importance of whatever it is that we are teaching.

So, teachers, think about the reading skills that fill your units of study. And think, "Why is it that this skill is so incredibly important that I'm going to devote months of my one year with kids, making sure that every one of them progresses in leaps and bounds toward being able to use this skill well?" Annie Dillard has advice for writers. "Write as if you were dying," she says. "If you had only one year left, what would you say that wouldn't enrage with its triviality." To me, that advice is good for teachers as well. "Let's teach as if we were dying," I say. Because actually, most of us only *do* have one year left with this child. What will we teach that won't enrage with its triviality?

## What Are the Skills and Strategies of Proficient Reading?

To rally kids to invest in the skills of proficient reading, we need, of course, to be able to talk and think about what that list of skills entails. It's easy to feel, once we've found a list of what reading entails, that we've found *the* list of the skills of proficient reading and then grip that list as if it is sacrosanct, written in stone, unassailable and complete.

The truth is that reading well, like writing well, calls upon a complex amalgam of skills. Interestingly enough, in the field of writing, there doesn't seem to be the same tendency to settle, once and for all, upon *the* list of the qualities of good writing. Instead, in the field of writing, there is a general under-standing that all the words we use to capture any quality of good writing are approximations. Does the term "show don't tell" suffice? Is this the same as "dramatizing rather than summarizing?" Will some quotes by authors help to bring this quality of good writing to life? And isn't it interesting that although "show don't tell" is important, so, too is the opposite. That is, it is also important for youngsters to learn the power of telling-not-showing, for some purposes. And that's just to talk about one quality of good writing, and there are many. How many? Who's to say?

In writing, the field is alive with constant new work around qualities of good writing. But in reading, many people assume that the conversation has ended and that somewhere there is a correct and complete list. But that's not how a field makes knowledge. No researcher has gone to the mountains and returned with the ten commandments of proficient reading. Instead, lots of different thoughtful people in lots of different parts of the world have read other people's lists of skills, surveyed studies that spotlight one skill or another, preferred one term over another for these mental activities that defy any attempt to be shoehorned into words, felt this or that was missing or redundant or unimportant in someone's list, watched more readers read and—based on that observation—added a new skill to their existing amalgam, and the work is ongoing. Although the list you hold perhaps bears the title, "The Skills of Proficient Reading," it should actually be titled, "Some Possible Ideas About the Skills of Proficient Reading." And you and your children are welcome to take your pen to that list—and go at it!

There are lots of open questions. Is *visualization* a better term, or *envisionment*, or *imaging*? Can one distinguish "determining importance" from "finding the main idea," and does the latter pertain to poetry and fiction or only to expository texts? Is "inference" a separate skill, or can every skill be done at a lower, more literal level and at a higher, more inferential level? Is "making predictions" part of "activating and making use of prior knowledge," or is it a separate skill in its own right? What word best captures a reader's relationship to "text structure"? Is this "attending to and uncovering text structure," or is this "story grammar"? Is "asking questions" really a skill, or might it better be called "generating and entertaining questions as one reads"? Why do so many researchers include "thinking aloud" on a list of comprehension skills? (Is that not more of a teaching method than a comprehension skill?) What is one to make of the conflicting views on "retelling" and "summarizing," with some people describing retelling as little more than regurgitating facts, while others saying that summarizing is "the most common and most necessary strategy" (Allington, 2006, p. 99). And why are skills such as reading with stamina and fluency missing from many lists, and what about the skill of "being adept with a wide range of diverse texts?"

My intention in pointing out that the conversation is ongoing and that there is no one sacrosanct and complete list of the skills of proficient reading is not to brush away the topic but rather to put it squarely in the middle of the table. I hope that you and your colleagues, like my colleagues and me, find yourselves constantly talking about the skills of proficient reading. I hope that frequently, you pause to ask yourselves, "What is our current best-draft thinking on the skills that are so important to reading that we have written those skills large in our curriculum and our assessments?"

My colleagues and I, for now, spotlight the following skills when supporting readers in grades 3–5.

- Stamina
- Fluency
- Monitoring for sense
- Envisionment
- Activating and using prior knowledge
- Prediction
- Empathy
- Inference
- Growing theories about characters

- Intratextuality (connections within a text)
- Intertextuality (connections across texts)
- Determining importance
- Using text structures
- Synthesis
- Summary
- Interpretation
- Critical reading

You will have your own list, with some terms penned in at the bottom—late additions—and some followed by question marks or stars or synonyms. The temptation will be to make your list very long, and of course there are many skills I could have added to the above list. You'll note that personal response isn't included, nor is asking questions, sequencing, learning new vocabulary, or making text-to-life connections. All of those skills and others could be added, but if the list is going to inform teaching, then we have to make some choices about what to leave off.

## How Do We Enrich Our Understanding of Reading Skills to Strengthen Our Teaching?

Hopefully, any word that we decide to use to represent a skill crystallizes a whole realm of experiences and associations that we have pertaining to that skill. If you and I were to teach social studies, and on our list of crucial content there was the phrase "system of checks and balances" or "Bill of Rights," then those crystal-lized phrases would represent, for us, a whole world of materials, information, ideas, stories, anecdotes, and concerns, and we'd draw on that whole rich repos-itory as we taught. In the same way, if you and I plan to teach skills of proficient reading, then each item on our list must represent a whole world of anecdotes, tips, examples, materials, pointers, qualifiers, stories, strategies, and the like. When our teaching comes from that sort of fullness, then it won't have that tinny, hollow feel that we've all experienced both as students and as teachers, when instruction comes from someone tonelessly executing an official script. How important, instead, for us all to know that teachers and learners alike read, and reflect on our reading, trying to reach for words to capture our experiences, and that we do this knowing that reading well will be vastly deeper and bigger and more human than words can ever say.

Yes, in the voice of Katherine Paterson, if we are going to teach "determining importance" or "summary" or "growing theories about characters" or any other reading skill well, we need to love that skill so much that we cannot bear to keep that love to ourselves. Someday, perhaps I will write a book in which I devote one chapter to each of the skills on my current list, but in the meantime, the more important thing is that *you* have a file going in your mind (if not at your desk) for each of the skills on your list. That is, the important thing is that you "collect around the seed idea" of whatever you are teaching or, as Piaget would say, to assimilate and accommodate information.

Doing so won't be new to you. Ever since you were a brand-new student teacher, as soon as you knew you'd be teaching something—the Gilded Age, perhaps, or writing memoirs—you became a magnet of the content that you were teaching. You'd walk through life seeing things everywhere about the Gilded Age or about memoir. In a similar fashion, you now need to do the collecting and connecting necessary so your files on interpretation and critical reading and envisionment and the other skills you aim to teach are full.

This shouldn't be surprising to hear—of course we need to become avid learners about whatever we teach—but I do think that sometimes, because the

teaching of reading is *so important*, we outsource learning about it. What irony. Here is the subject that matters most of all—arguably far more than, say, the Gilded Age—and yet, because it matters so tremendously much and because we want to be sure to teach this content well, we sometimes passively wait to be told The Right Way to teach. We sometimes neglect to throw ourselves head over heels into the project of collecting, combining, making, and remaking knowledge of the skills of proficient reading. How much better it would be if every teacher of reading approached that subject with as much chutzpa as we do when teaching kids about sea creatures or immigration or poetry or any of those other topics that turned our lives and our families' lives upside down.

## Read Professionally, Parsing Out One Skill, Even as You Know It's Enmeshed with Others

First, of course, you'll want to do some professional reading. This series has a bibliography that can send you to some sources, but it is also a wonderful thing to go to the people in your life whose teaching you admire and to ask them, "Which books on the teaching of reading have been especially powerful for you?" That way, when you read the book, it's apt to provoke the kind of conversation that will bring the reading to life. Perhaps you'll want to find places where people have written their understandings of particular reading skills. If you do this, you'll probably find that your own comprehension skills are taxed as you read what people say about particular comprehension skills. For starters, you'll probably see that it's not easy to distinguish any one comprehension skill from another.

### An Example of Parsing Out a Skill: Monitoring for Sense

Let's read the opening passage from Stephanie Harvey and Anne Goudvis's book, "Monitor Comprehension," from their important *Comprehension Toolkit*, and see if we can glean from this passage a clear sense of what the skill—monitoring for comprehension—is (and is not).

> When readers monitor their comprehension, they keep track of their thinking. They listen to the voice in their head that speaks to them as they read. They notice when the text makes sense or when it doesn't. We teach readers to "fix up" their comprehension by using a variety of strategies including stopping to refocus thinking, rereading, and reading on. All of the comprehension instruction suggested in the *Toolkit* helps readers to

monitor and use strategies to maintain and repair comprehension when it breaks down.

Monitoring comprehension is above all about engagement. When readers monitor their thinking, they have an inner conversation with the text. They merge their thinking with the information. Sometimes reading goes smoothly and sometimes it doesn't. Kids are more likely to stray from an inner conversation with the text when they are not interested in the content, find the reading too difficult, or don't have sufficient background to understand it. Readers stay on track when they question, connect, infer, sort and sift ideas, notice new information, etc. Engaged readers often show a range of emotions, responding with delight, wonder, sadness, even outrage.

I suspect that you come from this, as I do, unclear about the lines between comprehending and monitoring for sense. This is not because the writing is unclear. This is because comprehending and monitoring for sense are deeply interwoven. To fully separate them, in fact, would not make sense. But it's hard to develop a fat folder full of materials on the skill of monitoring for sense if everything in the folder is also in the folder for every other comprehension skill. As you read about reading skills, you'll find that the challenge to untwine one reading skill from another is a reoccurring one.

I've often pointed out that it doesn't make sense to think about reading comprehension as like a cake that can be sliced into, say, twelve pieces, into twelve component skills. If you think about what is involved in skillful prediction, for example, isn't that reader synthesizing what he or she has read, and doing so in ways that rely on determining importance and on text structure? Certainly the reader infers that which has not been explicitly stated. So yes, for good reason, passages describing one reading skill will refer to other skills as well. Still, if we are going to list skills of proficient reading at all, then I encourage you to work toward the goal of developing a set of reading comprehension skills that allows you to talk about skills in a way that is mutually exclusive and comprehensively exhaustive.

Let's depart for a moment and think about the parts of the United States. It's useful to have a way to talk about this topic in which the categories are mutually exclusive and comprehensively exhaustive, such as would be the case if you were talking about the north, south, east, west, and central parts of the country. You wouldn't want to talk about the United States by talking about the north, south, east, and rural parts. Those categories don't exclude one another, and they don't cover the whole United States. I'm not suggesting particular cate-

gories, but I am trying to say that when developing a set, it helps to aim to divide the main subject up in ways that are mutually exclusive and exhaustive. If monitoring for sense is one skill out of a dozen, then it can't contain questioning, sorting and sifting ideas, inferring, and the like. That is, the skill of monitoring for sense can't subsume within it all of comprehension and be any help to us as a category.

When reading about a skill, you'll need to do some sorting and sifting to isolate the portions of a text that illuminate that precise reading skill. When reading about the work of monitoring for comprehension, for example, the key word is *monitoring*. This particular skill involves watching over one's level of comprehension to gauge whether it's sufficient. Monitoring for sense needs to relate to the whole of comprehension on the one hand and to fix-up strategies on the other hand, but the actual skill entailed in monitoring is neither the whole of comprehension nor the work of repairing confusion. Just as the home inspector needs to check that the heating systems, the roof, the insulation, and the construction of a house are all in good order, yet doesn't make any repairs himself, the work involved in monitoring for comprehension will be work that gauges if the text is amounting to an understanding or if it is not. Does the reader need to stop herself and do a different kind of work, or can she go on, with the meaning-making systems all in order? In this way, monitoring for comprehension can be thought of as a discrete skill. If you sit down in this way and talk about reading skills and what exactly they do and don't mean, you'll find that what you are planning to teach, and how you would approach teaching it, begins to change.

## Examine Your Own Reading, Carefully Describing What Is Involved in One Skill

In addition to reading professionally to learn more about comprehension skills, you'll want to spy on yourself and your colleagues as you read, using whichever skills you are studying (and planning to teach). As you do this, I strongly recommend that you try to reach for the most precisely true words you can find to capture your own felt sense for what it means to use a skill, not relying on other people's words. Often you'll find that you are trying to describe something that isn't easy to describe. It may happen in a split second, or it may be something so cerebral that you aren't accustomed to putting it into words. Don't hesitate to reach for metaphor when that helps. And don't worry about using lots of different ways to try to convey what your mind is doing. For now, you aren't choosing one way to talk about the skill to your students. You are, instead, building up your own relationship to what you are teaching; you're digging the wells out of which you'll draw your teaching.

### An Example of Spying on One's Own Reading: Envisioning

So let's try it. Let's start with envisioning. We might begin this work by trying to note and jot the exact "something" that happens when the static black and white print on the paper evokes images in our mind. We'd pick a story—a narrative text rather than an expository or analytical one—and preferably find a part that is heavy in description and/or action, such as the excerpt below from *Charlotte's Web*. We might also pick up a pencil and mark parts that help us envision, parts that bring this text to life for us.

> When Mr. Arable returned to the house half an hour later, he carried a carton under his arm. Fern was upstairs changing her sneakers. The kitchen table was set for breakfast, and the room smelled of coffee, bacon, damp plaster, and wood smoke from the stove.
>
> "Put it on her chair!" said Mrs. Arable. Mr. Arable set the carton down at Fern's place. Then he walked to the sink and washed his hands and dried them on the roller towel.
>
> Fern came slowly down the stairs. Her eyes were red from crying. As she approached her chair, the carton wobbled, and there was a scratching noise. Fern looked at her father. Then she lifted the lid of the carton. There, inside, looking up at her, was the newborn pig. It was a white one. The morning light shone through its ears, turning them pink.

If you saw the scene unfurl sequentially, bit-by-bit in your mind's eye—Mr. Arable washing hands, then drying them, Fern walking down, approaching the chair, peering inside—then you will identify with the scores of teachers and readers who refer to envisioning as "watching a mental movie."

Accurate though this metaphor feels, it by no means encapsulates each and every aspect of what we refer to when we speak of envisioning a story. For example, did the mention of a woodstove not evoke a *felt* ambience? Did it not trigger the memory of a comforting smell? Did the mention of fresh breakfast not evoke coziness, and didn't the pit of your stomach stir slightly at the memory of coffee and bacon, especially if you're reading this just before lunch? Perhaps—and perhaps not—but bear with me. Did the image of light shining softly through its translucent ears not help you sense the baby pig's newness, its

fragility, its beauty? Could you sense the velvety texture of these newborn ears? Again, perhaps—and perhaps not—because we all differ as readers, not just in the level of attentiveness that we pay to different portions of the text but also in the associations that we bring to texts.

Regardless of whether your associations were identical to mine, if your envisioning evoked senses other than visual, you might decide to teach your students *more* than to merely watch the "mental movie" of their reading. Within the folds of envisioning, you might decide to talk of senses other than those of literal vision to suggest that to envision is *also* to pay attention to other senses—to note smells, textures, sounds, mood, and ambience.

On the other hand, if you felt like you too were seated in that kitchen as you read, alongside the mental movie metaphor, you might teach another, urging readers to "step into the world of their book." In the text we just read, a narrator's voice relates the story, but other texts might be told from a character's first-person perspective, granting us access to this character's thoughts and feelings, in which case envisioning might occur from the vantage of this character's take on the world. Envisioning in that case might be taught via yet another metaphor. We might urge children to step into the "skin" or "shoes" or "head" of a main character.

Then again, the way you envision the scene from *Charlotte's Web* above might totally differ in feel from the envisioning that helps you make sense of more complex texts, such as the start to Babbitt's *Tuck Everlasting*:

> The first week of August hangs at the very top of summer, the top of the live-long year, like the highest seat of a Ferris wheel when it pauses in the turning.

Of course, it takes little imagination to conjure the image of "the highest seat of a Ferris wheel when it pauses in the turning." Perhaps you see this seat silhouetted against puffy cumulus clouds and a blue sky; perhaps you see an excited child waving a cotton candy from that height. But for you to use this image to help make sense of this text might involve doing something altogether different from making the mental movie of a spinning Ferris wheel and different also from stepping into the shoes of someone watching or riding this Ferris wheel. You might, instead, consider a *still snapshot* of this image to understand the metaphoric reference to a calendar month. Again, your process might differ from mine, and both will be true, both will be effective, and *both are teachable*. How important it is then, to spy on ourselves as we use a specific skill and try to find the words that help us pin down what it is that we do each time.

## Consider Ways in Which Reading Skills Apply to All of Life

Then, too, when collecting stuff related to reading skills, I always think about the fact that reading skills are life skills—thinking skills. For example, when I think about what it means to love interpretation so much that I cannot keep that love to myself, I think about ways in which interpretation is part and parcel of living a life imbued with significance. We interpret when we pause in the midst of the hurly-burly to ask, "What's really important about this?" and "What can this teach me that relates not only to this moment but to many moments?"

### An Example of Seeing Reading Skills as Life Skills: Interpretation

When Katherine Paterson was asked, "What's essential about writing?" she told the story of a little moment like the ones that happen to all of us, all the time, but she framed the moment with ideas, and in doing so turned a little story into a statement about why writing matters. That's interpretation. As the story goes, Katherine's son David called, "Mom, Mom, come quick," and then she and her son crouched alongside a bug, watching as the cicada bug opened as if it had a waist-length zipper, then watching its wings emerge, transparent, all but the hairline veins of gold and green. As the cicada bug tumbled off and flew away, oblivious, Katherine Paterson wrote, to the wake of wonder it left behind, she thought, "What's this really about that pertains not only to that bug but to life itself?" She later wrote, "As I let that wake of wonder wash over me, I realized, 'This is what matters, because what good are straight teeth and trumpet lessons to a child who cannot see the grandeur that this world is charged with?" By finding messages and insights and illumination in the moments and objects, the comings and goings, which constitute life itself, she's engaging in the work of interpretation.

Interpretation is probably the single most important thing that I do as a writer and a reader. The other day, I decided to write about getting myself a new puppy, a story you'll read in another volume in this series. I knew I could start by telling how I woke up at 5 A.M. to drive through the early morning to the breeder's house. But before I could decide how to start the story, I needed to decide, "What's the story really, really about?"

> *By finding messages and insights and illumination in the moments and objects, the comings and goings, which constitute life itself, she's engaging in the work of interpretation.*

I ended up beginning the story about my new puppy by telling about a recent visit to my parents' house. A few minutes after arriving, I asked my mother how I could help. I know she saves projects for us kids to do; when the light bulb needs changing and she can't stand on a chair any longer, she saves the job for one of us. This time, it wasn't a light bulb that she had on her mind. "What you could do," she said, "is you could dig a grave for Flurry."

"For Flurry?" I gasped. I'd clearly been away too long. I hadn't even realized my mother's beloved dog had died. "Oh, geez, I didn't even know she'd died," I said, vowing to never again let so much time pass between my phone calls.

"She's not dead," Mum said. "But she will be soon, and we might as well have a grave ready."

So I went out and under the setting sun, I dug a hole under the big chestnut tree where all our dead pets over the years have been buried. And as I shoveled away, my mother's ancient dog, Flurry, my own ancient dog, Tucker, and my 86-year-old mother all watched on.

As I dug, I couldn't help but think that it wasn't just Mum who needs to ready herself for upcoming loss. Shoveling away at that hole, I thought about my dog Tucker, who is as old as my mother's dog, and I thought about my sons who are growing up and away, and I thought about my mother, too, who is not young. That evening, under the setting sun, I decided to get myself a puppy. Emma, my ebullient flat-coated retriever puppy, is my hole in the ground, my way of preparing myself for the losses that are around the bend for me.

That's interpretation. As I write and as I read, I pause to think, "What's the important thing that I'm trying to say?" and "What am I learning from this?" Interpretation is close to me here because I find that it is so easy for me to run, run, run through life, unwritten. I hurry here and hurry there, like the people in Eve Merriam's poem, "The Slow to Grow," never taking the time to pause, to think, "What's this really saying?" and "How can this change me?"

## Study Children as They Use Reading Skills

Of course, to develop a file full of insights about a skill that I want to teach, the most important work I do is that I watch kids as they engage in this work, and I try to understand what comes easily to them and what gets in the way. I think, for example, about intertextuality, about connecting one text and another. When youngsters know that this is valued, that we, teachers, celebrate times when they say, "This reminds me of…," then they'll perform on cue. And it becomes our job to study what they do and to try to figure out why it's not quite what we had in mind.

### An Example of Studying Children as They Use Reading Skills: Intertextuality

I remember one reader who read a provocative story about an injured boy who was found hurt, taken to an isolated community, and nursed back to strength, but who came to worry that he was a prisoner rather than a guest. Somewhere in the midst of this story, a gruff mountaineer—who may have been almost a jailor—enters the scene wearing a green hat, and the girl reading it said to me, "That's the same as in Amber Brown—the uncle in that book wears a green hat too." She went on to find five other ways in which her novel reminded her of various and sundry books, and each connection consisted of nothing more than a line drawn between the two texts: the sister in this book eats broccoli, as does the cousin in that book; there's a dog in this book and in that one.

It's always a good thing to be able to put one's finger on how what kids are apt to do isn't working, because this means that we have something to teach. Soon after the conversation with that girl, the teacher and I knew to begin work on intertextuality, teaching children that it helps to ask, "What's this book really about?" and only then to think, "What are some of the important ways that this book is like another book that I've read?" Then, too, we came to realize that the real power lies not in drawing a line between the two texts, but in the mental work that happens just after the connecting line is drawn. What does this similarity reveal? What does knowing about the situation in the one text prompt you to realize or consider about the other? Once the line is drawn, in other words, it should be that our understanding of both texts is deepened in some way.

# How Can We Teach Not Only the Skills but Also the Strategies of Proficient Reading?

You may find the terms *skill* and *strategy* confusing. Some people refer to the way in which a reader predicts what will happen next in a story as a skill; others refer to this as a strategy toward the larger skill of comprehension. The truth is the two words will always overlap like circles in a Venn diagram because first, many people use the terms interchangeably, and second, even when one distinguishes between a skill and a strategy, the same mental work can correctly be ascribed to both terms depending on how the work unfolds.

The word *skill* refers to muscles or abilities that a person has developed over time, usually after lots of practice. Some people refer to comprehension itself as the skill and to all the subordinate mental work that constitutes strands of comprehension—prediction, inference, critical reading, and the like—as strategies. Other people (and I count myself among them) will also refer to prediction and inference and envisionment, when done on the run as one reads, as skills. Strategies, then, become the step-by-step activities that a teacher can demonstrate to learners to show them ways to go about predicting, inferring, envisioning, or the like. Either way, learners sometimes deliberately use a strategy en route to a skill, choosing a step-by-step, conscious, goal-oriented procedure because the flowing, efficient, automatic work is not available to that person. Afflerbach, Pearson, and Paris, who have written about the difference that they see between skills and strategies, make a great point in noting that strategies are what readers turn to when they've realized that something is hard for them. Strategies are not, and should never be, considered the ends in and of themselves.

All this goes to say that when you are collecting ideas and techniques and insights and materials and anecdotes around the skills of proficient reading, you'll definitely want to think about some of the ways to help kids put reading skills into action. And you'll want to convey to youngsters that the non-negotiable, all-important work is that of comprehension. En route to comprehension, an individual person can choose, from time to time, any of a huge array of possible concrete, physical, goal-driven actions, but those actions are not the goal, and usually they are expendable and interchangeable.

Many of my colleagues have found it helpful to show students that readers can work toward a goal—say, drawing on a knowledge of text structure to read better—by using an array of scaffolds and supports. Our colleague Randy Bomer long ago created a chart that highlighted the way readers can do any particular sort of mental work by using any one of many different concrete scaffolds. Essentially, this chart has always reminded us that one could use many different scaffolds to support any skill.

Take envisioning. A reader could:

• Post-it places where she envisions (or where her mental movie breaks down).

• Sketch what it is she sees.

• Write into the gaps in a text, filling in what the author hasn't explicitly said but the reader envisions.

• Find another text in which she envisioned in some similar way.

• And so on.

My larger point is that a teacher will always want to have in mind a host of different possible ways, strategies, in which we can help readers work with any skill that matters to us. For example, if you wanted to help readers become more skilled at drawing on knowledge of text structure when they are reading stories and biographies, it would help if you had a repertoire of a half-dozen scaffolds, strategies, you could provide to readers to help them do this work, now and forever more. For example:

• You may want to teach readers that some people find it helpful to read stories, keeping in mind that it helps to learn about characters' traits, motivations, struggles, changes, and lessons. A reader could keep those key words on hand—on a bookmark or on a chart—and could read with an eye toward spotting information pertaining to those important aspects of a story. The reader could assign herself the job of talking about those aspects of a story with her partner at the end of a reading workshop.

• You may find it helps to provide readers with the summary scaffold:

| somebody | (who?) |
| wants | (what?) |
| but | (what gets in the way?) |
| and so | (how is that trouble addressed and resolved?) |

• You may want to show readers that a knowledge of story structure can help readers think about the sorts of work they probably need to be doing at the beginning of a book, in the middle of a book, and at the end of a book. Readers could then deposit Post-its or bookmarks at strategic places throughout the book. After the first chapter of a novel, readers could train themselves to ask certain questions:

• Who is telling the story?

• Who is the main character, and what is he or she like?

• What does he or she seem to want?

• What do you know about secondary characters so far?

• Where and when does the story take place?

• A different set of questions could be deposited at the middle and at the end of the story, helping the reader internalize the kind of work readers tend to do as they progress through a narrative.

Earlier, after I wrote about prediction, I pointed out that my message is really not about that one skill, and here again my message is not really about the strategies that you might have up your sleeve for supporting readers' work with narrative structure. Instead, my point is that as we ready ourselves to teach the skills of proficient reading, one part of our work will involve brainstorming specific concrete strategies that we can share with readers to provide them with the scaffolds they might need. All of this will help us approach our teaching feeling as if we're laden with goodies—with information and tips and strategies and materials and examples and stories—that we're eager to share.

No one said that teaching well would be easy. It isn't. This isn't about coming to work late, leaving early, putting your feet on the desk, and eating Doritos. Instead, this is about pouring all your intelligence and experience and imagination and energy into a gigantic learning project. The work will be hard, but it is important. Teaching in this way, you'll probably feel as if so much is being asked of you that you wonder if you can pull it off, yet I know that you'll find the resources in yourself and in others that will allow you to rise to the occasion. And your own teaching will be living proof that what we human beings want is the chance to work hard on goals that matter, on projects that require us to give all that we know, all that we are, toward causes that matter.

# CHAPTER FOUR

# Assessing Readers: Schoolwide Systems for Tracking Progress

From all sides, teachers are hearing that instruction must be data-based, grounded in the standards, and results-oriented. Pressure for results, as measured on standardized tests, has come to define the context within which many people teach.

Let's be clear. The hue and cry for data-based instruction can improve teaching and learning or destroy it. The original emphasis on standards-based reform in the 1990s was an effort that at least aimed to ensure that all students received the opportunities to learn that they deserved, and those reforms were at least in some states accompanied by efforts to use more performance-based assessments and to better prepare teachers so they would be able to bring all students to the same high standards. In states that developed performance assessments, teachers assigned more writing and more reading of whole books (in New York City, the hue and cry was that every child needed to read at least twenty-five books a year). A number of studies have shown that in the states that used enlightened assessments to assess standards, this first leg of standards-based reforms led to improved teaching and learning (Darling-Hammond, 2010, p. 69).

Since then, however, the push toward high standards has not tended to be accompanied by perform-ance assessments. Since No Child Left Behind (NLCB) legislation in 2001 mandated annual testing, most states have resorted to tests that are filled with easy-to-score multiple-choice questions. Not surprisingly, this—and also the increasing sanctions and pressures accompanying test scores—has led to a narrowing of the curriculum, to teaching that increasingly resembles testing, with more and more students spending substantial time on worksheets that look like the test items. In the process, real reading and writing, deep discussions, and higher-level thinking are all too often squeezed from the curriculum. This is most apt to happen in schools serving high-need students, resulting in an education that further penalizes low-income students by taking from them the opportunities to learn that they need to succeed in the twenty-first-century information economy.

The tragedy is that the standards movement—which was meant as a vehicle for giving all children a chance to learn—is widening the opportunity-to-learn gap. Linda Darling-Hammond, author of the important book *The Flat World and Education*, points out that when the national standards movement was first launched in the Clinton administration, a task force for the National Council on Education Standards and Testing (NCEST) noted, "If not accompanied by measures to ensure equal opportunity to learn, national content and performance standards could help widen the achievement gap between the advantaged and the disadvantaged in our society" (2010, p. 74). Those words appear to have foreshadowed the situation that we are now experiencing.

We've all experienced or heard about the scenarios that result. We've seen instances when a child's entire education is reduced to a curriculum of test prep, with students rarely reading a text that is longer than the passages on the state test and meanwhile spending more time answering questions than reading the passages. We've seen schools that literally broadcast a child's reading scores on giant wall-sized data charts and give prizes to children with higher scores and sanctions to those with lower scores—all in an effort to use competition and humiliation to whip young people into maintaining a laser-like focus on test scores. Of course, sometimes the effort to use competition and humiliation, prizes and sanctions, is directed at teachers and principals rather than kids. At times, the pressure to achieve a short-term bump in scores has even led some teachers to feel as if they are being pressured to abandon children with the deepest and most entrenched needs in order to direct the special services meant for those learners toward those whose scores are more likely to show quick improvement.

In a world that asks educators to be data-based, the evidence is now in. The push for ever-increasing scores on standardized tests has been no panacea. All the increased funding and increased pressures that accompanied NCLB have added up to reading scores that have flatlined, nationwide. The rallying cry for data-based instruction can demoralize teachers and students, can drive dedicated teachers from the profession, can turn reading into something that few would ever choose to do, and can dumb down the meaning of education.

But it doesn't have to be that way. We need only pick up the books that our kids are reading to be reminded that human beings have an extraordinary capacity to tackle difficulties. Surely the teaching profession can learn to respond to the pressure for data-based instruction while still holding tight to the highest of principles, and in the process we can surely find resources in ourselves and in others that we never knew were there!

A case in point: approximately three years ago, the word went out across the New York City schools that every educator was to assess learners not just with the one standardized test, but with three or four approximations of that test, referred to as *predictives*, with the scores from those predictives being sent home to care-givers. The intent behind this announcement was presumably a good one. Children and their advocates deserve to know how they are doing long before the all-important standardized test scores arrive.

On the other hand, hundreds of teachers and principals worried about this policy, fearing that it would make a school system that was already too driven by standardized tests become all the more so. The Teachers College Reading and Writing Project worked with several hundred of our schools and suggested an alternative. What if we developed an assessment tool that we made available to all schools at no cost that enabled teachers to conduct running records and other assessments (letter-sound knowledge, high-frequency word knowledge, level of spelling, and so on)? What if schools developed a common agreement about the levels of text difficulty that translated into a 1, a 2, a 3, or a 4 (with a 3 being standard) for children at each grade level at each of four times in the year? What if we developed letters that we could send home to parents that let parents know the level of text difficulty that was considered "standard" for that grade level at that time of the year and the level of text difficulty that the child was in fact able to handle with accuracy, fluency, and comprehension? Would that suffice?

The New York City Department of Education enthusiastically supported the idea that such an assessment system might be a choice for all schools, and now over 25% of New York City schools use this system, channeling all the students' data into a software program that the TCRWP has developed known as Assessment Pro. This allows a school to group students by need, to track progress of students in all sorts of cohort groups, to communicate levels of text difficulty across schools, and the like.

I tell you this to make two points. First, it is incumbent on all of us to find ways to live within the pressures of today without forsaking all that we believe is best for children. Some have critiqued the assessments that the TCRWP and New York City schools developed together as reductive—and of course describing a reader by identifying the level of text difficulty that child can handle is not a sufficiently rich description of that child's reading. But still, many educators in New York City schools are pleased that we can use this system rather than "predictive tests" to track readers' progress. And in fact, we will sometimes find that work that we might never have undertaken had we not been pressured to do so has unexpected benefits. There is no question but that the tremendous accumulation of data that we are compiling has catapulted my organization and the New York City schools to think about student growth (and impediments to growth) in new and generative ways.

Second, the extraordinary finding for us has been that there is alignment between the level of text difficulty a child can read and that child's scores on the standardized test. Remember— we have data from almost 60,000 children, over several years. These children are being assessed by teachers of kindergarten through eighth grade who are conducting running records, using leveled texts, within New York City's crowded classrooms. Many of these teachers have just learned how to conduct running records, and schools are still developing schoolwide consistency. Problems abound. And yet we have found extraordinary trends in the data. There is a very close correlation between the level of text difficulty that the reader seems able to handle and the reader's scores in the New York State standardized test. To illustrate the point, let's look at scores for third graders in the November assessment (and remember, the patterns you see here are replicated across our data).

*The extraordinary finding for us has been that there is alignment between the level of text difficulty a child can read and that child's scores on the standardized test.*

For third graders reading level I texts in November: 42% passed the standardized test with an average score of 646

For those reading level J texts in November: 53% passed the standardized test with an average score of 652

For students reading level K texts in November: 65% passed the standardized test with an average score of 657

For students reading level L texts in November: 72% passed the standardized test with an average score of 662

For students reading level M texts in November: 84% passed the standardized test with an average score of 671

For students reading level N texts in November: 92% passed the standardized test with an average score of 682

A larger chart, showing the average scale score in relation to the level of text difficulty that a child can read is an almost perfect rising curve.

You may wonder why I am so excited about this data. This is the reason: if it really is the case that the level of text difficulty that a student can read with 96% accuracy, fluency, and comprehension is a very strong predictor for the student's score on the state test, then instead of taking students away from reading great volumes of just-right books for the student to spend endless time in test prep, teachers would be wise to do everything possible to keep students "in books." In the schools from which we have data, students' abilities to read harder texts escalate during the months before test-prep begins to take over, and that incline stops when testing season gets into full swing. And no wonder. Too often, the all-consuming worry about the tests squeezes out time for reading. We already know that high-poverty students who do not have access to books in the summer sink three levels during the summer months. Too often, children also sink just before the standardized test because there is no time for reading just-right books. The data suggests it is a very bad trade-off to give up reading for students to do well on reading tests! It's an obvious point, but having evidence allows us to say this loud and clear.

Of course, running records are just one of many ways to assess readers and to use those assessments to inform teaching. In the assessment interludes within each of the books in this series, I write about some of the formative assessments that also inform teaching. Then, too, it is critical to say that running records not only help a teacher match readers to texts, but they also provide a glimpse into the readers' strengths and needs as well as enable a teacher to match readers to books.

Still, at the start of the year, one of the most important things that a school can do is to develop a schoolwide system for tracking readers' growth and matching them to books. After helping literally hundreds and hundreds of schools institute this system in short order, my colleagues and I have learned a host of tips that can help a school institute such a system.

# Preparing for Assessment before the Start of the Year

At the start of the school year, everything is urgent. Everything needs to be done at once. And the stakes are high because all of us know that a classroom culture is formed and identities emerge during those first weeks of the school year and that these developments set the stage for the entire year to come. The effort to assess each child carefully and to create impeccable records could easily consume the majority of a teacher's time and energy at the start of the year, and the problem is that this is also the time when the teacher needs to be establishing a productive work environment in the classroom, developing individual relationships with children, creating a culture of excellence even in places where that has not been the norm, and launching the learning life of the community. It helps, then, to prepare as much as possible for assessment before the children walk into our classrooms.

## Adopt a Schoolwide System for Leveling Books

The job of assessing readers and matching them to books is made immeasurably easier if there are systems in place throughout the school to support this. First, this means that classrooms throughout the school need a shared system for leveling books (as well as for assessing readers). Most schools that work with *Units of Study* in a reading workshop will probably adopt the Fountas and Pinnell system for leveling books, assigning books to levels of difficulty ranging from A to Z, although there are other good alternatives. Most educational publishers and distributors sell books that have been preleveled, although not all leveling is equally valid. Schools electing the Fountas and Pinnell system can use *Leveled Books K–8: Matching Texts to Readers for Effective Teaching* (2006) and the Fountas and Pinnell website, www.fountasandpinnellleveledbooks.com, as resources. Only books listed in these resources have been leveled by Irene Fountas, Gay Su Pinnell, and their trained teams of levelers. The first step in leveling a book is simply to look up a title to determine its level within the system; once a school has researched levels for many books, teachers can level other books by making best guesses, saying, "This book is a lot like others in this level." All efforts to level are fallible, and any level should be adjusted if, when children read the book, there is evidence that several readers who can read many, many books at this level with ease run into difficulty with this particular title.

In many schools, the classroom libraries need attention. Books in those classroom libraries are often wildly mislabeled. It is important for teachers (and/or for teachers and kids) to look across the books bearing a certain label—say, level S books—and make sure these texts all feel as if they are in the same ballpark of text difficulty. When books appear to have been leveled incorrectly, a system should be in place so that someone does the clerical work of finding that title on the Fountas and Pinnell website to correct the error. Locating a book's level of text difficulty is not rocket science; parent volunteers, teacher-aides, high school and college interns, publishers, and even kids themselves (after school) can be recruited to help with the clerical work of researching a book's level in the official Fountas and Pinnell resources or whatever other source you have chosen and affixing a dot with that level to the spine of a book. Many schools level approximately 60% of the classroom library, showing children how they can use the template of those levels to help them make appropriate book choices among books that have not been leveled.

## Adopt a Schoolwide System for Assessing Readers

You and your colleagues will need a shared system for assessing readers to match them to book levels. Again, Fountas and Pinnell and the DRA each have assessment tools in place that can help with this, as does the Teachers College Reading and Writing Project website. All three of these systems essentially aim to accomplish the same task. If texts have been leveled, A–Z (or 1–40), then the assessment tool essentially extracts snippets of those leveled texts, putting them onto forms so that a child can hold one form and the teacher another. The teacher's form needs to be written in such a manner that the teacher can record on it exactly what the child does when he or she reads the passage, allowing the teachers to later reconstruct the child's reading of the passage to ascertain if a text at this level of text difficulty represents the child's just-right level and to begin to develop some tentative theories about what it is that falls apart for the child at levels that are a bit too hard. The records of what the child does as he or she reads are called "running records," a term developed by Marie Clay, the founder of Reading Recovery. Clay has a short, accessible book on this topic, *Running Records for Classroom Teachers* (2000), and I suggest that people learn to conduct running records from the master by referring to this book. For now, my point is that the school will want to adopt an assessment tool that is shared among teachers at all grade levels because it is important that one teacher's assessments

are aligned with another's. It is hard on children and on their parents if one year the child is reading level R books, and the next year the child is directed to level N books!

You may ask, "Which assessment tool is best?" Frankly, it probably does not matter all that much which tool you select. The one on the Teachers College Reading and Writing Project's website can be downloaded and used without cost, and it is probably the most streamlined, time-efficient tool. Thousands of schools use the TCRWP assessment system and appreciate it. There are some downsides to it. First, the school system itself needs to do the duplicating work required so that teachers have the forms they need, in the binders that will keep the forms organized. This is still considerably less expensive than purchasing an assessment tool ready made from a publisher, but it is not free, nor is it effort-less. Then, too, the tool itself is made better because people using it are encour-aged to let the Teachers College Reading and Writing Project know if a question seems misleading or a selection seems too hard or too easy. This has led the tool to be refined over the years, drawing on wisdom from the field. On the other hand, this means the tool will be refined again, with slight adjustments being made in the spring of each year, creating up-keeping work for schools using the tool. Also, the fact that this is the most streamlined of the tools means that some hard decisions were made to postpone some aspects of this assessment for the sake of efficiency. I encourage school systems to research the DRA (Developmental Reading Assessment) and the Fountas and Pinnell models as alternatives.

## Engage in Conversations About the Use of the Assessment System and Running Records

I caution you to remember that selecting a schoolwide tool for assessing readers will not mean that your school community's assessments are in alignment. Instead, this requires shared conversations about assessments. You'll want to bring a child into a faculty meeting, to ask all the teachers in the school to record running records of the child's reading while one teacher works with this child in a fishbowl situation. The important part of this is that you'll want each teacher to analyze the running records separately, and then you'll want teachers to align their methods of doing this. You'll discover dramatic differences in judgment, and you'll need to come to a place of consensus. Don't rely simply on your personal preferences when doing this. Marie Clay herself has given guidance about issues such as, "If a child miscues on a proper name repeatedly, it is recorded as an error only once. But if a child miscues on the same regular word repeatedly (*look* for *like*), each miscue is counted as a new error," and "If the child mispronounces a multisyllable word but seems to know what the word means, is that counted as an error?" or "If this is an English language learner and the child doesn't use inflected endings when speaking English and he deletes those from a few words as he reads them aloud, do each of these instances count as an error?" So yes, absolutely refer to the source in response to questions such as these, but more than that, you and your colleagues will want to establish shared standards. Think not only about how to synchronize your judgments as to whether a text is too hard, but also think more specifically about what constitutes a just-right retelling or an acceptable answer to recall questions.

You will also want to establish shared protocols for conducting the assessments. For example, many teachers will hear a child reading an assessment passage and determine that the child's accuracy was 96% and that comprehension checks determine that this level text is just right for the child, and then declare the job of assessment completed. The problem is that the child might well have been able to read texts at several more challenging levels, so finding a text that appears just right can only be the first step. The next step is to continue assessing until a text is found to be too hard, so that the child's ceiling is established. A ceiling is necessary to determine the highest level of text the child can read with proficiency. More than this, until the child's running records contain a fair number of miscues, the teacher cannot analyze those miscues to understand what falls apart first for this reader when he is pushed to read at frustration level. For the teacher to help the child progress so that eventually he can handle texts that are, for now, just beyond his reach, it is important for the teacher to see which sources of information the reader continues to rely upon, and which he ignores, when the texts become too hard. That is, when a text is considerably difficult for the reader, does he stop thinking about what might make sense, stop relying on meaning, and zoom in just on phonics? Or does the child ignore what is actually written on the page and start fabricating the text, disconnected from the printed page, based on whatever comes to his mind? Until a teacher has collected running records of the child's work with a too-hard text, there is no possibility of analyzing patterns in that reader's miscues.

*Until a teacher has collected running records of the child's work with a too-hard text, there is no possibility of analyzing patterns in that reader's miscues.*

Your school will also want to develop some shared ways of actually getting through all these assessments. I've written about some of the ways to streamline running records in the conferring and small-group write-ups within the sessions, but for now let me say that while you assess your individuals, the whole of the class will meanwhile be reading books that you ascertain from whatever data you have—last year's book levels, test score levels—and your own artful judgment to be in the ballpark for particular readers. From a distance, you can scan the scene as readers read these leveled books, and you can look for signs of engagement or disengagement that will let you know whether the book a child is holding is at least roughly appropriate for that child. If a child has been reading *Sarah, Plain and Tall* with engagement in class, then you'll use your knowledge of that book to gauge that you might begin your running records at level R or S.

It is important that the school institutes systems for recording and storing running records. Teachers will give very informal running records on-the-run constantly, using any scrap of paper to record words correct and miscues, but at regular intervals across the year (at least at four predetermined times a year, and more for at-risk readers) the school will presumably expect each classroom teacher to record a more official sort of running record. The written record of those running records needs to be sufficient so that others can use the notations to reconstruct exactly what the reader did as she read. This way, people can retrieve the running records from an earlier time and, if necessary, reconsider the conclusions that were drawn based on those running records. For example, imagine that the fourth-grade teacher feels that one of her readers is reading six levels below the level at which she was last assessed. The teacher will want to know whether the child's reading abilities actually plummeted or whether her gauge for analyzing running records differs from that used at the end of the preceding year. If the running records were taken in such a way that the child's reading can be reconstructed, then this can be informative. This means not only that teachers adopt the notation system developed by Marie Clay, but also that each reader's answer to each question is recorded. It is not enough for the assessing teacher to deem a child's answer to be acceptable and to record just a check mark. Experience shows that the only way for a school to actually develop this sort of shared practices is for teachers to share their actual running records, not just the scores gleaned from those records. How important it is for principals to eyeball the running records that teachers collect, for teachers across a grade level to try reconstructing what children did during reading by viewing each other's records. This is time-consuming but worth every minute it requires. Once the school develops common standards for recording and analyzing running records, then this means that the records collected by one educator or another can all be compiled and shared, with the records for each child kept in that child's cumulative folder, available for specialists and caregivers to study. More than this, it means that children and caregivers are less apt to feel jerked about, willy-nilly, and more apt to feel as if progress is tracked in a seamless and professional fashion.

I need to insert an important cautionary word. When data about students' progress along a gradient of text difficulty is used as a way for educators to hold ourselves and each other accountable for teaching well, then it is not surprising that people at every level in this enterprise can feel pressured to inflate children's levels of just-right text difficulty. After all, parents respond warmly to teachers (and principals) who send home good news. It takes strength of character for a teacher to be willing to send home disappointing scores, especially to a hyper-engaged parent. Chances are good that the disappointed parent will be at our doorstep the next day, bearing recriminations. Then, too, even well-intended principals can inadvertently signal to teachers that if their children's scores are not strong, this means the teacher is at fault. I've heard of principals making announcements that every child is to be reassessed and to move up a level four times a year. These demands don't come from a bad place—the principal is right to be chomping at the bit—but the effect can be extremely troublesome because the entire data-collection enterprise can be compromised if pressure is great enough that teachers tinker with and fabricate scores. None of the charts or teaching plans or report cards or efforts to influence homework will be helpful in the least if the running records were tampered with from the start. There is an important saying: garbage in, garbage out.

Assuming, though, that teachers are aiming to collect accurate records of children's growth, it will then be important that a composite listing of each child's reading levels across time be collected, graphed, and examined by the classroom teacher and also, from time to time, by someone whose job it is to help maintain the assessment system for the school. Unless one person has the job of looking across the running records that individual teachers collect, it is unlikely that these will, in fact, be consistent from classroom to classroom. Once a consistent system is in place, the system is not all that difficult to maintain, but establishing this in the first place takes vigilance.

## When Implementing System-Wide Assessments, There Are Ways to Seize the Opportunities and Avoid the Pitfalls

As I described earlier, several years ago, a few hundred New York City schools, and many Teachers College Reading and Writing Project schools in the surrounding suburbs and across the country, adopted the Teachers College Reading and Writing Project's reading assessment tool, bringing this assessment schoolwide and district-wide. Because all these schools work within a shared, data-based system of formative assessments, we have been given an invaluable window into the opportunities and challenges a district is apt to encounter when it strives to implement system-wide assessment practices, and to do so in ways that lift the level of instruction.

These schools all decided to use Fountas and Pinnell book levels to level at least 60% of the books in classroom libraries and then used the leveled passages available on our website (at no cost) to ascertain each child's just-right level, doing these assessments at least four times a year. Again, as I mentioned earlier, the schools and the Teachers College Reading and Writing Project drew on state standards and on a knowledge of high-stakes tests to establish and agree upon a common scale for interpreting text levels, deciding which text levels were far below standards, approaching standards, at standards, or above standards for each grade level at each assessment period. That is, if a third grader in November is reading texts at level J or below, that child's reading is far below standards (1); if the student is reading K/L books at that time, the reader is approaching grade-level standards (2); if reading M/N/O, this is at standards (3); if P or above, this is above standards (4). Letters were written that teachers could use to inform parents about expectations and their child's progress in relation to those expectations, and suggestions (including book lists) were also sent home for ways caregivers could support a child's reading development. (These are also available on the CD-ROM.)

Once these schools had assessed all their children and begun informing parents of these assessments and of the relationship between the assessments and grade-specific expectations, it became very clear that it is best if teachers can work together for at least half a year and ideally longer, aligning their assessments to each other's, before letters begin going home to parents, saying, "Your child is in third grade. He should, at this point in the year, be reading texts that are characterized as level M/N/O in text difficulty, and he is, in fact, reading level…." Once these letters are sent home, all of a sudden the human cost for misalignment between one teacher and another or one grade level and another becomes especially great, with parents saying, "How is it possible that last year my son was told he can read level S, and this year he is being told he can only read…?" The best way to prevent this is for the school to embrace the learning that can result if every educator in the school works zealously, shoulder to shoulder with others, to develop shared ways of thinking about questions such as "How good is good enough?" and "What sorts of records can really allow us to capture what a child did as he or she read the text, in ways that will allow for shared analysis of that fleeting work?" and "What does it mean for a book to be well matched to a child?"

For teachers to develop assessment systems that are aligned, it is crucial for people to be willing to engage in hard conversations. If the fifth-grade teacher received records indicating that in fourth grade Randall read at level T, and the teacher thinks that at the start of fifth grade he instead is reading at level M (some summer regression is expected but not that much!), then this requires a conversation. The fifth-grade teacher in this instance needs to talk with her colleague, saying, "I know you thought Randall was reading at level T, but I don't know how you came to that conclusion because I'm assessing him as a level M." And if the fifth-grade teacher sees a pattern, with a number of kids from that one fourth-grade class entering fifth grade with what seems to the teacher to be exaggerated levels, there needs to be a way for some other professional to help adjudicate this and provide the extra professional development or extra collaborative conversations that are called for in order for children to progress more seamlessly from one year to another. We don't do kids any favors if, in the name of collegiality, we circumvent the hard conversations that are necessary.

*For teachers to develop assessment systems that are aligned, it is crucial for people to be willing to engage in hard conversations.*

One actually needn't wait for students to pass from one grade to another before spotting telltale signs that suggest a particular teacher might need help reading the data available in running records. A system of checks and balances is readily available to us all. That is—if a student's scores on last year's standardized reading test were extremely low and yet the child has been assessed as able to read texts that are at or above standards for her grade level, then this disparity should function as a blinking yellow light, signaling, "Proceed with care" and "Caution." Chances are good that the child is actually not able to read those challenging texts.

The good news is that once a school truly has shared systems for assessing readers and matching books to children, then all of a sudden the system itself can enable teachers in ways that make a world of difference. It goes without saying that there needs to be a schoolwide system for teachers to communicate to each other the levels of text difficulty at which each child can read. This means that when a teacher receives her roster for an incoming class, the teacher should receive the text levels at which each child can read and a record, too, of each child's progress over the past few years. For example, there may be eight readers in an incoming fourth-grade class that at the end of third grade were still reading level M books. The incoming teacher will absolutely want to look backward and see each of those readers' trajectory of levels. Some of those readers may have been stuck at level M since the end of second grade, when they were doing just fine, and the problem is that they have not progressed since then. Some of them may have entered the school just a year ago, and may actually have moved steadily up for the whole second half of last year, making fairly dramatic progress. These readers may not have had access to books that were matched to them until arriving at this school, and may be on a good course toward catching up. Of course, all this means that when one teacher communicates a child's reading levels with the next-year's teacher, it is important that not just the final, end-of-the-year levels be communicated, but also, the child's progress across the previous year(s).

There are ways to do this that are especially supportive. For example, in many schools, every classroom teacher spends time during the last week of school working with every child to develop that child's start-of-the-year book baggie. The classroom teacher who knows the child well works with him, filling the baggy with an old favorite or two and with a whole batch of books that promise to be just-right or easy (remembering that for children who do not read during the summer, there is always a notable slide backward) and, best of all, that promise to be as enticing as possible. That teacher—from the previous year—can even coach children to plan their progress through one or two of the selected books, using Post-its to mark Day 1's reading and Day 2's, using page-number patterns from the year that is ending to project progress through books in the year that is approaching. This system allows a teacher in September, who is trying to assess her incoming class, to watch those kids working with books that her colleague believed would be just right for each of those children (allowing that incoming teacher to align herself with the previous teacher's judgments) and meanwhile allows the teacher's running records to be informed by informal observations of children reading books that at least *someone* judged to be roughly just right for them. More important, it means that every child is able to get started from Day 1, reading books that have been carefully selected by the child and a teacher who knows the child well.

In schools that have developed a schoolwide system for assessing readers, professionals other than the classroom teacher can participate in the work of conducting running records and matching readers to books. Many schools hire the reading specialist or others who have special training in reading assessment to work with children during summer school or during the final two weeks of summer, conducting assessments and matching books to children. Some schools ask that these knowledgeable professionals conduct all the assessments for children who are especially at-risk, thereby making it especially likely that these youngsters' time in school will be maximized, with every moment spent doing work that has been tailored to those children. Sometimes schools ask that summer assessments be given to a random sampling of children from every classroom, because having these previously assessed children dotting a teacher's roster provides another way for classroom teachers to align their assessments with a schoolwide standard. In this situation, the teacher will have standards of measurement right there before her eyes. She can think to herself, "If Susie has been assessed as someone who can handle R books, then Deidre can't be an R as well, because her reading is considerably less strong." Even if a school is not able to use professionals to help during the summer, it is likely that at the very start of the year, some of the specialist teachers will not yet have their full caseload in place. Those teachers, then, can be brought into the work of assessing readers.

## Assessment Throughout this Series

As you read through this series, you'll encounter small "chapters" about the assessment practices you're likely to need at each stage of the curriculum. You may want to read or skim through these sections before you begin your year, so that you'll have an awareness of what is, and could be, on the horizon.

# CHAPTER FIVE

# Minilessons: The Methods that Undergird Explicit Instruction

When I was a brand-new teacher, my colleagues and I had a time in our day that we referred to as DEAR time—Drop Everything And Read. For fifteen minutes, the kids would all get out books and settle down to read, read, read. There was an emphasis on us, as teachers, reading during this time, too, so I'd settle down alongside the kids and sink into my novel. It was a peaceful time, a lovely interlude in the midst of a busy day. The room had a *Kumbaya* feeling to it.

Sometimes I try to explain the reading workshop to a teacher from my generation and her eyes will light up and she'll say, "Oh! I got it! So it's sort of like DEAR time, is that it?"

That's a sign to me that I have a lot more explaining to do. There are important differences between the DEAR times of yesteryear and today's reading workshop. And the biggest difference is that although it is crucial that we, as teachers, live in our classroom as richly literate adults, carrying our books and our love of reading with us, we've come to realize that youngsters need not only large stretches of time to read books of their own choice but also explicit direct instruction in the skills, strategies, and habits of proficient readers. That instruction happens during every minute of the reading workshop, from the first to the last minute, but it starts with the minilesson. So the reading workshop is not a time when the teacher can snuggle down with a book—far from it. This is the most intensive instructional time of our day.

That instruction starts with a minilesson. Just as the art instructor pulls students together to learn a new glaze or a new way to mix paints, just as the football coach and his team huddle over a new play, just as a writing workshop teacher convenes kids to show them techniques for exploring different leads in a fiction story, so, too, the teacher of reading pulls children together for a minilesson that opens the day's reading workshop and powers the curriculum.

# The Rituals and Procedures of a Minilesson

Minilessons are meant as intervals for explicit, brief instruction in skills and strategies that then become part of a reader's ongoing repertoire, to be drawn upon as needed. That is, every day in a reading workshop, as in a writing workshop, the teacher gathers the learners and says, "I've been thinking about the work you are doing, and I want to give you just one tip, one technique that I think will help with challenges some of you are having." Then the teacher demonstrates the new technique and helps students get a bit of assisted practice trying the technique in miniature ways, all within a ten-minute minilesson. After this, the teacher sends learners off to continue their important work, reminding them that they can draw on the strategy they learned that day as well as those they've learned on previous days.

I've often said that the most important words of a minilessons are the final ones: "Off you go." When minilessons are over and teachers say, "Off you go," it is important in any workshop that the kids know how to do just that. They need to know that after the minilesson is over, they can resume the important work they were doing the day before, drawing on all they have learned all year long and especially over the recent weeks.

Because children are gathering in and dispersing from the meeting area at the start of every day's reading workshop (and than again at the start of every day's writing workshop), most teachers that I know well have found it worthwhile to take a bit of time at the start of the year to make sure that children can move to and from the meeting area efficiently. Teachers literally teach children to walk directly from their work spots to the meeting area, sitting themselves down in their assigned spot, sitting on their bottoms instead of kneeling in ways that block other children's view. In some classrooms, teachers always ask children to bring the same materials to each day's workshop so that children are sure to have whatever they need on hand. In other classrooms, when teachers say, "Let's gather for our reading minilesson," the teacher is apt to gesture toward the white board that lists that day's materials. No one way of managing a reading workshop is more correct than another, but it is important for teachers to take seriously the challenge of managing workshop instruction, bearing in mind that

> *I've often said that the most important words of a minilessons are the final ones: "Off you go."*

this method of teaching calls for learners to do more self-management than some children have been asked to do before. I write in some detail about the management of a writing workshop in *A Guide to the Writing Workshop*, and the management systems you develop to support a productive writing workshop will transfer perfectly into the reading workshop as well.

Usually children sit in the meeting area alongside a long-term partner, clustered as close to the teacher as possible. This is not usually a time for children to sit in a circle, because conversations among the whole class are minimal. This is time instead for the teacher to teach as efficiently and explicitly as possible. So most teachers decide to ask their children to sit alongside a partner, at the teacher's feet, facing the teacher. Partners need to be able to read the same books. It is wonderful when a classroom has two copies of most books so partnerships can read the same book in synchrony with each other, but this requires the classroom to have a great many more books than would be necessary if readers were instead generally in swap-book partnerships, so the latter is more common. Because they swap books and read each other's books, just not at the same time, children can talk about the specifics of a book. However, it is easier to talk about the same book, so I strongly recommend that struggling readers be in same-book partnerships whenever possible. This allows the time a teacher spends working with one reader to do double duty, helping the other reader as well.

Although the teachers with whom I teach often worry over the *content* of their minilessons, the truth is that if you are teaching and learning alongside a classroom full of kids and engaged in an intense read-aloud book, you'll soon find that your mind will brim with ideas for minilessons. The biggest challenge is learning not *the content* of minilessons but rather the *methods*. And while the content of minilessons changes from day to day, the architecture of minilessons remains largely the same, and it remains consistent whether you are teaching writing or reading. The architecture of a minilesson (as we have taken to calling the design of a minilesson) is easy to learn and provides enduring support across any minilesson you might ever write.

Minilessons are only ten minutes long, yet within those fleeting minutes there are four component parts. The minilesson that follows illustrates the major components of most minilessons.

# An Example of a Minilesson

This particular lesson was written by Hareem Khan, one of the coauthors of *Constructing Curriculum: Alternate Units of Study*, and it is part of her unit. For now, I've taken it from its place and set it before us to that we can glimpse a reading minilesson, in its entirety, before considering its component parts.

## Connection

"When we were little, my sister always drove me crazy with the way she ate cereal. She'd eat one cornflake at a time. Or scoop up one, single, measly Cheerio with her spoon at a time. 'You're driving me nuts,' I'd say. 'You'll never finish the entire bowl in one sitting that way!' I love cereal; I respect it. To me, the way she ate cereal was an insult to the cereal. I'd say, 'How can you know the true taste of cereal till you take a proper mouthful!'

"Of course, now I realize my sister ate her cereal that way to get me all worked up. This was something *she* could control, and she'd flaunt that control in front of me. Little sisters can be like that, right?

"But sometimes I see people reading their books the way my sister ate her cereal. One word at a time. 'How can you know the real taste of the story if you don't eat proper mouthfuls of words?' I want to say. Or 'You'll never finish a big chunk of your book in one sitting if you read it one word at a time.'"

### Teaching Point

"Today, readers, I want to teach you that we read faster, longer, and stronger by reading groups of words at a time. When we set our goals to make this year the best reading year ever and to read faster, longer, stronger, we *didn't* mean we'd read one word, the next word, and the next word and do *that* kind of reading faster. To make meaning from the text, we read a group of words, then another group of words, and then another group of words."

## Teaching

"Readers, when we're really into a story, we don't read a word at a time. We don't pause after each word. If we pause at all, we do so after reading a whole group of words that makes sense. I'm going to show you how.

"Here are two sentences from page 50 of *Fantastic Mr. Fox*."

Mr. Fox ginned slyly, showing sharp white teeth. "If I am not mistaken, my dear Badger," he said, "we are now underneath the farm which belongs to that nasty little potbellied dwarf, Bunce."

"Let me tell you, first, how *not* to read these sentences."

Mr. Fox… grinned… slyly,… showing… sharp… white… teeth. 'If I am… not… mistaken, my… dear… Badger,' he… said, 'we… are now… underneath… the farm…'

"Readers, could you see how the way I just read that made it feel like I was eating one or two cheerios at a time? Wasn't it frustrating? Didn't you feel like saying, 'I need to hear not just *one* word, *one* word, *one* word but one *mouthful* of words, another *mouthful* of words if I'm going to understand!' This is because reading is like talking. We don't pause after every word we utter. We only pause after we've said a *group* of words that makes sense.

"Let me read the two sentences again, and this time watch out for the pauses. Note that I don't pause after every word. I only pause after a group of words that makes sense."

Mr. Fox ginned slyly,… showing sharp white teeth…. If I am not mistaken… my dear Badger,… he said,… we are now underneath the farm… which belongs to that nasty little potbellied dwarf,… Bunce.

"Did you see how I waited for a complete thought before I paused? I still paused often because it was a pretty long sentence. In some shorter sentences, I wouldn't pause at all. But in any case, I wait for a group of words to make sense before pausing so that I can reach across the group of words to grab meaning. It's almost like each word group is a complete thought. You see how meaning is in word groups, not in individual words?"

## Active Involvement

"Right now, find a passage you like—an important one, maybe one where there's some story tension. Signal to me when you've found the passage." I waited until many had signaled. "Try reading this passage to your partner, taking care to pause only at a spot where a thought has been completed. Try to make your reading smooth, like the read-aloud, so that your partner follows the meaning of the story clearly—so that your partner actually begins to have a mental movie from just hearing you.

"Here's a tip: you'll want to think about who is talking, too, even if the author doesn't tell you. You'll want to think about the character's feelings. Try reading the passage, then talk about the changing feelings of it, and then reread it to show those feelings."

## Link

"So today, you will continue to work on reading faster, stronger, longer. But your reading is not like this: 'Mr…. Fox… grinned… slyly… showing… sharp… white… teeth.' Instead, your reading is like this: 'Mr. Fox grinned slyly, showing sharp white teeth.' As you continue reading today, try to make the voice in your head work so you aren't just seeing the story. You are also learning the story."

# Components of a Minilesson

## The Connection

During the first two or three minutes of a minilesson, I often try to connect the content of today's teaching with the work the class has been doing so that this new bit of instruction does not come out of thin air but is instead contextualized, nestled into the prior work the class has been doing. Recalling what children have already been learning also reminds children of the whole repertoire of strategies that they've learned, so that at the end of this upcoming minilesson, children leave not with one single strategy in hand, but rather with an expanded repertoire at the ready.

Although minilessons are a form of whole-class instruction, when taught well, they have an intimacy and immediacy, and that tone is established in the connection. A connection might open like this:

- "Come close; I've been thinking and thinking about what the one most important tip I can give you might be, and it is this."

- "Readers, can I tell you a secret? I want to let you in on something that I do, something I haven't really told too many people about."

- "Last night, I couldn't sleep. I kept thinking about your work and thinking, thinking, thinking about what I could say today that might help. Suddenly, in the middle of the night, an idea came to me. I got out of bed and wrote it on a Post-it. You ready to hear my idea? This is it."

- "Last night, I was telling my family all about the cool stuff you've been doing. I told them…. Then as we talked about you, my sister said, 'Hey, Lucy, why don't you show them….'"

In these and other ways, I try to help children know that the teaching they're about to receive is important.

One goal of the connection is to make it likely that children connect with our words, our message. That is no small challenge! Over the years, I've developed a few techniques that I tend to rely upon.

*In the connection, I sometimes share tiny excerpts of student work.*
I'm always playing Johnny Appleseed as I teach, finding one youngster who does something that can nourish other readers' imaginations of what's possible. But I also keep a file of work from previous years and, frankly, from other people's classes. Kids are interested in other kids even if I need to preface my story by saying, "I'm going to tell you about something that one of last year's readers did." I save work that is funny, especially, and that represents problems many people encounter. Once the author of the problematic work is no longer in the school, I find it's quite effective to show children some of the work another child did that might be representative of work others are doing, allowing me to address some of the problems without making any of the students feel bad.

*In the connection, I zoom in on a very few tiny specifics, and I use the actual words someone said.*
Hareem didn't say that her sister ate tiny bites. She was more detailed. She ate one cornflake at a time. In one minilesson, I told children that the day before, Joel had given me a lecture on penguins. "Did you know that all the boys are called king penguins," he said. "All you gotta do is be a boy, and you're called King Penguin." I knew that detail would connect with listeners because it is a fascinating bit of penguin trivia, and also because I told the story using direct address. Chances are good I did not actually remember the exact words that Joel said to me, but when direct address is used to show characters interacting, the text tends to be livelier. This may seem unimportant, but actually minilessons are much better if we tell stories fairly well, and including the actual words that a person said and thought usually ramps up the liveliness of a minilesson in dramatic ways.

*In the connection, I often tell a story that will seem to the kids to have nothing to do with reading, but which, in the end, will become a metaphor for whatever I want to say.*

This was the case for Hareem's story of her little sister's infuriating eating habits. One of the minilessons in historical fiction begins with the story of how that day, when I'd come as a visitor to the children's school, I first met a five-year-old from my neighborhood. She gave me a tour of the school, showing me the swing that she'd fallen from and the child-sized drinking fountain. At that point, the principal appeared on the scene, and she proceeded to give me her tour of the school, taking me to an entirely new set of places: the mailboxes in the front office and the book room. The children, listening, will probably be entertained because they generally like to hear little true-life vignettes, but they'll think the story is unrelated to reading until suddenly, in the teaching point, I make explicit the fact that we can see a place through one set of eyes and see one thing, and through another set of eyes see something entirely different. This, of course, leads right into the fact that when reading stories, it is helpful to notice the perspective from which a story is told, and it is helpful, too, to consider how the story would be different had it been told from another perspective.

*When I tell stories in the connection, whether it is a true story from my life or a story about something a student said or did, I rely on what I know about writing compelling personal narratives to make my stories engaging.*

As mentioned earlier, I know that details help, so I share the littlest details. I also know that it generally works best to tell a story bit by bit, letting it unfold chronologically. Listen, for example, to the start of this story, and you will see that I'm telling my story very much as I would write it if I was in a writing workshop, working to write personal narrative well. "Yesterday I watched a tiny ant as he made his way across my paper. To see what he'd do, I lay my pencil across his path. I thought he'd climb over it, like one of those monster tractor toys that climb up and go over a hurdle. Instead, the ant turned left, walking patiently along the length of the pencil. My pencil felt so high to the ant that he didn't even consider climbing over it." Of course, before that story is over, I'll show students that actually this story has a lot to do with reading. For now I'll let you guess that connection!

*Sometimes in the connection, I try to involve readers in an activity that quickly crystallizes a lot of what they have learned.*

I might talk about how many of us keep lists to remind us of all we intend to do, and then proceed to show children a chart of all that we've learned thus far and suggest they take a second to scan the chart and to list a couple things from it they want to put on their personal to-do list. Or I might suggest readers sit quietly for a second and think, trying to recall three new techniques they've learned to accomplish a certain job, listing them across their fingers. Then I could ask them to tell a partner what they've recalled, and meanwhile I could listen in. Afterward, I might say back a few of the things I'd heard them say. If I want to teach readers that a wise interpretation of a story takes into account the whole story, not just the ending, in the connection to that minilesson I might recall what readers aim to do when we interpret a text. Then again, if I've already taught readers that when interpreting a text, readers think, "What lessons did this character learn that might pertain also to me?" and now I am teaching a second point about interpretation, I might want to use the connection to essentially start a chart called "What Readers Do when We Interpret Texts."

## Teaching Point

The teaching point is actually part of the connection. In the teaching point, we crystallize what it is we hope to teach in that day's minilesson. I work hard to make teaching points crystal clear and, when possible, memorable and worth remembering. Listen to a few of my teaching points:

- "Today I want to teach you that every nonfiction reader reads with energy, with power. One way that nonfiction readers do that is we rev our minds up for reading. Even before we shift into 'go' and read a sentence or a paragraph, we read the title, subtitles, we look over chunks of the text, and we think, 'I think this book is mostly about…' or 'And then it will also tell….'"

- "Today I want to remind you that thoughtful readers sometimes press the pause button, lingering to ponder what we've read and to let a bigger idea begin to grow in our minds. For each reader, there will be passages in book that seem to be written in bold, parts that just call out to that reader as being important. Often these are passages that harken back to earlier sections in the book and that

seem laden with meaning, and we read those passages extra attentively, letting them nudge us to think or jot ideas."

- "I'm going to teach you that whenever a person has lots of stuff— lots of ideas about a character, lots of information on whales—it often helps to organize that stuff and to find broad ways to label the piles. When reading nonfiction, we're given a whole lot of new information. Instead of trying to memorize all that information, it helps to create larger categories to help us sort the information. Then as we read, we put new little stuff under the bigger categories."

- "Today I want to teach you that whether you are reading fiction or nonfiction, it is equally important to talk about those texts with others, saying, 'Isn't it weird how…' and 'I wonder why…' and 'Did you notice….' But I want to add one more thing. Readers read differently because we're going to be in conversations later. We read holding conversations in our minds."

As you study those examples of teaching points and the scores of others in the series, you'll no doubt see that generally an effective teaching point conveys:

- What readers often try to do—the goal

- Ways we often go about doing it—the procedure

Very often, the teaching point starts with a sentence or two about a goal that a reader might take on, and then the teaching point conveys the step-by-step procedure the reader might go through to accomplish that goal. Notice, for example, the first teaching point above starts like this: "Every nonfiction reader reads with energy." That's the goal. It's followed by the way to do this: "Even before we read a sentence, we read the titles and the subtitles, we look over the chunks of text, and we think, 'I think this book is mostly about….'" That's the strategy, told in a sequential step-by-step fashion.

I wouldn't feel as if my teaching point earned its keep if it went like this: "Today I am going to teach you how to grow theories about characters." Such a teaching point wouldn't be worth posting as a bullet on a chart or reiterating several times within the minilesson. That is, a teaching point doesn't simply name the terrain that the minilesson will cover. It actually crystallizes the most important lesson from the day.

When working with teachers who are authoring their own minilessons, I coach them that if they hear themselves saying, "Today I want you to do…," then they'll want to double-check themselves, because those aren't the words of a teaching point but of a whole-class assignment. Seymour Sarason, a scholar who has written on school change, points out that very often in schools today, people take revolutionary new ideas and stretch, chop, splice, and twist those ideas so they fit into the ongoing assumptions and norms of their teaching. It is for this reason that American schools are characterized by a constant frenzy of change and by an underlying sense that the more things change, the more they remain the same. "New math," Sarason writes, "ended up as very much like old math" (Sarason, 1996). Reading workshops can end up as very much like traditional whole-class instruction if teachers don't guard against their teaching points becoming one-day assignments. If a teacher says, "Today I want you to reread the notes you have been taking as you read your nonfiction book, dividing those notes into categories," that is a one-day assignment. Children may all jump through the hoop of the day, but it is unclear that another time, when in the same position, they'll initiate using that strategy. How different it is if you instead say this: "Today I want to teach you that whenever you are reading nonfiction, it helps if you…" rather than "Today I want you to… ?" The difference is not just a matter of words. It's a difference of intent. In a minilesson, I'm hoping to teach readers something that they can do repeatedly, perhaps today, and certainly for the rest of their lives.

## The Teaching Component

Usually when teaching reading, one or two read-aloud texts will thread through more than half of the teaching sections of our minilessons. In the units in this series, for example, *Stone Fox* threads through the first unit, *The Tiger Rising* threads through the second unit, and *Number the Stars* through the fourth unit. Each of those units has another text or two that weaves through a few minilessons—usually this is a picture book or a poem—and minilessons fairly often revisit read-alouds that are familiar to the class from earlier in the year. Also, of course, some things can be taught without requiring a text.

### Determine the content and the teaching text you'll use.

If I'm writing a unit on character and using a text like *The Tiger Rising* as the touchstone for the unit, I'll read the text, noticing the reading work I do that pertains to character, and then I'll think, "Is the work I am doing with this text universal? Do I hope that all kids will be doing variations of the same work with their texts?" So, for example, I found that when I first met Sistine, I created a

portrait of her as a feminine girl dressed in a pink dress. She was named after Michelangelo's painting, featuring angels and white puffy clouds. Only when I got a bit farther into *The Tiger Rising* did I realize that Sistine was entirely different than I'd expected; this required me to rethink the way I'd read an earlier scene involving her. After spying on myself reading this book, I then thought, "Are my students, when reading whatever they are reading, apt to do what I've done? To create impressions of their characters and then, as they read on, find that something is awry—either their image of the person is off, or the person suddenly acts out of character?" My answer to that was yes, many students would probably be required to do similar work as they read, and so I had a teaching point—in this case about ways readers revise our ideas of characters as we read—and a chunk of text to use in the teaching or active involvement component of the minilesson.

### Determine the method you'll use.

Once I have decided generally what I will teach and the text or other material into which I'll embed my teaching, I need to decide on the method I'll use to teach. As far as I can figure out, there are only four main methods available to any of us. We can teach people how to do something in the following ways:

- Demonstration
- Guided practice
- Explicitly telling and showing an example
- Inquiry

To help teachers grasp what it means to teach using those four methods, I often ask them to get into pairs, and I then ask one teacher to teach the other how to put on shoes, and to do this bit of instruction using a specific teaching method. (I don't discuss what those methods might be just yet. I simply suggest teachers do this teaching using a specific teaching method.)

After two minutes, I stop the group and suggest that now the second teacher in each partnership teach the first how to put on shoes, only this time I ask the teacher to use a different teaching method. We continue this until people have had four opportunities to teach the one lesson—how to put on your shoes—and then I ask teachers to list the methods they have used. As mentioned earlier, I have come to believe we have only four options. One person may name one of those options differently than another person does, but the method would be the same.

### Demonstration

I think the most common way to teach someone how to put on ones shoes is to begin by first taking off a shoe and proceeding to narrate the step-by-step process of putting the shoe on. That's the method of demonstration. The teacher may have done the work previously—I may already have had both my shoes tied securely to my feet—but the teacher undoes that work (usually behind the scenes) so as to be able to redo the work publicly, this time naming the steps taken and tucking in little pointers. ("Sometimes you need to wiggle your foot from right to left a bit to get it actually into the shoe. Don't step down too hard on the heel of your shoe or it might fold in on you.")

### Guided Practice

Second, we can teach in a way that walks our students through the process. *Our* shoes can stay securely on our feet, and our attention can shift to the learner who needs to start, shoeless. "Okay," we say. "Start by pointing your toe." Then we wait for the sock-footed learner to do that action. "That's it. Now stick that pointed toe right into the shoe, all the way to the far end of it." That's guided practice.

### Explain and Give an Example

We could, instead, give a little lecture, complete with illustrations, to talk through the process of foot insertion into shoe. We could even use PowerPoint to make a chart listing the four stages of foot insertion, with pictures to illustrate each stage. That's the method I call explicitly telling and showing an example.

### Inquiry

Then again, we can simply say, "How do you think I got this shoe on my foot? Here's a shoe, here's a foot. Can you figure it out?" And that's inquiry.

### Plan the teaching.

Each of those methods can be used to teach readers within a minilesson. Let's go back to my example of the time when I created an image of Sistine that needed to be revised in light of further reading. Let's say this is the wording of my teaching point:

> "Readers, today I want to teach you that after you've made a theory of a character, then you read on, and as you learn more stuff about the character you say, 'Yep, I was right,' or 'Huh? That makes no sense.' When you have a theory of your character but he or she doesn't act according to your theory, you can rethink, asking, 'Might I need to revise my theory?'"

To plan how the teaching component will go, it helps to remember that 90% of our reading and writing minilessons rely upon demonstration. To devise a minilesson that uses the method of demonstrations, it's important to guard against simply telling people what you already did. Such a summary might start like this:

> "Readers, I want to tell you about how yesterday, when I was reading this book, I realized I'd created an image of Sistine that actually wasn't borne out as I continued reading…."

That's not teaching by demonstration. That's teaching by leaving your shoe on and simply looking back to explain (and perhaps showing an example). No, if I want to demonstrate, the first thing I need to do is to take off my shoe, to undo the reading work I have already done so that I can "put my shoe on" (that is, read the passage) in front of the learners.

Before proceeding, then let me share a few other tips.

***Kids will learn more if I don't try to demonstrate the entire process of reading the book or of thinking about a character, but instead home in on the specific kind of thinking I'm trying to teach today.***

I do not want to show readers how I grow a theory about Sistine, read with the theory in hand, and revise the theory all in one minilesson. So to demonstrate only the new part of my thinking, I already need to have this theory about Sistine that I know will prove erroneous. So we are getting closer to writing an effective minilesson. The teaching part could go like this:

> "Readers, you'll remember that yesterday we talked a bit about Sistine and how we could really picture her. I know for myself, I picture her with that frilly pink dress, and her name—Sistine—which reminds me of the angels in the painting for which she is named. Let me read on."

Then, of course, as I read on I could come to a place in the book which defies my image of Sistine.

***Kids will learn more if they see themselves doing what I'm trying to do.***

Brian Cambourne, the great Australian educator, once told me that people fly hang gliders on the field outside his office. On many days, he can look out his office window and see the people strapping themselves into harnesses and running pell-mell toward a cliff, whereupon they throw themselves over the cliff into the air. Brian pointed out that although he has watched this perhaps several hundred times, those hang gliders aren't functioning as mentors to him because he does not watch them as one would watch a mentor. He has absolutely no intention of ever strapping those machines onto his back and racing toward the cliff, so he does not vicariously experience what those hang gliding people are doing, nor does he learn from their actions.

This story hit home for me, and I am very careful to try to make it as likely as possible that when I do something in front of kids—performing, if you will—I try to get the kids to join me in the work so that they're trying to do the same thing, and watching me make moves that either match theirs or that show them what they could do. So in this instance, I'd say to the kids,

> "Readers, let's remember for a second what we know about Sistine. (I leave a space for them to think.) Hmm. I'm thinking about that pink dress, her name—Sistine—like the painting with the angels on it. I'm trying to crystallize my sense of what she's like. Umm, to me, she seems like a girly girl type, sort of feminine. Let's read on with that imagine in mind, picturing what else she's doing."

I'm hoping that you see that I've gotten the kids to join me in imagining Sistine in one way, and of course as I read aloud, I'll want them to join me in saying, "Huh?" when she acts in ways that defy our image of her. Then I'll go ahead and show readers how I handle moments of discordance.

*Kids will learn more if we are explicit with them about what we hope they notice and what they'll be asked to do with what they notice.*

Watch how I overlay the little demonstration written above with some explicit framing moves:

> "Readers, I want to remind you that it helps to pause as we're reading to think, 'What do we know about the character?' We already read a bit about Sistine. Let's remember for a second what we know about Sistine. Hmm, I'm thinking about that pink dress, her name—Sistine—like the painting with the angels on it. I'm trying to crystallize my sense of what she's like. Usually I find the author tells me details, but I need to come up with words for what the person's like. To me, she seems like a girly girl type, sort of feminine. Let's read on with that imagine in mind, picturing what else she's doing. Watch how I keep this picture in my mind, and as I read on, I say, 'Yep, this fits,' or I say, 'Huh? This does not fit one bit!' Let's see if our image of Sistine holds true."

Of course, later in this bit of teaching, I'll show children that when the character acts in ways that are totally surprising, I need to either change my image of the character or to realize that she's changing.

Although I've shown how you devise the teaching component of a minilesson using the teaching method of demonstration, I could have used different teaching methods, and as you read and use the series, you'll find minilessons that use those other methods.

## The Active Involvement Component

This is the time when you say to your kids, "Now you try it," and you provide them with just a little bit of guided practice. In the minilesson about characters sometimes acting out of character, I searched the book to see if there was a second example of a character who could easily be pegged as one way and who then acted out of character. Fortunately, the protagonist of the story, Rob, introduces himself to readers as a fairly timid character, one who cannot stand up for himself, but we no sooner crystallize this impression than Rob acts in ways that belie our expectations. This makes it very easy to create an active involvement section that is very similar to the teaching section, only now the kids will do 95% of the work.

You'd set them up to do this work by saying something like, "Let's think a bit about Rob. Yesterday we talked about how Rob is sort of a timid kid, right? Remember how he let the bullies pick him up and he didn't protest? So let's do what readers do, and carry our theory of Rob with us, and let's read on. Remember, we're going to see if we find more stuff that helps us add onto our theory of Rob—or whether we instead end up saying, 'Huh?' and changing our minds, as we did with Sistine."

Then you could read aloud, and at the perfect moment, when Rob has just acted in ways that belie your theory, you could show an astonished look on your face and say to the children, "Turn and talk. What are you thinking? Does this fit with your idea of Rob as a scaredy-cat? Turn and talk." After children have talked with partners for a minute or two, with you coaching into their efforts, you could repeat what one or two of them said.

The important thing to realize is that in this example you would have provided kids with lots of assistance, and that is your intention during this section of the minilesson. You would have first crystallized a theory about Rob that you knew was going to be relevant to today's passage. You would also have read aloud, so that understanding the text wouldn't be a problem for anyone. You would have selected the passage that does indeed upset the apple cart of the theory, and you would have created a talk interval at exactly the key moment. You would have channeled children to work in the supportive, safe harbor of a partnership. And, of course, after children have done the work, you'll use this to convey an example or two that is clearly within reach of most your readers.

In this example, the actual activity that children participated in was that of talking with a partner ("turn and talk"). You could instead have set children up to "stop and jot" or to "list across your fingers" or to be active in other small ways.

And this example involved children with a continuation of the text used in the previous section of the minilesson. You could, instead, have asked children to think about a character in their own independent reading book (or, if they are in book clubs, their book club books) and to read that book, looking to see if the character acted out of character. Alternatively, you could have turned to a second text during the read-aloud—to a poem, a picture book, or a different novel. You could even have turned to real life, setting children up to practice a reading skill by doing a bit of shared reading about life itself. For example, if you had taught children to use clues to predict, you could say to them, "Practice this reading skill, only instead of doing so with this book we've been reading, practice the skill away from a text. Right now, work with your partner and see if you can collect enough clues to figure out what we're going to have for lunch today."

There are a few principles to remember when constructing the active involvement sections of a minilesson.

### Set children up for quick success.

First, you will be aiming to give children a two- or three-minute interval to practice what you've just taught in your teaching point and your teaching component of the minilesson. This will only be possible if you take some time to set them up to have success in short order. For example, although theoretically I could have asked children to use their independent reading books as a place to practice the strategy of reading on to see if a theory about a character continues to fit the evidence or not, the fact is that it would have taken each reader a few minutes just to crystallize his or her theory of a character, and chances are that had each reader had time to read on in his or her independent book, there would be nothing in the passage the reader was poised to read next that would have had any relationship to the readers' theories. So in this instance, the only way to

provide readers with a really brief chance to experience the content of the mini-lesson was to do so in a shared text, with me articulating the theory of the character and then channeling readers to hear a passage that was preselected so that it would set them up to do the work.

### Find ways to scaffold the work.

There are other ways to scaffold readers, and as you read through this series, you might collect a list of possible ways to scaffold readers. You'll find that you use the same scaffolds in the active involvement sections of a minilesson and in conferences and small groups. For example, one scaffold you can use in all these instances is that once you've set people up to do the work, you can sometimes also set a few people up to be simultaneously doing the work aloud, publicly, so that if anyone is stumped, that person can shift from doing the work to watching another person do it. In this particular minilesson it would not have worked to ask for a few volunteers to do this work on white boards (which invite others to look on and create little displays of good work that can be posted afterward), but there are many minilessons where that does work.

Another variation of this is that while most children do some work in their notebooks or on Post-its, one reader can do the work on the easel.

Then again, while readers are working, you can call out brief prompts to remind them of what you want them to do or of the next step. Sometimes your prompts provide the actual words you think they might think or write to get themselves started. In this instance, for example, you might call out, "I used to think Rob was…, but now I'm realizing that maybe he's…." If you wanted to do so, you could leave a bit of time and then call out, in a voice over as children worked, "I think this because A, because B…."

### Tuck in more teaching points to differentiate your teaching.

It's also helpful to remember that kids are ravenous learners, and you can usually tuck some helpful tips into either your teaching or your active involvement. For example, if you are helping readers revise their theories of a character, you might tuck in the tip: "Remember, when you are trying to find the precisely right word to capture your theory about a character, it helps to try saying this one way, another, and another, 'til you get it right." In addition or alternatively, you could say, "If you are looking for the one word that will sum up your whole character, try using more than one word. Usually people are too complicated to be shoe-horned into one word. Sometimes it helps to compare the character to someone you know, to something else. So and so is like a melon, hard on the outside, soft on the inside."

**_Give every child a chance to be actively involved, not just listening._**

Finally, you want all your readers to be actively involved during this section of the minilesson. Had you asked the whole class to work together, joining you in thinking about ways your theory of Rob did and did not hold true as they continued to read, you could have asked everyone to do this in their mind, and then you could have elicited a few people's answers while the class watched on. Don't do this! That strategy may make you feel as if the whole class was actively participating because you'd be at the center of activity, but the fact is that when you call on two or three members of the class to do the work and others look on, this is a way to involve two or three kids, not every member of the class.

**_Extrapolate for children what you hope they can learn that will be applicable to their reading from now on._**

The active involvement section of a minilessons generally ends just as the teaching section ends, with you extrapolating what you hope the students have learned in ways that are hopefully transferable to another text and another day. This might actually occur within the active involvement section or it might be within the link, or it might be in both places. When it occurs in the active involvement section, it generally frames a time when you share what one or two students did as a way to provide the class with yet one more illustration. When restating what you hope children have learned that applies to another day and another text, you'll often restate the teaching point. I find it helpful to actually look back at the exact wording of the original teaching point and use those same words again. The goal is to make the minilesson and the teaching point stick, and one way to do this is by making the key words of the teaching point into almost a mantra.

## The Link

The minilesson ends with you restating what you hope children have learned, doing so in a way that is transferable to another day and another text. "Readers, from this day on, whenever you are reading a novel and you've developed a theory about a character, remember that your theory is tentative. It's your best guess. As you read on, you will learn more stuff about the character, and you'll say, 'Yep, I was right,' or 'Huh? That makes no sense!' When you have a theory

of your character, but he or she doesn't act according to your theory, remember, you can rethink, asking, 'Might I need to revise my theory?'"

Often at this point, the teaching point gets added to a class chart that compiles what you have been teaching.

Usually before sending children off to do their reading, you'll want to also recall other things you have been teaching that you hope they are doing today, perhaps gesturing to the same chart. You might say something like, "So readers, you've been learning so many things about what it means to not only read stories, but to read characters. You've learned to do A, you've learned to do B, and today I hope you have learned to do C. Today as you read, you can try any of these things."

Sometimes you'll also add on instructions: "If you do this work, bring it to your partner talks later." "I'm going to ask all of you to start today off by doing this for just a minute, and then you can continue…." "You'll see I've put some purple Post-its on your table. If you do this sort of thinking, leave a purple Post-it in your book where you were thinking that way, so we can find that place easily when I come around and when you go to share with your partner."

## Keeping Minilessons Mini

I actually am credited with inventing the idea of minilessons, some twenty-five years ago—with coining the phrase and developing the method. I've never been totally clear if that accreditation is accurate or not, but recently I've found myself eager to take the credit and to use it to establish Bylaws of Minilessons. You see, there is a prefix in the word *minilesson* that is too often ignored. That prefix is *mini*. A minilesson that consumes the entire reading workshop—not because it spills over, but by design—is not a minilesson. If, after ten minutes, there is no "Off you go!" or equivalent phrase that launches students into their own important work, then this is not a minilesson. If the "off you go" is just "Off you go to complete this activity we began together on this text I selected for the whole class," then it's not a minilesson. It's just a lesson.

I emphasize this because the truth is that when any new idea is incorporated into the existing norms of American schools, it will always be the case that the new idea is stretched, chopped, and tweaked until it fits the existing assumptions about how schooling goes. Since Colonial America, American schools have usually been characterized by a teacher who chooses the one-day thing that the whole class is going to do for a class period or part of one. The teacher shows the students what the teacher wants people to do, then gets everyone started, and then says, "You keep going while I come around and check on your seat work." Then the teacher reconvenes the class to report on how kids did at the teacher's designated task. That's a reasonable thing to do with a class period, but it is not how a reading or a writing workshop goes, most of the time.

The modus operandi in a reading or a writing workshop is different because the kids enter the class already having ongoing work that they're eager to get at and they have a repertoire of tools for doing that work. The teacher interrupts this work for the briefest time possible to name, demonstrate, and give a teeny window of practice time so that kids have one more item in their repertoire, and then the teacher releases the kids to carry on in their work. Now the teacher watches what kids are already doing and then intervenes to work in small groups or one to one to remind the students to draw on their full repertoire of tools, to invent new methods as needed, to help each other, and to launch a new project when the former one is completed. I'm a stickler about what a minilesson is and is not because I want to protect principles that are enduring and crucial to workshop instruction—principles such as choice, responsive teaching, and deep investment in long-term projects.

In a workshop, the message in the minilesson is, "Today I'm going to teach you one new thing to add to your repertoire." And then the message is, "So off you go. Continue your reading, and I know you'll use, when necessary, what you learned today and yesterday and three weeks ago while you read." If you look at a score of publications that advertise themselves as containing reading minilessons, fully half of the teaching is better described as reading lessons than as minilessons.

Now granted, my minilesson are not always contained within ten minutes. I confess sometimes they are too long. But if you read through this series, you'll no doubt find fifty places where I've encouraged you to trim, delete, bypass, anything to keep your minilesson just that—*mini*lessons. I'm convinced that we, as teachers, need the humility to realize that kids ultimately learn from their work, not ours. The only truly sacred part of a reading workshop is the reading part of it, that is, it what the kids do when we say, "Off you go."

# CHAPTER SIX

# Conferring with Readers: Intense, Intimate, Responsive Teaching

**W**hen people want to learn to do something, we consider ourselves very lucky if we can get ourselves a coach. A young person hopes to qualify as an Olympic swimmer. She gets herself a coach, and that coach begins to watch her swimming across time, noticing her needs and channeling her to work on them, noticing also her strengths and doing everything possible to maximize them. Someday, when that swimmer makes the team, when she walks to the pool and climbs into the water at the Olympics, the camera will scan to show her mother's face, and it will scan to show her coach's face as well.

When I wanted to get better as an organizational leader at the Teachers College Reading and Writing Project, I got myself a leadership coach. For an hour once a week, my coach talked to me on the phone about the work I'd been doing to become a better leader. She never actually observed me leading, relying instead on my hearsay, but she knew my goals. One of her first questions had been, "Where do you want your organization to be five years from now? One year from now?" She'd then asked, "What's standing in the way of that?" and "What positive steps forward could you take?" Having established a trajectory of work, she was able to start our weekly conversation by asking questions like, "How's it going?" and "What new work did you try?" and "How'd that go for you?"

Young readers, too, benefit from coaches who are invested in that young person's progress over time and who help that learner take all the instruction that is in the air of a rich reading workshop and use that instruction in ways that connect precisely to the learner, making sure that the learner is working with direction and feedback in ways that are making a palpable difference.

Conferring is every bit as important for readers who are working to become stronger as it is for swimmers, dieters, leaders, writers, runners, and teachers, too. The research is clear that one of the factors that contributes most to any educational achievement is feedback. Hattie's study may be the best known. He reviewed 180,000 studies involving 20 to 30 million students and found that of 100 factors that contribute to student achievement, providing learners with feedback rates is in the very top

5%–10% of influences. That feedback is especially powerful if the teacher helps the learner know where he is going, what progress he has made so far, and what specific activities he can do next to progress toward the goal. Ideally, learners also receive help refining and seeking more challenging goals. Learning is strengthened to the degree that learners share the challenging goals and adopt self-assessment and evaluation strategies (Hattie, 2008). Still, conferring with readers has challenges that are important to address.

There is, of course, the predictable challenge of how one can make time for one-to-one interactions when we teach twenty-some children. This issue is critical and real. Throughout the conferring sections that thread through the series I've written of ways to work most efficiently with the time we have, and about ways to conserve time. We overcome the challenge of limited time so as to confer with writers—and we can do so with readers as well. In reading, the challenge is not only to make time, it's also to know what to do with the time we have.

## The Importance of Conferring with Each Child About Reading, Not Just About the Text at Hand

We draw a chair alongside a reader and ask, "How's it going?" The child shrugs and answers, "Good. It's a good book." The child is sitting there, holding a two–hundred-page book that we only vaguely remember. What do we say next? We can elicit from the child what will probably be a somewhat jumbled and unclear summary of the book, but we're not sure that doing so will pay off. And other than that, we are not sure how to get a footing so that the conversation has traction, so that our teaching is worth taking the child away from his reading for that time.

It's in those moments—when we feel at a loss over how to teach well—that we long to go back to the days when the whole class read a book we knew well, say, *Skylark* (the sequel to *Sarah, Plain and Tall*). We knew *that* book backward and forward and could point out the four references to summer heat and dryness in the first two pages, showing kids that MacLachlan deliberately highlighted the drought because it will be central to the story. Then we could point out, too, all the references to people leaving the prairie for other places, and write "repetition" or "foreshadowing" or whatever else we want to make of this on the board, and onward we could go through that book, finding things on every page that we could teach.

When teaching reading, there is a place for instruction that is grounded in a specific book. I share the feeling that when a group of young readers and I gather around a book that I know well, it's as if I've hit payday. The opportunities to teach are almost overwhelming. There's so much to notice in a book and so much mental work that can be done. It's this richness that nourishes our minilessons, providing much of the content for them. What's more, when we thread a shared book through minilessons, the structure of minilessons saves us from the temptation to function as tour guides rather than teachers, to fool ourselves into thinking we are teaching if we simply point out the lovely sights in a book that others might miss as they drive past them; the structure of minilessons requires that we instead we make careful choices about what we will invest a bit of time in teaching. Because we just have one minilesson a day, we are required to think, "Of all that the book offers, what is particularly relevant to the work these readers are doing with their own books?" and we then to extrapolate and highlight just one kind of mental work and teach not our every observation in the shared book but the work that a reader can do to produce those (perhaps pointing out that when readers look at things that recur in a book, we see things the author believes are important, such as in *Skylark* when we see signs of drought. Readers could then notice that they can also see repeated references to people leaving the prairie). So yes, it is true that when we work together with a group of readers on a shared book, this shared focal point guarantees that we are never at a loss for something to teach.

But there must also be a place to teach young readers to apply all that they learn from those times when we lead work on shared texts (in minilessons, book clubs, and guided reading groups). In the end, if I were to ask each of you, my readers, "What is your real goal as a teacher of reading?" most of you would say that you want to help the young people in your care author richly literate lives. You want to help young people read their own books with increasing engagement, discernment, power, and responsiveness. If many of our ultimate goals have everything to do with kids' own reading, then we need to make sure that a fair percentage of our teaching time puts us face to face with kids' own reading. And that is what happens when we pull a chair alongside a reader during independent reading time. It is important to pay attention to what our students are doing as independent readers for lots of reasons. One reason is that this way, we essentially will have made an appointment to support that youngster's independent reading. Even if we are not as adept as we'd like to be at doing this work, kids notice what we notice. If we care about their independent reading, they'll care about it. And then, too, as we do this conferring, we learn to do it, and we become skilled at this, just as we may already be skilled at other aspects of teaching reading.

But also, it is important to pull our chairs alongside a child and help that child to use all we've been teaching while on the run as the child reads, because in the end, this makes it vastly more likely that all our teaching will be taught in the service of independent reading. If we are working with one child and another and another, and we see that most of our kids are starting and abandoning books, are not getting engaged in the through-line of the story when reading independently, we're going to think twice before making our minilesson into a chance to teach readers to notice the repetition of drought images in *Skylark*. Instead, we'll look at *Skylark* with our kids' independent reading in mind and think, "How can I find in this book—or not in this book—some real lessons that are actually going to pay off for the kids I have, not the kids I wish I had?"

Of course, stressing that conferring is critically important in the teaching of reading doesn't take away the fact that sometimes, when we pull a chair along-side the child and ask, "How's it going?" and hear in response, "Fine," we don't know what to say. We sometimes feel empty-handed as teachers, unsure of what we can draw upon in the absence of knowing well the book the child is reading. In the upcoming portion of this chapter, I'll help you feel less empty-handed.

# Resources We Can Draw Upon as We Confer

I always know that I'm working with a strong teacher if the teacher asks me, "How do I know what to teach when I confer with a young reader? I always feel sort of at a loss." The teacher who asks that question has made the enormous leap required to understand that when we confer, we are not simply helping readers implement the minilesson. Conferences are not little personalized reiterations of the minilesson! Instead, conferences are opportunities for new teaching, and often that teaching will not relate to the minilesson as much as it relates to the child's ongoing direction as a reader, to the skills with which the child is and is not yet proficient, and to the work that the reader's book asks the reader to do.

There will never be an answer to the question, "How do I know what to teach when I confer with a young reader?" because there are always a zillion possible teaching points. But there certainly are resources that a teacher can draw upon to imagine possibilities. In addition to drawing on the current unit of study and

the minilessons in it, the teacher can draw upon these resources (and others) when conferring:

- Previous conferences and small-group work, as recorded in reading notes
- The genre that the child is reading and the work that particular genre asks readers to do
- The band of text difficulty within which the readers is reading and the work that books in that band of difficulty tend to ask readers to do
- The child's readerly life—and the opportunity to glean evidence of that from the reading log and elsewhere
- The child's thinking about reading, as evidenced by Post-its and entries
- The child's place along the learning pathways of the major skills you are teaching in the unit
- The child's conversation (or otherwise, the child's work) with a partner about his or her reading

## Your Records of Previous Conferences and Small Groups and of Your Assessments of the Child

Records of reading are vastly more important than records of writing because when we work with writers, their writing is right there, in front of them and us. So the records are helpful, but the real focus is the writing. The records are tangential. But when working with readers, the reading can't be there, on the table between the teacher and the student. The book, even the book with the Post-its stuck onto it and accompanied by a reading log, doesn't add up to being the child's reading. How important it is, therefore, that we collect records of our observations, our assessments, and our conferences and small-group work and draw on these when we confer. If, for example, when conducting running records, we see that the reader could read accurately far beyond the level at which she could comprehend, then that note will be enormously helpful to us. And if the reader didn't seem to have trouble with literal questions, but rather with inferential ones, that'd be great to know. It doesn't actually tell us what to teach, in that almost any skill can be done at a literal or an inferential level, but still, this is helpful. And if we also know that on an informal assessment, we saw that the child tends to notice who did what, in large sweeping steps, and we know that during the last two conferences we have asked readers to record new learning that seems important about the setting of a story, then all of this, combined, will get us started on a direction for a conference. The records alone won't guide us, but this in combination with any of the below will be critical.

## The Genre that the Child Is Reading and the Work that Particular Genre Asks Readers to Do

If we do not know the book that the reader is reading, but we know the genre, then we can draw on our knowledge of that genre to ask wise questions, to gauge a reader's response. If this is a fiction book, we can ask, "Who is the main character? What does this character seem to really, really want?" Of course, a question such as that merits follow up. "Why does the character want this?" "How does this fit into what you know of the character's traits? What do you think might stand in the character's way of getting this?" Knowing that a child is reading a fiction book can lead us to scores of other lines of inquiry. We could, for example, ask about the minor characters. What role might these play in the book? We could ask about the setting—and whether the book might be different had it taken place in another setting. Of course, if we know the book is a particular kind of fiction text, that can steer our interests. If this is historical fiction, we might wonder if the child can talk about the unfolding time line of the historical setting, and then, once we learn about some of the events that are occurring in history, we could muse with the reader over whether different characters respond differently to events in the story. Do their different responses reflect not just their personalities, but also the groups they belong to? When the child is all excited that the pool that has been segregated for so long will now be open to all and the mother is wary, this might not reflect simply their different personalities, it might also reflect the groups to which they belong.

If, on the other hand, the child is reading a mystery, we can draw on our knowledge of that genre to ask the child whether he's found some parts of the book that make him suspicious. Of course, all of these questions will require follow-up work, and typically this will involve us saying, "Take me to that part," and "Can you read this to me?"

## The Band of Text Difficulty Within Which the Reader Is Reading and the Work that Books in that Band of Difficulty Tend to Ask Readers to Do

In one of the assessment interludes in *Following Characters into Meaning*, you will read that the Teachers College Reading and Writing Project has found it fruitful to think about levels of text difficulty as falling within bands, and those bands as having a few shared characteristics. For reasons I describe later, we do not think it is helpful to try to keep in mind fifteen characteristics for each discrete level of text difficulty, but it is enormously powerful to be able to look at the book a child is reading, notice that it is, say, a level O text, and then approach the child already anticipating some of the new work that readers of N–Q books are asked to do. For example, it is helpful to know that whereas before, characters tended to have two or three dominant and crystal-clear traits that endured, now characters are often more complex, even ambivalent, and they are apt to change across the text. This knowledge, then, can prompt a teacher to ask, in a conference, "Have you noticed that your character sometimes has complicated feelings, where she feels partly one way, partly the other way—like she partly likes a person, partly doesn't, or partly likes to do something and partly doesn't? I'm asking because books that are about as challenging as this one often have really complicated characters. The main characters usually aren't just one way. Like you. You are outgoing some of the time, but sometimes I notice you get sort of shy. Is the character in your book complicated in the same sort of a way?"

Of course, there are at least half a dozen other traits that pertain to books at this band of text difficulty, and this is just one band of text difficulty. Then, too, teachers will be informed by whether a child has just entered or will soon be leaving one of these bands of text difficulty, because sometimes we can teach readers to begin doing the intellectual work that they'll soon need to do. When you read the assessment interlude in *Following Characters into Meaning*, you see lots of other ways in which knowledge of the child's band of text difficulty can help you have ideas for some of the work that a reader is apt to be required to do. The powerful thing about this teaching, of course, is that you'll be addressing work that readers need to do not just in this book, but in lots of books.

### The Child's Readerly Life and the Opportunity to Glean Evidence of that from the Reading Log

Stephen Covey, in his important books on leadership, cajoles all of us to remember "first things first." It is important as a teacher to have priorities, and for those of us who are responsible for a child's growth in reading, few things are more important than keeping an eye on the actual amount of reading that a child is doing. So plan to look at the child's reading log. Notice even just the record of the reading that has occurred on the day of your conference. If the child has had eleven minutes so far today to read, has the child read at least seven or eight pages? If not, then you'll want to research the patterns in the child's reading log, looking for whether on the whole the child reads at least three-quarters of a page in a minute. That's a rough rule of thumb, and sometimes it proves problematic, but most of the time if a child hasn't been reading at that rate, something is amiss. So talk to the child. Say, "When I sit with you and look over your reading, one thing I notice is whether you are reading about seven pages in ten minutes. Usually (but not always) if a reader is reading less than that, something's going on that is not quite perfect." Then, of course, you'll want the child to read aloud so you can listen for fluency and so you can make sure the child isn't being stumped by tricky words every other minute. You'll want to examine whether the child might be doing too much writing about reading. Is the child engaged? Of course, this is just one of many things you can study. You might notice the amount of reading the child is doing at home. If the child seems to not get to reading very often, you'll want to make a gigantic point of celebrating the child's accurate records. This is a true scientist, collecting real data. That is so key. Then, with all the support in the world (so you don't lead kids to falsify their logs) you will want to talk about what gets in the way for the child of doing more reading, and what ideas the child might have for remedying this. You might notice that the child seems to read the assigned amount each night, but never gets lost in a text. Take that up, then. Or you might notice that the child's reading volume escalated when reading a particular author or genre. Again, take that up.

> *When we are teaching a skill, we are helping readers to move along a learning pathway, becoming more adept at whatever it is we are teaching.*

### The Child's Thinking About Reading, as Evidenced by Post-its and Entries

One of my favorite ways to confer is this. I sit beside the reader and say, "Will you walk me through the thinking you've been doing as you read?" and then gesture to the child's Post-its or entries, as if clearly they are abbreviated markers of the child's thinking. The important thing for me is that I want to start earlier in the book and tour the progression of the reader's thinking. I do not read every Post-it with great care, but I graze along through them, and as I do, I'm thinking, "What patterns do I see in this reader's ways of responding to a text?" Most of us have a fairly limited repertoire of ways to think about books. Some people are always reading on the edge of their seats, in a plot-driven and active way, anticipating what will soon transpire in the story and hoping and worrying about it. Some people read as writers, noticing the decisions an author has made and wondering at the author's reasons for them. Some readers read with pen in hand, recording the important points to take away from a book. I find it is helpful to say back to a reader what it is that the reader tends to do a lot. In life, it is a gift when someone helps us see what our characteristic ways of engaging tend to be, and I think it is a gift to do this for a reader, too. I then make a point of trying to build upon whatever the child is already doing. (My instinct is to take the child to whatever he or she is not doing, but I know better than to let my knee-jerk deficit thinking actually control what I do.) I can often suggest that if this reader could work on becoming even better at whatever it is he or she often does, then maybe the reader could teach others. You won't be surprised to hear that after making a fuss about what the child tends to do as a reader, I do often suggest that it is also helpful to expand our repertoire and to deliberately take on a way of responding that isn't second nature to us. Perhaps two partners can trade "ways of responding."

## The Child's Place Along the Learning Pathways of the Major Skills You Are Teaching in the Unit

As you read this series, you will see that I think it is always important for a teacher to think of skills as pathways, not as end points. When we are teaching a skill, we are helping readers to move along a learning pathway, becoming more adept at whatever it is we are teaching. This means that it is helpful for a teacher to be able to look at the skills that a child is demonstrating as he or she reads and then to think, for at least the most dominant skills, "What would be required for the child to progress a bit farther along the pathway of this skill?" For example, imagine that a child either tells you or shows you (through Post-its and entries) that she fairly often notices a small point in a book and then says, "This reminds me of…" and then makes a personal connection. As far as you can see, that work—drawing a line between a detail in the book the child is reading and a detail in his or her own life—is what the child does when making a personal connection. You, then, will want to think, "What might it mean to make personal connections in a more advanced way?" That is, you need to have in mind a learning pathway that will help you know what you might teach next. In this instance, I'd probably think that I could help the reader know that once a reader says, "This reminds me of…," then the reader mines that personal connection for all sorts of help. If a character in the book is going to the dentist and worries tremendously about it, and the reader says, "This reminds me of when my brother was scared to go to the dentist," you'd want to help that reader to know that the personal connection then gives a reader some help anticipating what might happen next or filling in details in the reader's image of what's happening. So one possible next teaching point might be to help readers that saying, "This reminds me of…" is the start, not the end, to a reader's thinking. Then again, if the reader seemed to make personal connections about extraneous details in the text, the more immediate goal for me might be to teach readers that it can be distracting to think, "What have I experienced that reminds me of this?" to every little detail in a text. It's more important to follow the trail of a story than to constantly be leaving the story to rope in every parallel text imaginable. But at the same time, this reader could be shown that it is very powerful to ask, "What is this text really about?" and then to ask, "Have I read other texts that are like this one in deep and important ways?"

My bigger point is that when teaching reading, it always helps to have in mind the learning pathways along which children are traveling so that we can be diagnostic teachers, thinking, "If…, then…."

### The Child's Conversation (or Otherwise, the Child's Work) with a Partner About His or Her Reading

Imagine that a child is reading quietly. You want to get a sense of the child's thinking about her book. One option you have is to say to the child, "I know this is quiet reading time, but while I'm here, would you and your partner mind talking about your book as you usually do during partner time? I tend to miss out on hearing how you talk together, and I'm dying to get a sense of it." Then you can listen as the two readers externalize their reading, and you can decide whether you want to work with just one child or both and whether you want to work on the reading itself or on the ways of talking that the partnership seems to have established. For example, you might hear that a child has a ton of random little one-sentence-long thoughts about a book, and you could take that up as an individual matter and confer with the child to suggest she snowball her ideas a bit more, staying with them longer, almost having conversations in her mind about them. Or, alternatively, you could address this as the work of the partnership and show the readers how they can help each other to develop their wonderful but undeveloped ideas, turning sentences of thought into passages of thought.

## The Architecture of a Conference

Conferences have a consistent architecture we have come to rely on to help ensure they are on target and lasting interactions with children:

- **Research:** This may involve questioning the reader, looking at his or her work, or thinking back over all you know of the reader, his process, goals, text level, and all the other data you have collected about him and his reading.
- **Decide and Compliment:** This involves making a decision about the most helpful lesson to teach this reader, and it includes offering the reader a *compliment* that is meant to support and instruct.
- **Teach:** This phase may take various forms, depending on the method of teaching you choose. This phase includes a teaching point and the reader's *active involvement*. This phase will also be where you help the reader *link* your teaching in this moment to her ongoing independent reading work.

### The Research Phase

Think for a moment about a time when you went to an expert for assistance. Think about a time when you interacted with your minister, your rabbi, your doctor, your hairdresser, your fitness coach, your principal, or your staff developer, a time when you hoped that person in authority would help you. How did you hope the interaction would begin?

You walk into a doctor's office, and you probably expect the doctor to say something general like, "How's it going?" You don't expect the doctor to bypass that and to start immediately peering into your cracks and crevices! You go to your hairdresser or barber, and you expect the opening comment will be, "So how have you been liking your hair lately? Do you have any special thoughts about what you want?" Similarly, if your principal comes by to observe your teaching, you no doubt hope she'll start by saying, "What have you been working on lately?" and "How's it been going?"

Your conferring will be light-years more powerful if you draw on your memories of all the many times someone has conferred with you, using all that you want from those interactions to guide you as you frame your interactions with your kids. Because the truth is that kids are not all that different from you and me. If a child has been reading and working on becoming a better reader, then it makes sense that you need to do some research before you can teach in a way that will really make a difference. So chances are good that you'll begin your reading conference by asking something basic, such as, "How's it going?" or "What have you been working on as a reader?"

### Listen Wholeheartedly

Think about times when people have asked you questions such as, "How's it going?" or said things like, "Fill me in on what's been going on." My hunch is that you can recall times when the question alone led you to reflect to create dawning insights about yourself. Other times, the same question led you to provide a perfunctory answer: "Not that much has been happening, really. I'm just continuing to…." The difference in the two probably has less to do with the words out of that person's mouth than with your felt sense of whether the person was really interested and sympathetic. We all know there are ways in which a person can listen, leaning in to hear more, nodding in ways that convey, "Say more," signaling for us to amplify what we've said, responding with gasps or little interjections that make us feel heard and understood, that make us want to talk. A good reading conference begins with deep listening.

### Draw on All the Information You Have

Journalists have a rule of thumb that guides their research. "The more you know, the more you can learn." Conferences profit from information. So if you know a reader has been starting and abandoning books, then you wouldn't ignore that information and begin the conference by asking, "How's reading been going for you lately?" Instead, you'd probably want to say, "I've noticed you started and stopped three books in the last few days. That's unusual for you. You aren't usually a picky reader. What's been going on for you, do you think?" Then, too, if you began a line of work during a previous conference, you're apt to bring readers to that vicinity and to say, "I know last time we met we talked about…. How's that been going for you?"

Of course, as you try to ascertain what it is that this particular child has been doing as a reader, you'll use whatever reading records you maintain to help you recall what you have taught and observed during previous interactions. You'll rely on those records more in reading conferences than in most other forms of one-to-one instruction. After all, when you draw yourself alongside a *writer* and ask, "How's it going?" whether the child can articulate how it's been going or not, you have the evidence right before you. You can see what the child has done in living detail. But when you ask a *reader*, "How's your reading been?" there won't be any reading sitting there on the table for you to look at. There will be some evidence—reading logs, Post-its, perhaps entries in a reader's notebook—and it will be critically important for you to pore over these, deducing whatever you can from them. But ultimately, you will rely on your record keeping and your cumulative work with this child more in reading than in writing. And you will need to mine whatever children do say or show you for all it's worth.

### Follow Up on Information Readers Offer

When I studied research methods early on in my professional training, I was taught that it is always important to "unpack" what an informant means with follow-up questions. If a reader says, "I've been finding evidence to support my theory about sharks," you might, for example, say, "When you say that you have been 'finding evidence,' what does that really mean? What sort of evidence are you looking for?" Alternatively, you might say, "Could you tell me what you mean when you talk about your theory about sharks. What, exactly, is a theory?" You might feel foolish at first asking questions such as those, because of course you know what the terms mean. The child is only using them because he's

parroting back terms you've taught! But you do *not* know what the youngster means by any of these terms.

Another way to unpack what a child really means is to channel the child to shift from telling to showing. So if the child says that she is collecting evidence to back her theory, you could say, "Could you walk me through that work?" Alternatively, if the child doesn't have evidence of the work or is just about to embark on it, you could say, "So will you get started doing that right now while I watch?"

### Help the Child Understand Her Role in the Conference

Of course, you can follow all my advice, do all these things, and the child can look at you like you are crazy. "What do you mean, What am I working on as a reader?" the child might say or think. "I'm reading. I'm on page 92. What am I working on? Page 93."

Alternatively, when you ask those sorts of questions, the child could easily launch into a prolonged retell of whatever it is she is reading. Taking a giant breath, she can get started. "Well, see, in my book, there's this guy, and he…." If you know the book, conceivably you can extract from the retell some information about the sort of thinking the child has been doing as she reads, but frankly if you do not know the book, you're apt to feel a bit at a loss. The child can go on and on and on and on, and try as you might to will yourself to listen with rapt attention, you can feel your eyes roaming the room, checking on who is and who is not working.

So, an important comment: first, if you ask the question, 'What are you working on as a reader?' or any substitute for it and the child launches into a retell of the book, you need to stop the child. It is okay to hold up your hand like the crossing guard at your school does to stop oncoming traffic. "Wait, wait," you'll want to say. Then you need to not just steer the child in a different direction but to explicitly say why you are doing this. "When I ask, 'What have you been working on as a reader?' I'm not really wanting to hear the whole story of your book from beginning to end, though there will be times when I ask you to retell the book. When I ask, 'What are you working on as a reader?' I'm wanting to know what new stuff you are trying to do to get to be an even stronger reader. I'm wondering if you have been trying any of those things on our chart. Like, for example, have you been…," and then I might fill in some of the answers I anticipate the child producing.

Much of what we do as readers is done with automaticity, inaccessible to conscious meta-cognitive thinking, so it will not be utterly surprising if your children are not particularly articulate about their reading goals and strategies. As Marie Clay points out, "Most things we do as readers need to operate below the conscious level most of the time, so that fast and effective processing of the print is achieved and attention is paid to the messages rather than to the work done to get to the message" (Clay, 2001, p. 127). It will help, then, if you show children how to take on conscious deliberate goals, to work in purposeful and strategic ways to take on new challenges as readers, and to be able to name what they have done. There will be times when a child can't name what he's doing as a reader, so you'll say, "Will you do that work right now, as I watch," and then after the child does whatever it is—say, orienting himself to get ready to read an expository article—you can name what you have seen the child doing, "So to me it looks like you are the kind of reader who doesn't just pick up an article and sort of drift into reading it," I say, feigning a sleepy, passive approach to the text. "No way! You turn your mind on to high even as you just get the article into your hands. And it looks to me like when you look over the article, you are already thinking about what the big ideas might be that it will teach readers. Am I right?" and the narrative could continue, either with you continuing to talk through what you have seen the reader do or with you passing the baton to the reader, who could resume the narrative, taking up the story where you leave off.

### Readers Benefit from Teaching You About Their Reading Work

Inviting children to reflect on and articulate what they have been doing as readers allows them to articulate their strategies, which is helpful to them for a number of reasons. This puts them in a position to teach others, which of course is important in a learning community because this means that young people as well as the teacher can be the source of knowledge. As Peter Johnston writes in *Choice Words*, "The side benefit of the 'How did you… ?' question is that as children articulate their strategic action, they teach their strategies to other students

*Your conferring will be light-years more powerful if you draw on your memories of all the many times someone has conferred with you, using all that you want from those interactions to guide you as you frame your interactions with your kids.*

without the teacher being the authoritative-source-from-which-all-knowledge-comes. It arranges for instruction without hierarchical positioning. Naturalizing this sort of conversation opens the possibility that students will continue such conversations among themselves, thus increasing the level of 'explicit' instruction without increasing the extent to which children are being told what to do" (Johnston, 2004, p. 32).

There are other reasons as well that asking a child to teach us what she has been doing as a reader can, in and of itself, help that child. To really understand this, imagine that I came to your school. You know I'm an authority, and you expect me to come and teach you some things about using these *Units of Study* really well. I arrive early in the day, before the kids have come, and we're alone in the staff room. We each get coffee and then sit for a minute. "So," I say. "Can you fill me in on your teaching of reading—how's it been going for you over the last year or two?" You talk, I lean in closer, blown away by what you are saying. "Whoa," I murmur. "Geez." Then I ask a question or two. "So how has that really affected your interactions with kids, do you think?" "Has anything helped?" and then, a follow-up, "So why do you think helped so much?" After some more talk, "So how do you think these *Units of Study* are going to fit into that whole story of you and your teaching reading?" And finally, "While I'm here, are there things I could do that might help, do you think?"

A conversation like that reverberates. Later, afterward, we ask ourselves the same questions that the teacher asked us. How *has* my teaching changed over these years? What *do* I want for myself? What might be the first steps I could take?

When I realized, about fifteen years ago, that my lifework is not just teaching but also leading—and leading a very large organization—I decided I needed a leadership coach who would help me rise to the challenge of this role. There was nothing in my training that prepared me to lead a giant organization, and I frequently found myself feeling like I was feeling my way in the dark. For three months, I talked to this coach once a week for an hour on the phone. Years have gone by, but I still find myself asking myself the questions she asked me, and I still find the questions themselves as important as anything else she taught me. "Where do you want your organization to be ten years from now? Five years from now? What's getting in the way of it being that? What positive action could you take right now toward that goal?" Her questions to me have become my questions to myself.

## The Decide, and Compliment, Phase

If you return to the memories of times when people in authority have come into your life, assessed your work (or your hair or your physical fitness) and then intervened in ways that aim to help you improve, my hunch is that some of those times ended up being incredibly destructive, and others were incredibly helpful. It's important to think, "What was the difference? Why did the one interaction hurt me for life, and why did the other help in ways that still matter to me?"

Part of the answer will come from all that we have already discussed. If another person is going to help you and me do our work better, it's important that the person first listen to what we have been trying to do, to our assessments of that work, and to our goals. My coach couldn't really help me become a better organizational leader until I'd thought about what I wanted, and then once she and I had some direction in mind, we could build from that base.

But I think that mostly, the way we feel about a coaching or conferring interaction will depend on whether the person in authority gives us the sense that we have the capacity to do the work, to rise to the occasion. If someone watches us teach or if that person reads our writing or studies the records of our reading or hears about our marriage or looks over our hair and then, having seen us, says, "Geez. This is a bigger problem than I realized. I don't know…," then this one interaction can seal the deal, making us totally convinced that we are not cut out to be a teacher, a writer, a reader, a wife, a beautiful person. Marie Clay has written extensively about the fact that sometimes, without meaning to do so, we can actually teach children that they can't solve problems, can't help themselves, can't get better. Clay's classic paper, "Learning to Be Learning Disabled," shows that just as a teacher can help a child learn to be an active agent of his or her own learning, a teacher can also teach children to be passive victims, filled with self-doubts (Clay, 1987).

After researching what a child has already done and has been trying to do, I try to do two interrelated, intertwined things. I compliment and I decide. Sometimes I decide first, then compliment, and sometimes the sequence is the reverse. But either way, I take a few moments to name what the child has already done that I hope he or she continues forever more, work that I hope becomes part of the child's identity. And I think, "Out of all that I could possibly say and teach, what will help the most?" That decision influences the compliment, of course, as well as the teaching that follows.

In this section, I'll discuss the decision first and then the compliment.

### Decide

To an outside observer, a conference may seem fairly relaxed. But for me, as the teacher, conferences are the most intellectually rigorous times in my day. I listen with every cell in my brain activated, and I am thinking, thinking, thinking. Malcolm Gladwell, the author of the bestselling book *Blink: The Power of Thinking Without Thinking*, talks about how an expert can thin-slice and, in the blink of an eye, make critical judgments. As I write this, my husband has just had knee replacement surgery. The day after he came home from the hospital, he had a horrific fall, his screams echoing through the house. My husband decided (don't ask me why) to not tell the surgeon about this. Three days later we went to John's regular post-op appointment. They took X-rays, hung them on a board. The surgeon walked into the exam room, glanced at the X-ray for a split second, and said, "We need to go back in." In the blink of an eye, he saw that there'd been a fall, that things were no longer right. In a reading conference, I'm also trying to make judgments with equal speed and accuracy. To do this, I need to know:

- What goal is the learner aiming toward?
- What does that goal look like in concrete terms?
- Where, on that pathway toward her goal, is she located?

This means I need to crystallize a sense of the skills or constellation of related skills that this reader either is—or should be—working on, and I need to think, "What can she do with ease, with support, and what seems still out of reach for her?"

I describe these instructional and learning pathways in more detail in the assessment sections of the *Units of Study* books and on the CD-ROM. For now, let me emphasize, as the authors of *Breakthrough* point out, "Instruction is powerful only when it is sufficiently precise and focused to build directly on what students already know and to take them to the new level. While a teacher does and must do many things, the most critical is designing and organizing instruction so that it is focused. Without focus, instruction is inefficient, and students spend too much time completing activities that are too easy and do not involve new learning or on tasks that are too difficult" (Fullan et al., 2006, p. 34).

As I listen to the reader and take in all the evidence I can see and all that is available in my reading records, I'm theorizing, predicting, and connecting this reader to other readers I've known, determining priorities, imagining alternate ways to respond, and lesson planning! I'm practically building the learning pathway as I help readers travel along it. All this must happen while I smile genially and nod warmly enough that I keep more data coming my way. This is not easy. You are wise if you realize that this invisible aspect of a reading conference is the most challenging one of all.

A few words of caution: there are two temptations to avoid when making the decision of what to teach the reader.

*It is tempting to listen just long enough to know the kind of work that reader is engaged with and then to leap to an instant conclusion about what one will teach.*

We must try to avoid doing this. The important thing is not just to identify the area within which one will teach (i.e., finding the main idea in an expository article), but rather to disentangle what it is that the learner knows to do and does do from that which she doesn't know to do. The real decision involves not what terrain one is teaching in, but rather what *precisely* it is that the learner doesn't yet know how to do and seems ready to learn.

*It is tempting to first study and name what a reader is doing and then send the reader off to new territory, in a new direction.*

If I read over a reader's Post-its and notice that she does a lot of raising questions about the main character, then my instinct is to say, "I love the way you are asking questions as you read. Now, though, can I teach you that in addition to asking questions, you can envision/predict/read critically, and so on?" When a learner seems to be "all about" one line of work, instead of redirecting her, we should try to honor the learner's intention and, as much as possible, to help the learner do whatever she has set out to do just a bit better because of our time with her. We want to do this because it is important that learners have a sense of agency, authoring learning lives for themselves. So, if she tended to ask lots of questions about the main character, I might look over those questions and show her that there's one kind of question she's not asking too much, and that's "Why?" When characters do something or want something, an astute reader can usually discern why the character has said or done this, and to do so, we

generally need to locate earlier parts of the text that link to the part we're reading now. So this is important work. Alternatively, I could notice that the reader asks questions that are so important that they are worth entertaining, and I could teach the reader to do that. Or I could show the reader that the questions she is already asking could encompass minor as well as major characters. One way or another, I try to stay with and extend and build off from a reader's own intentions rather than redirecting her.

## Compliment

As I listen to readers, another key decision revolves around the question, "What is it that the reader has already done (or almost done) that I could compliment?" I know that I can teach as much through finding and recognizing and celebrating good work as by issuing challenges, so the compliment portion of a conference is an extremely important one.

### Make the compliment transferable.

The trick is that I want to extrapolate something transferable out of the reader's work. So if a reader's book tells of a character journeying from one town to another and the reader has recorded the names of the towns on Post-its that dot the book, I'm not going to say, "I love the way you recorded the towns your character visited," because I don't really want to say, "Whenever you read a book, remember to do this." But I could recast what the reader had done, saying, "It's really helpful that you think about the main things that are happening in your book, and record them so that later you can look back over your jottings and recall in your mind the time line of big events in your book." That compliment could be transferable. That is, I could say, "Whenever you read a book, remember to do this."

### Make the compliment centered on new learning.

There are a few ways to make a compliment especially significant. One is that I try to compliment work that feels as if it represents the cusp of a learner's trajectory. If the learner has just begun to do something and is still a bit shaky at this new work and I can celebrate the work, that's powerful. Peter Johnston (2004, p. 13) has written, "Focusing on the positive is hardly a new idea. It is just hard to remember to do it sometimes, particularly when the child's response is nowhere near what you expected…. Much more important is noticing—and helping the students notice—what they are doing well, particularly the leading edge of what is going well. This leading edge is where the student has reached beyond herself, stretching what she knows just beyond its limit, producing something that is partly correct. This is the launching for new learning." Sometimes, when I try to notice and name what the student has done that represents the leading edge of the student's learning, I end up complimenting what the student has almost done or is just about to do. In this instance, for example, I might say to the reader, "I am blown away by your decision to mark the important steps that your character made on her journey—the big things that happened, the places she visited. I know you did that so you can look back over the whole journey, sort of retelling it in your mind and to others, and that is just so smart— to not just read forward but to stop from time to time to recall the path the book has taken so far."

### Make the compliment personal.

Then, too, I can make my compliment more significant if I personalize it. I tell teachers that in general, when I am complimenting a child on doing something, I do not want to re-use the words of my own teaching point. If I have taught readers that when predicting, it helps to think, "What do I know about how stories like this tend to go that can help me think what might happen next in this story?" then I do not want, in a compliment, to say, "I love the way you thought, 'What do I know about how stories tend to go that will help me think about what will happen next in this story?'" I might as well say, "I love the way you did as I told you to do," and no child is going to phone home and share that compliment with a parent! Instead, the challenge is to find new words to use to capture what, precisely and uniquely, this learner has done. If I'd told everyone to mark the main way stations along the character's journey, for example, I would need to think more precisely about why this particular reader had done that work especially well.

### An Example of a Reading Compliment

Listen to a compliment that I've used in this book, just to give you a sense for how this portion of a conference tends to go.

When I spent a bit of time with Kobe on the last day of this part in the character unit, I definitely wanted to support the hard work he'd done to lift the level of his predictions and his envisionments. So I said to him, "Kobe, you are so determined! I remember that first day when you and your table looked over your envisionment Post-its and you told me the group had decided that yours just repeated the stuff that was in the book. Other kids might have gotten all discouraged and said to themselves, 'I'm not going do this kind of thinking. It is not my

style.' Others might have folded their arms in a huff and said, 'I'm not the type to envision.' But you—you have been so determined, and bit by bit, you have worked harder and harder. Look at the difference in your envisioning. At the beginning, you just wrote, 'He is a good basketball player.' Now look at your envisionments!" We looked together at the progression in his work.

Then, continuing, I said to Kobe, "To me, you are a lot like Sassy, in *Dancing in the Wings*. Remember how when Mona and Molly told her she had no talent, that there was no way she'd get picked to go to the dance festival, she didn't let them discourage her? No way. Remember how that very night she dreamed that she was dancing on the Milky Way and she went right on to those tryouts and didn't let Mona and Mollie's snickering get to her? You are just the same as Sassy because the two of you never give up."

## The Teach, Active Involvement, and Link Phases

After complimenting the reader, I name my teaching point and teach. This aspect of the conference feels a bit like a minilesson. The difference comes in that in a conference, just as in small-group work, the time spent teaching is less and the time spent guiding children's active involvement is more.

For me, it is important that I do not just slide from researching and teaching by asking leading questions. For example, if I've noticed that the reader asks lots of questions and I start the conference wanting to learn how the reader comes to generate those questions during reading and what the questions then do to alter the reader's reading, I could easily turn the tide of my questions so they are not really inquiries any longer but nudges, asking things like, "And do those questions affect how you read on? Do you ever carry one of the questions with you as you read onward and try to answer it? Have you ever thought of coming up with possible answers?" I try not to do this. I used to think this was a subtle way to allow a reader to feel as if she was still in charge, as if she was making all the decisions and that masking my instruction by embedding it in questions allowed the reader to keep the ownership reins firmly in her hands. Over time I've come to realize that when our teaching is especially subtle, the kids often miss it. They may end up doing the work we want them to do in that one instance, but if we are not explicit, the chances that they learn something they can use again another day is unlikely. So in the example above, now I'd be much more apt to conduct my interview, perhaps give a compliment, and then to crystallize whatever I wanted to teach about questioning into a single, straightforward teaching point. "One thing I want to teach you is that it helps for a reader to not only generate questions, like you are doing, but to also carry those questions with us as we read on. Then as we read, we come up with possible answers to those questions. We sort of think, 'Could it be… ?' And then we read on to see if that tentative answer works."

After I've named the teaching point, I tend to do a tiny demonstration. I often carry with me the class read-aloud and a short stack of other books that my children and I know well. When I'm super prepared for conferences, I've gone through those books, mining them for possible illustrations of teaching points, jotting these on Post-its so that I'll be able to say, "For example, watch me do this in this book." Then I demonstrate (read about demonstration in the discussion of minilessons on p. 54) and name what I have done in the demonstration that I hope is transferable to the kids. The conference then turns a bend as I say, "So try it." As the reader tries what I have just demonstrated, I coach into the reader's work as I coach into their active involvement in a minilesson, giving lean pointers that help them do the work successfully.

The conference ends with me suggesting the reader try this not only today, with this book, but often. I might give the reader some sort of a cue card or reminder—a bookmark, perhaps, containing a summary of what we've just gone over together, or a special color of Post-its so that when the reader does this work over the next few days, we'll be able to see the traces of it and to talk together about them. I might suggest that for a time, the work we've done affect what this reader does with his or her partner.

By then, it is time to record what I've taught and learned and to scurry on to another reader, another lesson—for the child, and for me.

To see examples of all I have written about in this chapter, I suggest you read through some conferences inside this series and watch some conferences on the DVD. Most of all, I suggest you try holding some conferences, or some new and improved conferences, on your own or with a colleague. After each reading conference you hold, give yourself the luxury of processing what went well, what didn't go so well, and what you want to try and work on as you improve the intimacy, responsiveness, and effectiveness of your conferring in the reading workshop.

# CHAPTER SEVEN

# Small-Group Work: Developing a Richer Repertoire of Methods

When I was a young professional, fresh on the scene, I was invited to be one of ten young women featured in a "Young Women to Watch" article in *Ladies Home Journal*. I was asked to appear at a certain address downtown to have my photo taken. I spruced myself up—clean hair, new pink suit—and arrived at the appointed address, a New York City loft, my first time ever in one.

"Come, come, sit here," the people told me, and I sat in a chair, expecting to say "Cheeeese" and to be on my way. To my surprise, the chair on which I sat was suddenly cranked backward, and I found myself leaning so that my head was positioned over a sink, with a team of people surrounding me, one sending a stream of water over my already clean hair, another massaging shampoo into it. Once that process was completed, a man arrived with a suitcase. I wondered if this would be a new outfit to replace my new pink suit but no, the entire suitcase was filled with makeup. A full hour later, I was standing against an entire wall of cascading, shiny, white fabric, one foot slightly in front of the next, face cocked upwards and turned to the side, chin up an inch—no, less, that's it. As I held that position, I felt someone's hands fumbling at my back, around the waistline of my skirt, and realized he was releasing the top button of my skirt so that it would ride a bit lower on my hips, then adding clothespins to alter the drape of the skirt just so. "Head up again, eyes here," the photographer called. And then he said, "Just relax, be yourself."

There was, of course, no way under the sun I was going to be able to just relax after having been subjected to these intensive efforts to remake me, and make me, in certain ways. And here's the point of my story: I think that many teachers have been subjected to equally intensive efforts to remake our small-group instruction so that it is just so. There have been so many books written on how to lead small groups in the precisely right ways that too many teachers approach a little hub of readers, gripped by anxiety over doing this The Right Way. Meanwhile, the whole point is to be personal, to be intimate, and to be responsive.

# The Point of Small-Group Work: Responsiveness

When I lead large conference days on the reading workshop, there are always two topics around which anxiety runs especially high: time and small-group work. Often I sense that teachers have been schooled to lead one specific kind of small-group work (usually one interpretation or another of guided reading), and they want to be sure they can bring that very specific sort of instruction into the reading workshop. Of course, my response to this question is that by all means they can bring that form of small-group work to the reading workshop. Each one of us needs to teach readers in the ways we know how to teach and the ways that have worked for us. But I encourage teachers to know that over time and with practice, they'll probably develop a more expansive repertoire of ways of working with small groups. Some native Alaskans, lore has it, have twenty-six words for what I refer to with just one word: *snow*. They're such experts on snow that they don't think of all that white stuff as just one monolithic thing. And I'm convinced that with increasing expertise, teachers, too, come to realize that all our small-group work need not be labeled by one label (e.g., guided reading), nor does it need to employ any one method. After all, if a method is powerful enough to use with a whole class—as in whole-class shared reading, read-aloud, interactive writing, word study—why would that method not also be powerful when used with a small group of learners?

The whole goal of small-group teaching is responsiveness. So it is critically important that each of us tries to outgrow any feeling that we need to cling to one rigid template for small-group instruction. If you have been trained that every small group begins with a text introduction, followed by a time in which readers each read while you circle among them, listening to one child and then another and coaching into one individual's reading, and then another's, with you ending the small group with a teensy book talk followed by a little teaching point, you need to understand that yes, indeed, that is one way that small groups can go. Many people refer to that format for instruction by using the term "guided reading." But others do entirely different things under the guise of guided reading—(it is a term that has vastly different interpretations in one school and another) and in any case that particular ensemble of work is going to be effective at accomplishing some goals and not effective at accomplishing others.

The one thing we know for certain about young readers is they are not all the same! At a conference at Teachers College, Dick Allington recently reported that most teachers who lead small groups have only one format for how those small groups tend to go. The irony is that the biggest reason to work with small groups instead of the whole class is precisely so that we can tailor our teaching to our students. So one wonders what the reasons would be for anyone thinking that The Right Way to lead small groups is to do the same thing in every small group! There are abundant ways in which you can work with small groups, and this is especially true because this is a format in which you will sometimes work in out-of-the-box ways, trying something bold that you have never tried before just on the off chance it might help. After all, your small-group instruction will be your forum for working with students for whom in-the-box sorts of teaching may not have done the job.

## Consider Shorter, More Frequent Small-Group Coaching Sessions

The first and most important thing to say about small-group work is this: Do it! One of the reasons to lead a well-structured, streamlined reading workshop—one in which readers know how to carry on independently as readers—is that this provides a perfect context within which you can lead flexible small groups. For a major chunk of the school year, your children will be reading in book clubs. These will be roughly homogeneous groupings of children working with multiple copies of the same book. How can you *not* support these groups? When your class is working in book clubs, then a good deal of your teaching will inevitably support those groupings of children. And earlier in the year you simply will have too many things to say, to show, and to support, for you to teach everything through one-to-one interactions. In a typical day's reading workshop, you will probably aim toward working with two small groups and holding three or four conferences, some with individuals and some with partnerships. I can see you adding up the minutes, thinking, "Two small groups—that is thirty minutes right there, and three or four conferences…," but let me jump into your thinking and point out that both conferences and small-group work can vary tremendously in length—and in format and content too.

In general, though, small-group work will be more powerful if you do smaller bouts of it across time than if you have one gigantic small-group session every few weeks. It helps to work with a particular small group for something like ten minutes, twice a week, for two weeks, rather than to work with that group for half an hour only once every few weeks. The extra advantage of working with a group for more shorter bouts of time is that you can then ask (and expect) children to do some work related to the group between your meetings, allowing the group work to influence their reading for broader stretches of time.

## Plan with Learning Pathways in Mind

It is helpful to approach a small group with a sense for the developmental pathway readers progress along when learning the skill you hope to teach. This way, if you have a sense for what beginning, intermediate, and proficient work with the skill entails, then you are more ready to see where a particular learner is in that progression and to be able to help her go from where she is to where you hope she will go.

### Set Readers Up for Success

For example, if you will be helping four readers find the main idea while reading a nonfiction text, you might prepare for this group by thinking about some of the easiest ways for a child to be successful at this work. Perhaps you decide that the first step is for readers to be able to recognize the main idea when it is explicitly stated in headings, front matter, and topic sentences that frame an expository text. You might, then, duplicate two small articles, each containing a very clear infrastructure of headings and subheadings, and you might use one of these articles as a teaching text to show children how you orient yourself to an article by looking it over, thinking, "What's this mainly about?" and then read on to confirm what you glean from the text features and topic sentence. You could then coach children to try similar work with the second article.

### Set Readers Up to Move to the Next Step Along the Line of a Particular Skill

To be ready to respond to the differences you see in the students, you'll want to prepare for teaching this skill (or any skill) by thinking also about what the next step in a skill progression might be. You might, for example, decide that the slightly more challenging work along this same pathway involves locating and extracting the main idea when it is embedded in a paragraph, rather than highlighted in headings. It's more challenging still if the main idea has been left implicit or if it is an umbrella idea that spans large and disparate parts of a text. My point, though, is that the best way to plan for a small group is to think about

what a line of development in the skill you aim to teach might entail. As you teach, then, you figure out where each learner is along this progression and help the learner take the next step or two. Always, then, you use your knowledge of learning pathways and your sense of a child's zone of proximal development (Vygotsky, 1978) to support each child's progress.

## Plan to Decrease Scaffolding, Little by Little, and Vary Scaffolding for Each Learner

In addition to planning small-group instruction by thinking about the learning pathways along which readers develop proficiency in a skill, it is helpful to anticipate using the gradual release of responsibility model to progress from providing heavy scaffolding to providing light scaffolding as learners become more proficient with whatever it is you are teaching. The concept of scaffolded instruction was first used by Wood et al. (1976) to talk about children's language development. Referring to the temporary structures that are installed and eventually removed from around a building under construction, they suggested that with varying amounts of scaffolding, learners can be successful. This can become an important principle of teaching. Teachers provide learners with maximum support for something that is just beyond their reach, and then gradually remove that support so learners can function with increasing autonomy (Pearson and Gallagher, 1983).

> *If I've cordoned myself off with just a little group of four readers, I want to spend most of my time seeing what each can do and then teaching in response to what I see.*

When I'm planning a sequence of small-group work designed to help a cluster of readers extend their skills, I know that I will move from more to less scaffolding and that I'll vary the amount of scaffolding I provide different learners based on my on-the-run assessments that occur as I work with individuals in the group. Always, the goal will be to teach toward independence, so as a cycle of small-group work ends, I try to make sure that before I sent readers forth into the world, they have begun incorporating whatever I've taught them into their independent work.

## An Example of Responsive Small-Group Coaching

Recently I decided to work with a small group to help them see that details that occur on one page of a text pertain to the larger text. I came up with this goal after being flabbergasted at how many readers of MacLachlan's *Skylark* read that a ravaged coyote approached the house and did not seem to notice that this had something to do with the fact that drought had brought life on the prairie to a standstill. For too many readers, the coyote was just a coyote, and its presence had no connection to the fact that yet another set of neighbors had just packed up and moved away.

When I convened the group of four readers in hopes of reminding them that what happens on one page in a book is utterly linked to what happens on other pages and of making sure they are not reading as with blinders on, I knew I'd want to begin by spending a minute or two telling them why I'd convened the group and what I hoped to teach them and then doing some teaching, followed by providing them with guided practice.

### Choose what and how to teach.

The important thing for you to realize is that a teacher always has choice not only of *what* we will teach but also of *how* we will teach. In this instance, for example, I could have decided to teach readers by using a read-aloud as a small-group strategy. That is, I could have said to this group, "Can I read this with you? I want to show you the way we can think about passages that seem important." Then I could read a bit of the book aloud to the small group. And as I read, I could sometimes say things like, "This seems really important—let's slow down and think, right?" or "Oh my gosh, this goes with what we were talking about earlier in the book, doesn't it? Lots of times, important passages set us thinking about earlier parts of the book, don't they?" I could sometimes say, "Huh? I'm trying to figure why he did that? Let's look back, right, because usually the answer's there. It just takes a second to see it." Of course, throughout the read-aloud I could progress from demonstrating to scaffolding, so that after a few minutes I'd say, "So what are you thinking now? Turn and talk," and then after they talked, I could say, "I loved the way so many of you were thinking, 'How does this part fit the earlier parts of the book?' That's such a smart question to ask." In time, I might pass the read-aloud baton to kids, letting children know that just as I sometimes read to them, they can read to each other. And I could point out that when something important happens in a story, it sometimes helps to pause and to think, "How does that connect with what I've already read?" The child who had agreed to read aloud to the others in the small group could now determine places in the text that were suited to pausing and synthesizing.

Of course, there is nothing magical about using reading aloud as a method of instruction for a small group. It is just as possible for me to adopt and adapt any other method that I use in minilessons, tweaking the method so it fits the new format. Later, I'll show how the same teaching point could have been taught differently. Whatever method a teacher chooses, teaching almost always begins with the teacher naming what it is she wants to teach, just as we name our teaching point in a minilesson. Letting kids know why we've convened them is common sense.

### Keep demonstrations, or other teaching, short so that small-group time can mostly be for guided practice and coaching.

After saying, "I pulled you together because I'd like to teach you…," I often demonstrate whatever it is I hope children will learn. Let me stress at the onset, however, that any demonstration I do while leading small groups will always be quick because the structure of small-group work is especially conducive to a teacher observing, scaffolding, and supporting individual readers. If I am going to do a long demonstration, I might as well do this within the minilesson with the whole class benefiting. If I've cordoned myself off with just a little group of four readers, I want to spend most of my time seeing what each can do and then teaching in response to what I see. So I start off expecting that at least 80% of my time with any small group will be time when the kids are actively engaged in their reading work and with me, watching and supporting what they do.

### Use familiar texts when demonstrating.

Because I want my demonstrations to be two or three minutes long, I am apt to return to a text the readers knows well, because this way I don't need to explain the story's content. Working with familiar texts allows me to zoom in on a page smack in the middle of the text, one that is conducive to what I want to teach, without the kids being disoriented. I'm apt to teach into students' own independent reading texts most of the time when coaching, but sometimes I give all members of the group copies of a particular text I've chosen.

### Condense, but keep, all the parts of an effective demonstration: name the teaching point, enact it, and name what you hope they've seen.

So on this day, because I had read *Stone Fox* aloud earlier in the year (in Unit 1), I brought that book with me to the small group. "Today I want to remind you that when I'm reading a page, I sometimes stop to think, 'How does this part fit with what went earlier?'" I said, naming a teaching point. "So watch." And then I read three or four sentences from a page—sentences that told that even though the potato crop is turning out to be a good one, Grandfather is still really

depressed. I wanted to show children that first I read, and then I paused to do the work I was asking them to do. After pausing, I articulated what I was thinking, trying to do this in ways that were somewhat transferable to other books. "I'm just trying to think how this part connects to stuff that has happened earlier," I mused as if I was thinking aloud. "Oh yes, I'm remembering that yesterday we read about how the grandpa owes a ton of money! So that part that we read yesterday may connect to this passage, where the grandpa doesn't cheer up, not even when he hears the potato crop is going to be good. *Wow! Now* I understand this part about Grandpa still being upset because now I'm remembering that Grandpa owes a ton of money. That may explain why he isn't jovial now. One good crop probably isn't enough money."

By this point, the demonstration was over, and I needed to name what I had done just as I do in the minilesson. "I'm hoping you see that when I'm reading one part—especially a part that feels important—I pause and think to myself, 'How does this part go with things that happened before? How does the part clear up questions or add to thoughts we were having earlier?'"

### Use a rhythm of guided practice or coaching—one that allows space and time for readers to work in front of you.

Now I wanted to let the members of the small group try this. I might have decided to have them try this first with another section of *Stone Fox*, in which case I would have again read aloud and gotten them started doing this sort of thinking, exactly as I would have done in a minilesson. But I tend to want to focus more on kids' own work during our fleeting small groups, so I said, "Now pick up your book and begin reading where you left off, but as you read, do what readers do and ask, 'What information am I learning that clears up questions or adds on to something I learned earlier?'" In small-group work as in any other teaching, I trust repetition, and I often repeat anything I hope students will internalize.

### Intervene in ways that lift the level of the work each child is doing, differentiating according to the child.

As children began their quiet reading, I circled among them, turning like the hands of a clock to the children who are sitting at 12:00, 3:00, 6:00, and 9:00. To one child I said, "First, what you just read right here, does it fit with the last chapter? Tell me about that."

I wanted to make this work easier for the next child, so I rephrased that question, asking, "What are the things you are noticing that are continuing from earlier in the book?" This child was reading *Number the Stars*, so I said, "In the last chapter we found out about the list of Jewish people at the synagogue, and now we are finding that the community has been talking. Is the fact that they are meeting to talk related to the list that contains everyone's names?"

If I had wanted to prompt this child in ways that were more challenging than either of these ways, I might have said, "Can you tell me some of things your character is doing that make you wonder, 'Why might she do this or he do this?'" Then I could have added, for transparency's sake, "I'm asking because usually the causes—the reasons—are earlier in the book. Asking 'Why might she be doing this?' is a way that helps readers realize that the beginnings of our books connect to the middles and to the ends and so forth."

Of course, if the reader struggled with a question, then I might have decided I needed to provide scaffolding, and I might, in that instance, have stepped in and asked more targeted questions. "Have you thought of why she is doing this? Might it be because she thinks it is her responsibility to protect Ellen?" If I essentially end up doing the work for the reader, then I need to channel the reader to do the next bit of work. For example, in this instance, had I felt that I needed to provide the reader with a lot of help, I might then have suggested, "You could read on to confirm or to get new information." In this way, then, I worked with each reader in the group for a minute or two, scaffolding them to attempt work that felt within reach.

***Make an appointment to check in again on this ongoing work that they will continue.***

At the end of this small group, I suggested we meet again in two days and that until then they take some time to do this sort of thinking, asking, "How does what I am reading go with earlier parts in the book?" I asked them to use purple Post-its when they did this work over the next few days so that I could quickly ascertain how many of them were doing this and how much they were doing, and over the next two days I nudged the one child who did not have many purple Post-its to remember to do this work.

***Follow up with the group and help the members take next steps.***

A couple of days later, when I reconvened the group, the first thing I did was to suggest the children work with their partners within the small group, telling each other about the instances when they'd done this work, talking about their purple Post-its. I also asked them to start with the part they were reading and then to

show how they looped back to an earlier part in their mind as they read that part. For the reader who needed more clear scaffolding, I gave her a sheet of paper that said:

> What I just learned here is _____,
> and that goes with _____,
> and kind of goes with this _____.

As I coached on this day, I nudged children to see that the one passage they were reading linked not just to one thing, but to many things. "What else does this connect with?" I asked. "Is there a possibility that this might fit with something earlier? Okay, then read on and see."

After a few days of supporting this sort of work, I pointed out to readers that what they had been doing is called synthesis, and that readers needn't stop other skill work to synthesize. For example, readers can predict by first synthesizing lots of passages, across the whole book.

## Use Small Groups Flexibly

Of course, this detailed description of one small group is meant to illustrate principles that apply to other topics and other ways of working. Small-group work can support instruction in any lesson that might be taught to the whole class or in one-to-one conferences. And any method of teaching that is powerful enough that you use it while teaching your whole class is also a method you will want to draw upon some of the time when working with small groups of readers.

If a few readers have a hard time participating in whole-class book talks, for example, then in a small group we could do a tiny read-aloud and help students become comfortable participating in an interactive book talk involving just the small group. The same principles could apply to this small group as to the one supporting synthesis. I might, for example, begin by showing children a transcript of yesterday's whole-class book talk and use that transcript to teach the idea that one person says something, and then we all think about that idea in light of the text, and someone says something else—pertaining both to the idea on the table and to the text. And again we hold that new idea in mind and think between it and the text. Instead of demonstrating by playing a part in a book conversation, I might bring in a transcript of a discussion and then point out what a classmate did that worked. The discussion transcript might show the start of a conversation, and I could then coach the children to think about something they might say to extend that conversation. I could further scaffold the students by suggesting that two readers talk together to come up with something they could say.

Sometimes for small-group work, you'll decide beforehand to investigate and teach into a particular aspect of readers' work. You might, for example, decide to devote one day's reading workshop to addressing the volume of reading that children have been doing. This would mean that before or during the reading workshop, you would survey your students' reading logs, contrasting the amount of reading they are doing now with what they did earlier in the year, and you'd engage children in conversations about making time for reading and pushing themselves to read faster and more. In many of the schools that we know best, children progress up levels of text difficulty in the first semester of the year and seem to become stymied in the second portion of the year, and an investigation into the volume of reading they are doing may yield reasons for that: children may be creeping through books. If you begin by investigating a specific topic, you'll end by teaching it.

I could continue. Small-group work could support children thinking about how to make more time in their lives for reading. It could support them working to read with intonation. And small-group work can not only support any topic of study, it can also involve any method of learning to read. In the examples I've described, small-group work has involved reading aloud, turn and talk, using cue-cards as scaffolds, and Post-it-ing. It can also involve acting out roles, participating in shared reading or interactive writing, writing in response to reading, word work—the works!

# CHAPTER EIGHT

# Reading Aloud: The Lifeblood of the Reading Workshop

Reading aloud is the best way we have to immerse children in the glories of reading, showing them both how and why one reads. "Great literature, if we read it well," Donald Hall has said, "opens us to the world and makes us more sensitive to it, as if we acquired eyes that could see through things and ears that could hear smaller sounds." Together with our children, we gulp down stories—stories that allow us to thunder across the finish line at the Kentucky Derby, to live in a thatched hut, to work at the mill. Together with our children we experience what it means to lose—and to find—ourselves in a story. Word by word, chapter by chapter, we are led into another time and another place.

Paradoxically, we are at the same time led deeper into our own lives, our own souls. We read *Charlotte's Web* and weep as Wilbur the pig comes to realize that "friendship is one of the most satisfying things in the world." We talk and talk and talk and through the talk come to understand that Charlotte's generosity has been as good for her as it has been for Wilbur. "By helping you perhaps I was trying to lift my life a little. Anyone's life can stand a little of that."

"Read to them," Cynthia Rylant says. "Take their breath away. Read with the same feeling in your throat as when you first see the ocean after driving hours and hours to get there. Close the final page of the book with the same reverence you feel when you kiss your sleeping child at night. Be quiet. Don't talk the experience to death. Shut up and let those kids think and feel. Teach your children to be moved."

We read not only because it is good for our children as readers, but also because it is good for all of us as people. We read because this is the best way that we know to come together in a community of care. I think, for example, of a teacher in Queens whose classroom had for years been one of those rooms where everything seemed to be done perfectly well but there just was no chemistry. The teacher had a lovely author's chair at the front of her meeting area, lovely charts around her room, a daily reading workshop and writing workshop, but it often seemed like her children were going through the motions when they were reading and writing.

Then one day, when the Teachers College Reading and Writing Project staff developer arrived in this teacher's room, everything was utterly different. The room was charged with energy and intensity. During writing workshop, kids were pouring their hearts out onto the paper, and during reading the room felt brim full of care and investment. "What happened?" my colleague asked.

The teacher nodded, knowingly. "Can you believe it?" she said, scanning the room.

"What'd you do?" my colleague asked, big-eyed with amazement.

"We read together," the teacher said. "That's all. We read sad, sad stories, like *A Taste of Blackberries* and *Bridge to Terabithia*." Then she said, "I think I'd been pretending that stories have happy endings. Reading those sad books, it tapped into the pain in children's lives and in mine. I started telling the children about how my parents are moving and it's killing me. I told them about all my years of plastic surgery on my face and how I always thought I was ugly, and they started telling me their stories, too, and writing them."

A tiny little boy had written about seeing his father go into diabetic shock, and a little girl had written about seeing her father released from jail and how she hugged him and he hugged her and "it is like the greatest love of all."

How powerful it is to read aloud, right smack in the midst of the hopes and heartaches of a classroom, amid friendships that form and dissolve, invitations that come and do not come, clothes that are in or out of fashion, and parents who attend or do not attend the school play. Here, children work out their life and death issues. Doing so with books at their side is a way to help them make sense of it all. Ralph Peterson, author of *Life in a Crowded Place* (1992) suggests that we respond to the challenges of elbow-to-elbow classroom living by using ceremony, ritual, and celebration to create a sense of community in the classroom, and he further suggests that one way to create that sense of community is to read aloud poems and stories as a way to cross the threshold, to mark the classroom as a world apart. It may be that every day the class joins into a shared reading, perhaps of a poem such as Shel Silverstein's "Invitation," which invites dreamers into the circle. As the poet Julius Lester says, literature can "link our souls like pearls on a string, bringing us together in a shared and luminous humanity."

And so we read aloud. We read aloud several times a day; we read to greet the day, to bring a social studies inquiry to life, to learn about molecules or gravity, and to fall through the rabbit hole of story.

# Choosing Books to Read Aloud

So how does one choose the texts to read aloud? My advice is this: choose carefully. Spend your summer reading one book, another, and another and mulling over your decisions. Think about books that will bring your class together—to laugh together, to be outraged together, to cry together. Think about books that are more complex than those readers can read on their own, books that can take your children toward more complex understanding of stories.

But think, too, about books that match those that your strugglers are reading. By reading a book like *George and Martha* aloud, you use reading aloud and grand conversations to elevate the books and the authors that are fundamental to the reading lives of some of your strugglers. When you read one of these "simpler" books, emphasize the way the books make you think and think and think, perhaps saying something such as, "I want to read to you one of my all-time favorite books. It's a story that can really make you think, so turn your brains on to high and get ready." If you follow that with a reading of *Poppleton*, or a *Pinky and Rex* book, or Katherine Paterson's *The Smallest Cow in the World*, you will have made an important statement.

As you mull over your choice of books, you'll want to consider the length of books. Chances are good that you might want to read aloud powerful, complicated books such as *The Great Gilly Hopkins*, *Where the Red Fern Grows*, *Roll of Thunder, Hear My Cry*, or one of the Narnia books, and if you make reading aloud a mainstay in your classroom, by all means turn to books such as these. But if you tend to have a bit of trouble actually finding twenty to thirty minutes a day for reading aloud, then you'll want to opt for shorter books such as *Fig Pudding*, *The Hundred Dresses*, *From the Notebook of Melanin Sun*, or *My Name Is Maria Isabel* because you won't want your read-aloud to drag on over too many days.

It's helpful to think about the band of text difficulty within which most of your children tend to be reading (or will soon be reading) and to make sure that for a fair proportion of the year you are reading aloud from within that band. I describe these bands of text difficulty elsewhere, but for now let me simply say that the challenges readers will tend to encounter when reading K, L, and M books will be notably different than those they'll encounter when reading N–Q books, and those are different than those readers will tend to encounter when reading R–T books, and those are different than those readers will encounter when reading U/V books. For example, if your read-alouds tend to be books from within the U+ bands of text difficulty, as you read aloud, you and your children will need to spend a fair amount of time wrestling with subplots, with gaps in time, and with shifts in perspective. Readers will often know more than the characters themselves. If your children are meanwhile reading mostly in the N–Q band of text difficulty, the challenges they'll need mentoring with will be more like those involved in understanding that the main character is not just one way and learning to notice ways in which the character changes from the beginning to end, often by resolving some of her ambivalence. Granted, you will often want reading aloud to invite children into heady intellectual work, and more complex books are especially supportive of that work, so you won't want to limit yourself to only reading aloud books that are similar to those your children can read, but there will be advantages to some alignment.

Then, too, you'll need to think about the relationship between your read-aloud books and your reading units of study. You will usually weave a chapter book and a few shorter texts into a unit, building many of your minilessons around those texts. For example, the historical fiction unit weaves in and out of Lois Lowry's beautiful novel, *Number the Stars*. When you plan curriculum around a book, your reading aloud time will be reined in, held in check by the fact that particular parts of the book will be perfectly aligned to lessons you want to teach—and those lessons sometimes require prior work. And so, for example, in the historical fiction unit, it takes seven or eight days between the day you read aloud the first page of *Number the Stars* and the day you will need to start Chapter 4. This is a particularly problematic example of the fact that your unit of study can rein in your read-aloud, but there are other instances when the progression of minilessons holds the read-aloud in check. The answer is to consider the way a read-aloud book progresses within a unit and to sometimes maintain a second read-aloud.

When selecting books that will thread through your units of study, we often choose a picture book, or otherwise a brief book, and then a chapter book. When teaching historical fiction, we generally start by reading aloud *Freedom Summer*, or *Baseball Saved Us*, or "New Day Dawning," a short story by Joyce Hansen that is contained within Sandy Asher's anthology, *But That's Another Story*. Then we shift to a novel. In a unit of study on mysteries, we often start by reading aloud "Who Waxed Mad Max?" a short mystery story by Gary Blackwood, again from Asher's anthology.

We might also read aloud a *Nate the Great* or a Cam Jansen mystery before moving on to a full-length chapter book.

# Using the Read-Aloud to Teach the Skills of Proficient Reading

In the classrooms I know best, although texts are read aloud throughout the day for multiple purposes, there is one time, several days a week, that children refer to as read-aloud time, and this is an instructional, interactive read-aloud. This is often at an entirely different time than the reading workshop—perhaps after lunch, or at the end of the day—and it generally lasts at least twenty minutes and often more like half an hour.

The book that is weaving its way in and out of a unit of study is sometimes read aloud during this time, with the teacher pacing that read-aloud so as to not read past the portion of the book needed for an upcoming minilesson.

Other times, we read other books aloud—a second chapter book that is woven through the unit and other texts of all lengths and all sorts. On the DVD, you'll see a great many examples of these read-aloud sessions, and I highly recommend you watch these because you'll learn more from seeing them than from anything I can say.

I absolutely recommend you plan your interactive read-aloud.

## Spy on Ourselves While Reading

To do this, you need first to read the book (or the portion of the book) that you will be reading aloud to your children and spy on the work that you do as you read the text. Ideally, you'll do this in the company of some colleagues, and you'll each note the work that each one of you does, and this way you'll come both to cumulate ideas for the reading work that portion of the text supports and to form a consensus about some of the especially essential work.

Let's imagine, then, that you were going to read aloud the first chapter of E. B. White's classic, *Charlotte's Web*. You may have read the book before, but you'd try to resurrect a "first" reading.

> "Where's Papa going with that ax?" said Fern to her mother as they were setting the table for breakfast.
>
> "Out to the hoghouse," replied Mrs. Arable. "Some pigs were born last night."
>
> "I don't see why he needs an ax," continued Fern, who was only eight. "Well," said her mother, "one of the pigs is a runt. It's very small and weak, and it will never amount to anything. So your father has decided to do away with it."

> "Do *away* with it?" shrieked Fern. "You mean *kill* it? Just because it's smaller than the others?"
>
> Mrs. Arable put a pitcher of cream on the table. "Don't yell, Fern!" she said. "Your father is right. The pig would probably die anyway."

Perhaps you and your colleagues might come up with a list like this.

- The story begins in action and dialogue. We might cue children in to envisioning who is talking and what is happening.
- The story presents a problem at its very outset: a runty pig is going to be killed, and a little eight-year-old girl is upset—outraged even. She confronts her mother. We might decide to scaffold children's ability to predict by anticipating whether this pig will die or whether it might be saved. (The picture of a beaming pig on the cover of the story should already give children a strong sense that this pig will not only live, but that it will probably be featured as a main character.)
- We might use this text to model that characters have different voices and different speaking styles, and that seeing a mental movie while reading requires that we hear these characters' distinct voices in our own heads as they speak. We might use just the dialogue to develop initial ideas about these two characters. Fern and her mother haven't been explicitly described, but hearing them speak already helps us form an image of who they are and what they're like.
- We might teach children to pick up context clues to figure out the setting. There's mention of a hoghouse and a pitcher of cream being set on the table, so we might guess that this opening scene is set in the kitchen of a farmhouse.

> Fern pushed a chair out of the way and ran outdoors. The grass was wet and the earth smelled of springtime. Fern's sneakers were sopping by the time she caught up with her father.

- This part of text might support helping kids develop a strong sense of setting—and also support the reader's ability to envision and actually step into the world of the book by calling to mind the textures, smells, and sounds being described.

> "Please don't kill it!" she sobbed. "It's unfair."
>
> Mr. Arable stopped walking.
>
> "Fern," he said gently, "you will have to learn to control yourself."
>
> "Control myself?" yelled Fern. "This is a matter of life and death, and you talk about *controlling* myself." Tears ran down her cheeks and she took hold of the ax and tried to pull it out of her father's hand.

- There is definite action and drama right from the outset of the book. The story doesn't lazily unfold. It steps right into action. We might begin work on synthesis and prediction from right here, teaching readers to note the problem and predict how it might be solved.

> "Fern," said Mr. Arable, "I know more about raising a litter of pigs than you do. A weakling makes trouble. Now run along!"
> "But it's unfair," cried Fern. "The pig couldn't help being born small, could it? If I had been very small at birth, would you have killed *me*?"

- We might note the potential for teaching interpretation right from the start. While different from a retrospective end-of-the-book interpretive stance, we do get an inkling, at its outset, that this story might advocate a humane treatment of animals or that it might deal with issues of justice. We could set readers up to view upcoming text with this lens to see if this will be a recurring theme.

> Mr. Arable smiled. "Certainly not," he said, looking down at his daughter with love. "But this is different. A little girl is one thing, a little runty pig is another."
> "I see no difference," replied Fern, still hanging on to the ax. "This is the most terrible case of injustice I ever heard of."
> A queer look came over John Arable's face. He seemed almost ready to cry himself.
> "All right," he said. "You go back to the house and I will bring the runt when I come in. I'll let you start it on a bottle, like a baby. Then you'll see what trouble a pig can be."

- Could this book be about standing up for what one thinks is right? Could it be about bringing about a change by taking action? We might note the opportunities that this book provides to interpret a larger story.

> When Mr. Arable returned to the house half an hour later, he carried a carton under his arm.

- We'd pause to confirm the prediction that the pig was saved after all. But what next?

## Choose the Skills to Teach

After (or before) spying on ourselves to see the work that we tend to do as we read the passage, we need to decide on the purpose of this read-aloud. While reading those three pages, we will have envisioned, predicted, monitored for sense, made personal responses, asked questions, inferred, developed theories about the characters, and the list could go on and on. So it is important to decide whether this read-aloud will support readers drawing on their full repertoire of reading skills, as called for by the story, or whether the read-aloud will bring readers along a sequence of work, in which case we'll probably select a small cluster of related skills to highlight. Then we'll plan on demonstrating those skills and on channeling readers to use the same skills themselves, first with more and then with less scaffolding.

Such specificity is important—crucial even—to our teaching. Riding a bicycle might require the seamless cofunctioning of many different actions. A biker pedals, steers, balances, distributes his weight on a slope, monitors speed and momentum, and occasionally brakes. Yet while teaching someone to ride a bike, we'd tackle *one* of these actions at a time. In fact, we'd start with training wheels so that balance and weight distribution are *off* the instructional radar completely when we start, so we might begin exclusively with just a few cluster skills: pedaling and steering—and ringing the bell. Teaching reading, in many ways, is no different than teaching swimming or dance or tennis or painting. When any of these activities are done proficiently, the effect is that of effortless synchronization, but to the practicing novice, each component skill might be taught with focus and exclusivity to eventually achieve the fluidity or fluency that over time and with practice becomes automatic—second nature.

When we do teach one or two specific reading skills at a time, we might attempt passing the read-aloud text through the sieve of just these skills. That is, even though reading a text as rich as *Charlotte's Web* will often lure us into focusing on envisioning, on interpretation, on critical thinking, and on empathy—often all on the same page—if our instructional aim at a given time is synthesis and helping readers grow theories about characters, then we'll allow the teachable moments on envisioning or critical thinking or empathy to slip away as irrelevant for the moment and hold on *solely and exclusively* to those teachable moments that help in synthesis and growing theories about characters. We'd plan for our teaching to shine a spotlight on one skill—or one related cluster of skills—at a time.

## Spy on Ourselves as Readers Again, with Particular Skills in Mind

Let's imagine how this might go. Let's imagine that the two skills we decide to teach at a particular point in a unit of study are synthesizing and developing theories about characters. We'd do this work by spying on our own reading, noting the thoughts we have when we read to develop a theory about a character and also how we *synthesize* this theory across the book.

To begin, we might note our own reaction to each new character as he or she is introduced, with the view of making this public to our readers. We'd probably begin with the part of the book where a main character first steps into the story—as Charlotte the spider does, when she first calls out friendly "Salutations!" from her web in the barn door to Wilbur, the pig in the manure pile below. Wilbur has no idea who Charlotte is at this point and neither do we.

> Wilbur jumped to his feet. "Salu-*what?*" he cried.

We'll probably note, right away, that each time a new character enters the story—particularly one so important that the book title features her name—our radar is especially alert. "Is she a goodie or a baddie?" we wonder, calling on our knowledge of conventional story structures that divide heroes from villains. Our reading at this initial stage is rich with anticipation. We sense that this part needs our attention—if this were a movie and we missed this scene, we'd need to rewind before we could make sense of the rest of the story. "Who is she? What will she do?" The reading voice in our head is alerted anew; it watches with a kind of bated breath.

> Salutations are greetings," said the voice, "… it's just my fancy way of saying hello…"
> At last Wilbur saw the creature that had spoken to him in such a kindly way.

In this state of heightened alertness, we hone in on all the little clues that the text provides about the personality and nature of this newcomer to the story. We pluck out the word *kindly* and, like the first defining brushstroke on a blank canvas, we use it to begin creating the picture of Charlotte in our minds: kind, quirky, has a peculiar way to greet people.

> "My name," said the spider, "is Charlotte."
> "Charlotte what?" asked Wilbur, eagerly.
> "Charlotte A. Cavatica. But just call me Charlotte."

The more Charlotte talks, the more this canvas fills up, because she has such voice, such presence. I think I like her.

> "I think you're beautiful," said Wilbur.

"Wilbur likes her too!" I note.

> "Well I *am* pretty," replied Charlotte. "There's no denying that. Almost all spiders are rather nice-looking. I'm not as flashy as some. But I'll do."

"Quite a personality," I think, as I read. "She's not entirely immodest, because she admits that there are spiders flashier than she is, but she *is* confident and assertive. Knows how to take a compliment, too!" Though I'm having this thought silently as I read quietly, I'll say it out loud, as an aside, during my read-aloud. Then I'll slip back into reading in Charlotte's voice:

> "I wish I could see you, Wilbur, as clearly as you can see me."
> "Why can't you?" asked Wilbur. "I'm right here."
> "Yes, but I'm near-sighted. I've always been dreadfully near-sighted."

"She needs glasses," I think. "And she's a bit of a chatterbox—a nice one." Again, this is the kind of silent thought that I have as I read to develop a theory about a character. During the read-aloud I will insert such a thought as part of an accompanying "think-aloud."

Note that I'm developing a theory about Charlotte, about a character. Because I'm using this specific sieve as I read, filtering out only the skill that I want to highlight—that is, developing a theory about a character—I'm allowing other "teachable points" to fall away. I'm making no effort to offer any *predictions*, though I have a few predictions up my sleeve. Nor will I alert myself to how I'm *monitoring* for comprehension here. And by no means will I pick up the conversation of how E. B. White, in making this spider spunky and beautiful, defies familiar spider stereotypes where they fall out of dusty cobwebs in dark haunted houses, inspiring shrill, terrified shrieks from hysterical ladies. I'll reserve that observation for when I use this text to teach *critical reading*. For the moment, I'll stick solely to highlighting the specific skills I want to teach—developing theories about a character and synthesis.

I haven't accumulated enough information about Charlotte yet to *synthesize*, but I know that work is about to follow. Though first impressions often last, I know that developing a theory about a character across the story arc will usually require readers to *revise* our first impressions as the character reveals greater nuance, depth, and complexity. As new information about the character piles up, I'll want readers to retain and revise the old. And so it is with deliberateness that I read this following new thing about the likeable Charlotte:

> "Watch me wrap up this fly."
> A fly that had been crawling along Wilbur's trough had flown up and blundered into the lower parts of Charlotte's web and was tangled in the sticky threads. The fly was beating its wings furiously, trying to break loose and free itself.
> "First," said Charlotte, "I dive at him… Next, I wrap him up." Wilbur watched in horror. He could hardly believe what he was seeing, and although he detested flies, he felt sorry for this one….
> "You mean you *eat* flies?" gasped Wilbur.
> "Certainly… Of course I don't really eat them. I drink them—drink their blood. I love blood," said Charlotte, and her pleasant, thin voice grew even thinner and more pleasant.

If you, like me, are mesmerized by how the curtain is suddenly lifted away from the spunky, likeable spider with her friendly chatter—to reveal a darker, more sinister queen of the web, you too will flag this part. If there had been background music to this reading, it would have switched at the point where Charlotte says, "I love blood," from a merry little ditty to a lower, more ominous chord. I'll let the mood of my entire read-aloud change to match Wilbur's sentiments.

> "Don't say that," groaned Wilbur. "Please don't say things like that!"…
> He was sad because his new friend was so bloodthirsty.

This is the perfect chance to teach that we *synthesize* our theory of a character based on the changing, occasionally conflicting information we receive about a character. Needless to say, I'll bring this up in my think-aloud when I'm reading to the children.

In this way, I'll go through the read-aloud text, armed with tiny Post-its or flags, and perhaps a pencil, to enter small instructional think-alouds in the margins. I'll sift through upcoming text with the same sieve, picking up and marking off the parts that will further synthesize this developing theory of who Charlotte is. Along the way, I'll have important teaching points to insert. "Even though she's good and noble, she's complicated," I'll tell kids. "Characters aren't just one way." "We constantly revise our first impression of a character to reach a more complete picture." "We try to see this character through the eyes of the other characters." Do note, again, that each teaching point deals with just two skills—developing a theory about characters and synthesis.

I know I've picked the text well if the upcoming story supports the work I'm trying to do. A page or two later:

> Wilbur lay down and closed his eyes… "Charlotte is fierce, brutal, scheming, bloodthirsty—everything I don't like. How can I learn to like her even though she is pretty, and of course, clever?"
> Wilbur was merely suffering the doubts and fears that often go with finding a new friend. In good time he was to discover that he was mistaken about Charlotte. Underneath her rather bold and cruel exterior, she had a kind heart, and she was to prove loyal and true to the very end.

I'll use a special new Post-it flag to mark this part. "Characters are complicated!" I'll remember to nod, when reading this. In this way, as Charlotte goes through her short life, weaving miracles of literacy with her spinnerets, I'll follow her alertly with a pencil so that when I read aloud her story to children, they'll have synthesized a theory about who she is and use her reference point to understand the scores of *other* characters they'll read about on their own.

## Reading Aloud a Variety of Genres Across the Curriculum

Picture an animated teacher leaning in toward a group of rapt students, book in hand, reading aloud. Sometimes, the reading has to stop a second because everyone needs to chuckle at a part. At other parts, the reading slows and children's faces twist with dismay. Mouths open, eyes dreamily riveted, they hang on to every word.

There is good reason why this image has such appeal. Read-alouds are an enormously powerful tool in teaching reading because they dramatize, and therefore make visible, the internal work of proficient reading. Step into classrooms where read-alouds occur and you'll see that the most rapt audience belongs to the teacher who can muster up the greatest drama. This teacher will often alternate between voices, and even accents, so you know which character is talking, turning squeaky one second, adopting a baritone in the next. Goose will have her own fast-talking, phrase-repeating speaking style, and I suspect Templeton the rat will be decidedly nasal. When Charlotte tiredly announces that she won't be returning to Zuckerman's farm, our reading teacher's voice will turn quiet and her shoulders will droop. When Thing One and Thing Two run around with a kite that goes bump thump, thump bump, her voice too will race with all the adrenaline that Seuss unleashes in that tale. Much like Oscar-deserving actors, therefore, teachers who read aloud most effectively adopt the characteristics of their character—*become* their character and enter the story.

What a powerful tool this is to bring to science! To social studies. To history. Narrative reading can be exhilaratingly close to actually experiencing, and you'll work for kids to develop experiential engagement with nonfiction texts, just as you do with fiction. We teach children that they can climb into their character's skin in a fictional world. Imagine texts where readers climb into the skin of a caterpillar as it eats its way out of its cocoon to become a butterfly, experiencing the thrill of metamorphosis. You can expect that the child who can climb aboard a red blood cell to ride the roller coaster of arteries and veins in a narrative science text will create his own visual-spatial map of the circulatory system.

You'll certainly want to bring this magic to expository nonfiction. There are few ways more effective in demonstrating that expository and narrative texts sound, feel, and are structured differently than reading these different kinds of texts out loud. In fact, you can actually read expository texts aloud in ways that highlight specific text structures, where you might state the *boxes* in a stronger tone and proceed to count out *bullets* on your fingers. Or, while reading, you might motion one way and another with a hand, wherever similarities and differences are being enumerated. You might read aloud a part and then stop to restate its main idea to the side.

On the other hand, if your instructional focus, while reading expository nonfiction aloud, is on decoding, you'd probably take care to pronounce content-specific technical language clearly so that students have the chance to hear a variety of words spoken aloud. You might even decide to pause and fuss over such words, demonstrating an effort to acquire content-specific technical lingo as you meet it on the page. And of course you'd want to verbalize the internal thinking that you engage in where you attempt to pronounce and decipher a hard word where it appears.

Then again, if your instructional focus is on synthesis and retelling, you might choose to pause every once in a while and paraphrase text chunks, taking care to link new information with information that appeared in preceding paragraphs. A read-aloud is a great place to isolate and scaffold specific skills that are crucial to each genre.

## Making Read-Aloud More Interactive

Reading aloud in a way that is spellbinding is an acquired talent, one that requires practice and planning. The teachers best at the art have been known to practice in front of the mirror, to record themselves, to rehearse their pauses and to rehearse also the thump-bump scary parts, the balloon-floating happy parts, and the slow, sad, knot-in-the-throat parts. The teachers who read aloud best use their hands, their eyes, their posture, their voices, and their hearts. But no matter how thrilling the dramatic impersonation of characters and no matter how prosodic and engaging your reading is, to optimize instructional potential you'd want also to provide children with the chance and space to actually respond to the texts you read aloud to them.

Think about this for a second. It is no longer a secret that reading is a two-way process, one that depends on the reader's response as much as on the author's intent. When we think aloud our own response to a text as we read it, we're certainly demonstrating to readers how *we* as teachers and proficient readers may respond. In fact we've been talking so far about how we'd tuck all instructional agenda into our think-aloud so that we can model the skilled thinking that we hope children will later engage in independently, with their own books.

But this is hardly enough. Imagine for a minute that someone was teaching you to drive. Of course, it would be helpful to actually be in a moving car with a proficient driver, hearing a steady commentary on why he's choosing to brake, why he's accelerating *just so* during an overtake, what he'd do at a busy round-about. The next step, however, is for us to actually take our *own* spot behind that wheel, for us to actually have our proficient driver egging *us* on with advice and encouragement when we enter the traffic flow on *our* first busy roundabout. A read-aloud accompanied by your out-loud thinking might serve as a great demonstration, but instruction is scarcely complete without the learner's active involvement.

In order to pass the baton to children, to go from you pausing to think aloud to you engaging the children in responding to the text, you'll become adept at saying, "Stop and think," and then leaving a pool of silence, or saying "What are you thinking? Turn and talk," sending children into partnership conversations. Sometimes, instead of saying "Turn and talk," you'll say "Stop and jot," and duck your head to do this while others do as well. Of course, there are many variations on these prompts. Instead of saying "Stop and think," you can say, for example, "Oh my gosh, what's going to happen next? Predict, will you? Make a movie in your mind of what will happen next." Then, after the pool of silence, "Let's read and find out." That is, any of the prompts can be made more specific. "Stop and jot" could be "Stop and jot. What's this *really* about?" Still, the three main invitations you'll give will be to think, to talk, and to write.

Each of these three prompts invites children to develop and articulate their own independent response to the text, and each does this in a different way. Silent thinking is the most introspective of the three methods and perfectly suited for especially moving or poignant parts. The turn-and-talk differs from the stop-and-jot in that it incorporates a social element, allowing peers to model, imitate, or reinforce each other's ways of responding to text. The stop-and-jot itself differs from a written response. It allows children just a moment in which to scribble a few words, quickly catching the images or thoughts that bubble to the surface of their minds before they're dragged back into the flow of the continuing read-aloud. When you plan, then, you'll think about not just the specific skills that you'll teach during a read-aloud, and not just the *points* at which you'll nudge children into responding, but also about the various ways to scaffold their response—through silence, through talk, or through pencil and paper.

Of course, there will be days when you pause more or less—or not at all. Indeed there will be days—and books—that remind you of Cynthia Rylant's advice to end with quiet reverence, to "be quiet" and not "talk the experience to death." There will be other days—and books—that will invite, almost beg, questions, discussions, hot debate. You and your children will decide which those days and books are for your community. The best thing about a read-aloud is that it can be tailored to fit time, need, and instructional agenda; when done often and done well, it can be the binding cement that holds your community of readers together.

## Supporting a Whole-Class Grand Conversation

When you finish reading for the day (and sometimes in the midst of a day's reading), you'll want to support your children in talking together as a class about the text. You'll use those whole-class conversations as opportunities to teach children to grow ideas about texts, to hold themselves accountable to what the text actually says, to mine passages of the text for meanings that may not at first be apparent, to think across texts, and to use their higher-level comprehension skills to comprehend with depth, harvesting all the insights and feelings, understandings, and knowledge that the texts can yield. These conversations are enormously important. If I had more time, I'd write one more book for the series—one that supported reading aloud and whole-class conversations.

For now, let me tell you the way I tend to launch whole-class conversations early in the year. I read aloud a chapter, pausing half a dozen times to think aloud for a few sentences. Perhaps once or twice I pause to support children in thinking to themselves about something I got them started thinking about. Then I suggest they talk to a partner ("Turn and talk.") before I resume reading.

I come to the end of the chapter. At this point, I'll need to decide whether I want to channel the conversation in a particular direction or when I want to let the children develop an idea. Let's imagine that I choose the latter alternative, as I'm prone to do. I'll probably close the final page of the chapter and say, "Oh my gosh, my mind is on fire. Isn't yours? So many thoughts right now. Whoa! Turn and tell your partner what *you're* thinking. Go!"

The room will erupt into conversation, and as the children talk, I crouch among them, listening in. Frankly, I'm hoping to overhear a child who is full of an idea that I believe will pay off easily in a whole-class conversation, but I don't let on. Just to let you in on all my secrets, I confess that there have been times when I enter into a conversation and get a couple of kids going on a question or an idea that I'm all excited about. If the children have two or three minutes to talk about that idea, I know I can call on them to share their thinking, and the origins of the thinking will have slipped from their minds.

In any case, after children talk for a few minutes, I convene their attention and start the whole-class conversation with an invitation that will become part of the fabric of the classroom. "Who can get us started in a conversation? Who's got an idea to put on the 'table' (there is not really a table—we're just sitting in a circle)."

Later, I may take the time to put a magnifying lens up to this particular juncture, showing children how to sift through their various thoughts to find a thought that is (as my colleague Donna Santman likes to say) provocative, compelling, and central to the text. It is, after all, worthwhile to teach readers that it is helpful to pause a bit and think, "Will this thought that I have pay off? Will it be an important one to develop?" If readers become skilled at this, their conversations about books will head toward interesting terrain, and so will their writing about books, and, frankly, their thinking about books. A comment such as, "My Uncle Dave has a hat like the one the main character wears" isn't one that the class as a whole could think about for a long while! And if a character is missing from a book, and the book doesn't really provide much information about that character, discussing him won't yield much.

At some point, if children have trouble getting started in lines of thought that will pay off, I might step in to teach them that there are some universal questions that almost always work when we're thinking about a text.

---

## Questions Readers Ask of Books

- Is this a journey? So many books are, so it is interesting to think if this book qualifies as a journey. If so, who is traveling, and where? Is it an external journey, or is it also an internal journey? Will the protagonist end up where he or she started or somewhere new?

- Why did the author decide to write it this particular way? Why is it titled this? Why might it start this way? Why might it contain whatever characteristic bits of craftsmanship it contains (the italics in Baby, the quotes from Pushkin in Letters from Rifka, the free verse format in Love that Dog and in Home of the Brave). How might these decisions go with what the book is really, really about?

- Is there an object in this book that takes on special importance? A place? A name? A saying? How does that object (place, name, saying) connect with what the whole book is really about?

- What lessons does the protagonist learn, and what do I learn alongside him or her?

- Think about one of the minor characters. What role does he or she play in the book? Why is that character here? How would the story have been different had that character not been here?

---

I would rather children not reach for one of these ever-ready invitations to think, but that they listen, question, conjecture, notice, hypothesize, and that they are willing to cup their hands around a fleeting thought and to put that fleeting thought at the center of a conversation.

In any case, once I have nodded to a child who signaled with a thumbs-up that he could get a conversation started, I'll probably make sure that members of the class look at that child, giving the child their attention. "All eyes on Tyrell," I might say, and signal for Tyrell to wait until he has his classmates' attention. I might also coach Tyrell to say his idea to them (not to me, not to his collar, not to a hand held over his mouth).

He puts his idea out there. Now I want the others to ponder it, and I want the idea to spark thoughts in them. I'm apt to model the way I listen deeply, taking in the idea that someone else has put onto the table. "Hmm," I say, as if the idea is a new one, dawning on me as I reflect on it. I repeat it to myself aloud, making sure that my mind is going ninety miles an hour as I think about my response to that idea. I know that children can see and feel the wheels of my brain spinning, and I know that I'll help them think in response to this idea if I actually do so as well.

If I think the children don't have much to say in response to this idea yet, I'll give them a few minutes to develop some thinking. I might say, "Let's take a second and jot our thoughts about this, okay?"

If I want to support children as they do that thinking, I might say, "Can I have a few of you jotting on white boards?" and then I can pass a white board out to three or four children, dispersed throughout the group. That essentially makes eavesdropping inevitable. Alternately, I might say, "Can I have a few readers thinking on our easel and our white board?" And then a couple of children can jot their thoughts on some large space at the front of the circle. Then again, I could do that myself. Or I could start jotting, and after children have started jotting, I could reread a few relevant sections of the read-aloud passage, helping them ground their thinking in the texts.

Then again, if I want to support children's thinking, I could suggest that instead of writing, they talk with each other. That means that in the end, if one of the two partners has a thought, that person can carry the other partner.

In any case, I'll soon say, "Who can talk back to the idea?" and I'll reiterate the idea. The next speaker may address her comments to me, in which case I'll signal that she needs to speak to the group and to the original speaker. Now a second, related, idea will be on the floor. I'll probably raise my eyebrows and scan the group, asking without words for someone to add on, and when one child catches her breath like she can hardly contain the idea that has come to her, I'll try to refrain from calling on her with words, using a gesture instead. I'm hoping that before long one child will speak and another and another, without me needing to emcee the entire conversation.

This portion of the conversation, again, merits more instruction. Another time—or even this time—I'll want to help children talk back to each other. There are lots of ways in which I can help them with this.

## Ways to Help Children Talk Back to Each Other's Ideas in a Book Talk

- I might repeat the ideas on the floor and then say, "One way to develop an idea is to say to yourself, 'I agree (or I disagree) because, for example (and then we retell a part of the story that goes with—or doesn't go with—the idea)." Then I could say, "So pick up your pen, and let's talk on the page right now. Try writing, 'I agree or disagree because....' Then retell a part of the story that builds your case."

- I might say, "Readers, one way to grow an idea is to repeat it in our own words and then use a thought prompt to get ourselves to say more about it, to think more about it. Right now, I'm going to repeat the idea that is on the table right now, and then Partner 2, turn to Partner 1 and (1) repeat the idea in your own words and then (2) grab one of these thought prompts, any one, and say it next, seeing if an idea comes to you as you say that thought prompt. It might, and it might not—but try." The thought prompts could be, "This is important because...." or "As I say this, I realize...." or "The surprising thing about this is that...." or "This connects with...."

- I might say, "Get with a partner. I'm going to help you say more about this idea. Partner 1, repeat the idea, and then, after a minute, I'm going to say something. Whatever I say—repeat it, and then keeping talking and thinking about the idea." Partner 1s could then have two minutes or so to say the idea before I call out, "In other words...," and wait for Partner 1 to reiterate the idea in different words. "The interesting thing about this is...." "What I wonder is...." "One answer might be...."

- I might transcribe a conversation among children that jumps from topic to topic without developing any of those topics and display this to the class, suggesting we "rewind" and try again, this time using thought prompts to develop an idea before jumping to a new idea.

As the conversation unfolds, there will be other ways that I support the conversation, and all of these are "conversational moves" I might later teach children to do for themselves. So, for example, after children have talked for a bit,

I might say, "We've been talking for a bit. You know how, when we read nonfiction, we read until our minds are full and then we stop and think, 'So far, what the text has said is…,' and then we say it back? Well, I find that it helps to do that in a conversation, too. Let's see, so far, what we've said is…" (and then I say back the conversation). Of course, another time I might, at that point, suggest, "Turn to your partner, and Partner 2, say back the conversation, and Partner 1, you add in bits you remember as well." Alternatively, I might say, "We've been talking for a bit. Let's take a second to crystallize what we've said so far. Use writing to capture what the main ideas are that we've said so far." Again, I could, if I wanted to, provide some scaffolds do this myself on the easel, working alongside the others in ways that I know the kids will learn from and emulate, or I could, alternatively, say, "Partners, help each other to do this."

There are other conversational moves I'll make and teach the children to make on their own.

- For example, if someone has put a theory into the air, I'm apt to say, "What do you base this on?" or "Can you show us what part of the text made you think this?"

- Later, if an idea has been stated and no one but me seems to feel the need to ground it in a text, I might make a tiny gesture to one child, surreptitiously hinting to him that it would be great to ask his classmate, "Where in the book did you see evidence of that?" If the child needs me to be less subtle, I'm happy to whisper to a child, "Ask for evidence," and then, when the child does as told, I'll give a thumbs up.

- Then, too, if a child takes the conversation to left field, saying something totally unrelated, I'll try to make it clear to the class that it is okay to say, "I'm not sure how that goes with this idea," and if, in fact, it doesn't go with the current line of thinking, to say, "Can we talk about that later, 'cause right now we're talking about...."

All of these conversational moves are turns of thought. Teaching students to *talk* well about a book teaches them to *think* well about a book. What could matter more?

# CHAPTER NINE

# Writing About Reading: Deepening and Clarifying Ideas About Texts

Take this opportunity to step back for a moment, pause, and think about what you believe about writing about reading. What is the purpose of responding to reading with some writing? How does writing about reading look, in classrooms, at its best? Give yourself the job of researching the writing about reading that your students are doing. Look in your classroom and also across your school. Be an investigator, if only for a day or two. Watch kids' engagement as they write about their reading and watch their pace. Talk to them about that writing. What are they aiming to do? What does good work entail? Why are they doing this? How does this help their reading? Look back over the work they've done to notice how their writing about reading seems to have changed over time, looking not at the fancy piece they did with tons of input from you but the everyday writing they do about reading.

You will probably see what I see all too often. In far too many classrooms, youngsters aren't clear why they are writing about reading. If pressed, they think it is for you, so that you can check on whether they did the reading. They do not know what is entailed in doing this well, and they have no expectations that the writing is supposed to be for them. They don't think it helps them read, save perhaps for the fact that helps them recall names and places. And it is not unusual for students' writing about reading to look pretty much the same one month and the next.

If you give yourself the job of sorting the writing about reading your students are doing into piles—one pile for the writing that feels like deadwood and the other pile for writing that has life to it—you may be surprised to notice how much of it doesn't feel as if it is serving much of a purpose. It does not have to be this way.

In this chapter, I'll suggest ways you can make the writing your students do in the reading workshop more vital and more supportive of their reading. Writing can be a powerful tool for thinking, and your students can certainly use writing to deepen their thinking about reading. But I want to emphasize that in your reading workshop, your first goal needs to be to support your children's *reading*. If you are going to ask students to write about their reading, that writing must support their reading, and if you are not vigilant, their writing about reading can instead compete with and replace their reading.

## Holding Fast to Reading as a Priority

Ultimately, people learn to read by reading. Our data reveal an extraordinary alignment between the levels of text difficulty a student can handle and the student's score on the standardized test. The way that students progress up levels of text difficulty has everything to do with time spent reading. There is a mountain of evidence available to suggest that the one thing that readers need above all is time for reading—not only to become better readers, but also to conquer the high-stakes tests. In the name of "holding readers accountable" for reading, it is all too easy to create conditions in which there is very little time for reading.

Certainly, until readers are reading a huge volume of texts, carrying books between home and school, making time in their lives for reading, getting engaged in storylines and arguments and lines of thought that make them want to read on, your most important goal needs to be to support your students' progress toward becoming avid readers. Telling students to write regularly about every little bit of reading they do will definitely not help that cause! And even after your students are reading up a storm, the writing that you ask students to do in response to their reading must not interfere with that reading.

There is another reason why I recommend you be cautious about the amount of writing you expect of your readers. It is this: If our goal is to make sure we help kids make richly literate lives for themselves, if we really want children to initiate reading in their own lived lives, then we would be wise to think about what people do who love to read and read a lot. Perhaps you are such a person. If not, you will have someone in your life who is totally head over heels for reading. Think about it. How much writing about reading does that person do?

The truth is that not many people read a chapter in an enthralling novel and then pull out the computer to write about that chapter. Instead, we read a chapter, and our response is to read the next chapter. We are more apt to pause

*When we write, we put our thoughts on the page, we hold our thoughts in our hands, and we set our thoughts on the table before us and invite others to join us in thinking about those thoughts.*

to write after reading a chapter in an informational text, but still it's safe to say that some of us would not choose to read if every text we read needed to be accompanied by entries and essays; book reviews; and letters to an author, a classmate, a teacher.

## Tap the Power of Writing to Support Thinking

On the other hand, when readers comprehend deeply, what we do is we think deeply about texts. We generate ideas, organize these ideas, prioritize, develop, question, and extend those ideas. Writing has always been one of the most powerful fulcrums a person has for this sort of thinking, and also for thinking about our thinking. When we write, we put our thoughts on the page, we hold our thoughts in our hands, and we set our thoughts on the table before us and invite others to join us in thinking about those thoughts. Writing about reading can be an important part of a reading curriculum.

When you read the books in this series, you'll see tons of examples of writing about reading. The writing will consist of jotted notes, time lines, informal records of thoughts, quick entries, and less frequent elaborated developed essays. Much of the writing about reading won't be fancy or long, but it will brim with ideas. When you look at this writing, you may wonder two things in particular. First, you may think some of the writing seems strong, considering it's done very quickly, and you may wonder how it got to be that way. You may think, "My students' writing isn't as fluent as the writing I'm seeing, yet my reading workshop is not all that different than the one you are describing. What am I missing?" Remember that the reading workshops described in these books exist side by side with strong writing workshops. The readers who populate these books work every day in writing workshops; day after day, they are given time to practice their writing, and they participate in units of study similar to these, only in writing. The work these students do during the writing workshop has enormous pay-offs during reading time, making their writing fluent enough that it can more easily function as levers for thought.

Then, too, you may wonder whether these writers ever work on full-blown literary essays. Sometimes, especially in the final book of the series, their entries almost do resemble little literary essays. You may ask if they are ever developed into full-fledged essays. The answer is absolutely, but for students to learn to write literary essays, they need to devote some time to drafting and revising those essays, and this work is done in their writing workshop, not their reading workshop. This process of learning to write literary essays is described in the sister series, *Units of Study for Teaching Writing, grades 3–5,* in particular in the book, *Literary Essays: Writing About Reading.* I also address this in one of the assessment interludes in the final book of this reading series.

But yes, the literary essays that students draft and revise during the writing workshop are written about texts they have read and talked about during reading time. Their abilities to write literary essays are far stronger because students can draw on muscles that they have developed during the reading workshop. Their abilities to read well and to talk and think about texts make all the difference in their abilities to write well about their reading.

Because reading, talking, and thinking well about books is necessary for a student to be able to write well about reading, I can say with confidence that even if you approach your school year especially determined that by the end of the year your students must be able to produce effective on-demand literary essays when standardized tests require this and to write more substantial literacy essays when called upon to do this, you still need to launch your reading workshop in such a way that your kids do relatively constrained bits of writing about reading until they've become accustomed to reading, reading, reading, with engagement. Then, as the year unfolds, you can carry your students through an unfolding sequence of work that sets them up to eventually be able to write more extensively, yet still quickly. Students will especially write at length about reading during the second half of the year when they are in book clubs and have audiences for that writing.

In the upcoming chapter, I'll detail ways in which you can help students write about reading in ways that support their reading. Specifically, I'll think with you about ways in which writing can help students think about their texts, ways it can help them engage deeply with their texts, and ways it can help them communicate with others about their texts.

> *As children's reading changes, the challenges children need to address change, and so too will the role that writing plays change.*

## The Writing Readers Do Should Scaffold Their Thinking

Writing can help a person construct a reading of a text. That is, the text passes by a reader, like a filmstrip running through the projector, and writing gives the reader a way to hold onto one chunk of the text and another long enough to see the relationship between those chunks. In this way, writing helps readers make lasting understanding out of the temporal experience of reading.

For some children, it is a challenge to see even a small chapter book as a single coherent text. On the page that the child is reading at one moment, for example, Henry is getting a dog with floppy ears named Mudge. The reader may not easily connect this dog with the earlier section of the story when Henry asked his parents for a dog and they said, "No dog"—until they thought about Henry's life with no brothers or sisters and looked into his face and caved in. Without holding onto the start of the story while experiencing the middle of it, this reader will not wonder how the parents are feeling about the dog now. The initial reservations that those parents felt may be long gone from this reader's mind. If the start of the book has vanished from the reader's mind, the reader will not wonder if the dog will suffice as the company Henry wanted. The page he is reading is simply about getting the dog, and that—and only that—is what is on the mind of this reader. For a reader such as this, then, writing about reading is a way to extract portions of the text that the reader wants to hold onto, allowing the reader to cumulate those portions of the text. This child can't afford a long detour away from reading. His reading is fragmented enough as it is, so the writing that is apt to work best will probably be a Post-it with a word or two on it, just enough writing so that later the child can use these Post-its to recall and cumulate the crucial information. Once the child has recorded key phrases as he reads, then looked back on those records and therefore on those parts of the book to see that these parts fit together, and once the child has become accustomed to talking between those Post-its (and those parts of the text), the child may not, for a time, need to do this work. It will become second nature (that is, until the child moves to substantially more complex texts, when the need to do this will resurface—as it does for me when I read really complicated, fragmented expository texts).

As children's reading changes, the challenges children need to address change, and so too will the role that writing plays change, because a decision to write about reading in a certain way allows a child to formalize his or her commitment to thinking about reading in that way. For a time, you and a child might decide that the most important thinking this particular child could do would be to regularly lean forward enough to make predictions. If this child is accustomed to reading with blinders on, thinking only about the current page, then it will help for this child to make a commitment to regularly thinking, "What might happen next?" and to jotting predictions, and then reading on until the reader is able to think and jot, "I was right," or "Wow! What happens is surprising!" Of course, it could be that you and this reader decide instead that it would be powerful for the reader to read, think, and jot not predictions but theories of a character, starting with the question, "What kind of person does this protagonist seem to be?" Whether the child starts by conjecturing predictions or theories of a character, either way the child needs to learn to read on, carrying that thinking, that writing, with him, and then to think between the upcoming text and his initial conjectures about that text, remarking to himself either, "I was right" or "Wow! This is surprising."

Once readers easily construct predictions and theories of the protagonist on the run as they read, reading on to see if those hunches hold true, the leading edge of these readers' reading work will need to change. And as the thinking that readers are learning to do changes, so, too, the writing that you'll want them to do will change. It may be that the reader cumulates when reading relatively straightforward narrative texts, but reads scientific texts as if he is made of Teflon, with the information rolling right off. You may suggest this reader sketch, label, and caption so as to build a mental model while reading texts that ask readers to retain and add to their developing understanding of a particular case-in-point. It is likely that as readers become more skilled, one of the most important things you will want to do is show them how they can use writing to grow theories of all sorts about the texts they are reading.

Usually, when we want to show readers how they can use writing to help them think, we start this by inserting tiny intervals of writing into the read-aloud time, where we pause at particularly rich sections, wonder aloud in ways that prime the pump of the children's thinking, and then say, "Let's write fast and furious." We duck our heads and begin to do that writing. This is usually, at first, a few sentences of writing: a Post-it, a time line, a list. As children become more fluent and more accustomed to thinking on the spot in this way, we will some-

times suggest they write in their reading notebooks, pushing themselves to write a whole page in three minutes.

This work can then be transferred to independent reading time. You can suggest children read and, from time to time, pause to jot. During a mid-workshop teaching point you can say, "If you haven't had a chance to think yet about (whatever sort of thinking you are especially supporting that day), read on and do some of that thinking in the next five minutes. Then you'll have a chance to share that thinking, that entry, with your partner." During that mid-workshop teaching time, or at the end of the reading workshop, during the share, you will sometimes say, "Partner 2, select one of your entries that seems especially talk-worthy, especially thoughtful, and put it on the table between you and your partner. Then talk at length about the part of the book you'd marked and your thoughts. After that, let's have the two of you talk as long as you can about that one entry. Go!"

Of course, telling students to "talk long" or "write long" about a thought is not the same as teaching them how to do this, and if you don't intervene to teach them, you'll find that what they do in their talking and their writing is jump from one thought to another, another, and another, skimming the surface of the text and of their thinking in ways that create a jumble of underdeveloped ideas. You will absolutely want to show them different ways to elaborate on their thoughts. One thing they can do is to learn to return to the text to illuminate the way their idea is grounded in specific parts of the text. For example, you may want to teach students that it can help to illustrate an idea by summarizing the portions of the text that illustrate that idea. Once students are accustomed to doing that, you can show them that they can summarize these portions of the text in ways that pop out the aspect of the text they are trying to highlight. (I refer to these as "angled summaries.") You may also want to teach them that citing portions of the text is a start, but that ideally readers then "unpack" these examples by discussing what the example shows. Transitional phrases such as "This part of the text shows… (and then the reader would refer back to his or her original idea, explaining how the passage relates to that idea)" or "This is important because…" or "Notice the way that…" or "I'm starting to think that…."

Of course, if you want to teach your students to use key phrases to extend their thinking, you'll probably bring this work first into your read-aloud and then into oral conversations. After reading a portion of a book aloud, you'll ask, "Can someone get us started thinking about this book?" When a student says an idea, it is as if that student has put a single Post-it or entry on the table at the center of this giant book club (the class). "Let's talk off this idea," you say. "What are you thinking?" Then, to prime the pump, you might say, "Turn and tell your partner what you are thinking about the idea that so and so has put on the table before us." You might then reveal a chart of thought prompts and say, "Try using some of these thought prompts to get you to say more, think more."

### Prompts that Can Help Readers Go from Sentences to Paragraphs of Thought

- To add on…
- In other words…
- On the other hand…
- For example, in the text…
- Another example of that is…
- I agree because…
- I disagree because…
- One place where you see this is…
- The part of the text that really shows this idea is…

Once readers have become accustomed to talking with a partner for a long while about a single Post-it or entry, it is a small step to encourage them to sometimes prepare for those conversations by selecting a provocative Post-it or entry and then writing long off of it, doing so by conducting a "conversation in the mind" even before they convene with another reader. You may, for a time, create a bit of time each day (three minutes, not ten!) for your readers to rehearse for partnership and club conversations. You can say to readers, "Take a few minutes to reread your jottings and choose one idea (or two that go together) to bring to the conversation. In fact, get started having that conversation in your mind, before you actually pull together with your partner." This won't be a small deal, because it means writing with depth and elaboration about a small idea yields much more sophisticated writing than that which skims the surface of ten ideas about a text. Of course you will want to do this sort of work across the curriculum after students have read science and social studies texts as well as during your language arts classroom.

That is, although the writing that readers will do will often be brief and quick—Post-its or quick entries, or the most informal graphic organizers imaginable, such as quick time lines or sketches, lists, or theory scratched into a boxes and bullets outline—all of this on-the-run jotting can hold elaborate and new and interesting thoughts. You and your students will want to look at whether their writing does brim with thoughts, because that will be an important goal. Trust me—it won't all be thoughtful writing even after all this teaching. Expect that. The important thing is that students sometimes review their writing and notice that some of it is not helping them read in more thoughtful ways, and they are reminded that such writing isn't useful. I sometimes tell students that their writing needs to hold a lot of "TPWs" (or thoughts per word). We all know people who talk all the time and say very little. Well, there are students who write on and on and on and say very little, too. In a reading workshop and in content area classrooms, too, when the moments for actual reading are as precious as gold, then it is important that kids learn to write the shortest possible notations that can still hold their ideas.

When you and your students reread and reflect on the writing and thinking they are doing on the run as they read, you may notice that some of your readers, including some of your ELLs, could benefit from some help writing and thinking in ways that incorporate literary language. If you have charts of literary language for character traits up in the room, you might suggest your readers reread their jottings for just a second and make substitutions, inserting *furious* into a Post-it in place of *mad*, *miserable* in place of *sad*, and so forth. The precise words that describe mood, character traits, and emotions are not the words we use in social language, so the children may not incorporate these words in their writing and conversation until you have small, home-grown lists available.

Of course, when writing about nonfiction text, your students will need to refer to charts of academic language rather than literary language. Your charts may contain optional ways to think otherwise—*in contrast, on the other hand*, or *then again*, and your charts may contain ways to refer to example—*for instance, for example, one illustration of this can be found....*

One of the powerful things about writing is that it can allow people to think across and between multiple ideas. You will, by the second or third month of your year, probably want to teach your children that sometimes it helps to cluster related Post-its and entries to make theory charts. You'll learn about these toward the end of the second unit of study. If students are growing theories as they read forward, they should be able to talk long about those theories (and then sometimes write long about them, too). This will again mean helping them to cite and categorize and compare and contrast evidence and to unpack that evidence.

When your children are reading nonfiction, you'll encourage more outlining, of the most informal sort in the world, and summarizing and explaining and questioning. Eventually the writing they do will involve making and writing off from graphic organizers that synthesize information across text sets.

The fourth unit in the series aims to help readers read complex novels in which it can be challenging for readers to keep track of characters, their visible traits, and the problems they seem to face, so the writing that students do may return to the writing they were doing early in the year. They may begin making very short jottings of characters' names and traits. How many of us, in college, wrote lists of characters inside the front cover of our novels or turned to the list that was in *Anna Karenina?* Our *Anna Karenina* is a young reader's *Roll of Thunder, Hear My Cry.* As I was reading this young adult novel alongside the children, I found myself needing to clarify several times that TJ was not a member of Cassie's family. I finally had to make a quick list of the names and ages of Cassie's siblings, and post it inside the cover. This act is important. These time lines and character lists and charts are not tools that emergent readers use and grow out of. Rather, this sort of writing is the work that readers do whenever we are tackling books that have new complications. I don't generally make maps as I read. But when I read a novel that follows a journey, I love it if the publisher provides a map, and if there isn't one, I'll try to sketch it.

## Your Conferring Can Make It More Likely that Children's Writing Supports Thinking

Often, you'll want to sit with a child and say, "Walk me through the thinking that you've been doing as you read this book," signaling toward the child's reading notebook or Post-its. Expect that the reader will show you one day's responses, the next day's, and the next. When I do this, it helps me if I tell myself beforehand that I'm not going to respond to any one entry or Post-it but am instead focusing on the patterns I see across the student's work.

When you are looking for patterns, for the sorts of thinking that this particular reader does often, be prepared to say something such as, "What I notice is that you are always comparing what you learn about this topic with things you already know about. It seems as if you make these comparisons as easily as you breathe, and they really help you." Then again, you could say, "What I am noticing is that you really identify with that main character, don't you? You seem to be the kind of reader who reads with your heart on your sleeve. You empathize with characters. You are always worrying about whether things will work out for them. That's a real talent to have. It is a big deal to be the kind of reader who really truly walks in a character's shoes, especially now when you are reading historical fiction. You could very well say, 'I'm not like him. I mean—he wears a loincloth and hunts with a bow and arrow. I'm nothing like that.' But instead you see ways in which you and characters from even long ago have a lot in common. That is a huge gift that you have as a reader."

Simply attending to children's records of their reading is, in and of itself, an important thing to do. When you study children's entries and Post-its assuming these are the records of their thinking, this helps children see that their responses to reading merit attention. It is equally or more important to help *children* reread and think about their own and each other's responses to reading. By doing this, you can help them become more invested in their thinking about books, and this, more than any specific skill-development work, will make a world of difference toward encouraging deeper and more reflective reading.

Of course, you can also coach children to lift the level of their writing about reading. When you do this, you'll want to be clear whether your goal is a coherent, clear written essay or is a reader who reads with his or her mind on fire, generating and developing ideas of all sorts, at a rapid clip. Obviously, in the end, you will want both. You'll want your students to be able to write to grow ideas and also to write to present those ideas, but as children are in the act of reading and talking about texts, you will presumably place a priority on the sorts of writing that enriches their reading. This means that you won't expect their writing to address a single coherent thesis statement—not yet, not at this point. Instead you will want to see evidence of lots of thinking. You'll want to see evidence that the reader has been making connections, seeing patterns, asking questions, growing and testing and applying insights, and so forth.

In the end, then, your hope is that *you* won't be the one assigning students to write about reading or telling them the sort of writing that they need to do. Books will pose particular sorts of challenges, and readers will bring unique aspirations to their reading. The writing they do is really an externalized form of the thinking they do. It is important that readers have ownership over the kinds of writing they decide to do as they read. Your job is to teach readers to figure out what they're struggling to make sense of and to coach them to invent or recall a writing tool that helps them do the mind work they want to do.

Before moving to the next section of this chapter, I need to remind you of the cautions I emphasized early in the chapter. Remember that writing about reading can take far too much time, especially for the very children who most need tons of time to read. So teach your students to write fast and furious, to "write short" often and to "write long" occasionally, and keep your eye on the reading logs. Are your students reading at least one book a week (and more for your strugglers)? That is generally a minimum amount of reading for them to be doing, and ultimately your job during reading is to support reading.

> It is important that readers have ownership over the kinds of writing they decide to do as they read. Your job is to teach readers to figure out what they're struggling to make sense of and to coach them to invent or recall a writing tool that helps them do the mind work they want to do.

## Let Students Know There Is a Place for Creative Writing in Response to Reading

Do you remember the olden days of language arts instruction, when most of the writing that kids did was first-draft-only "creative" writing, interspersed into instruction around whole-class texts? On Monday, the class read Whitman's "Song of Myself," and then on Tuesday, during class time, everyone was told to write their own "Song of Myself."

Much of what educators now advocate as guiding principles of the reading and writing workshop are beliefs that were created in direct opposition to that approach. Leaders of the *writing* workshop make compelling arguments against assigning children to spend fifteen minutes writing the ending to (or an adaptation of) someone else' story. "That is not how writers go about writing!" people argue. "Writers create literature through a process that involves rehearsal, drafting, revising, and editing," they say. "Requiring kids to crank out an ending to someone else's story, and to do this in a first–draft-only fashion, within fifteen minutes is anathema to everything we know about good writing."

Meanwhile, leaders of the *reading* workshop approach have equally compelling arguments against the practices of yesteryear. No one argues more compellingly and with more data than Dick Allington, who shows that children in the classrooms of effective teachers read ten times as much as children in the classrooms of less effective teachers, and who shows, too, that time spent reading matters so much that it dwarfs every other factor accounting for reading achievement (save for the presence of a good teacher).

On the other hand, let's remember that children in our reading workshops are not simply readers. They are also writers and historians and scientists and artists. And if we want them to read wholeheartedly, bringing all they are to all that they read, this means that presumably we will want to acknowledge that just as there are times when a child walks down the street, sees an old homeless woman dumping cat food onto paper plates and swarms of homeless cats emerging from everywhere, and reaches for her writer's notebook to record what she's seen, so, too, there will be times during the reading workshop when reading fills a reader with feelings and memories and images and words that are too good to be lost forever. And so, yes, there will be times when a particular child responds to reading not in her reader's notebook but by writing creatively in response to reading. If the reader is lucky enough to keep a writer's notebook, she'll probably do this writing in her writer's notebook. Of course—the place for such response does not really matter. There will be times when a child who is responding to reading in his reader's notebook will break into song! (Not really, but almost. You've seen the responses to reading in which suddenly a bit of creative writing bursts forth.) And just as our children might respond to reading as writers, they will, from time to time, respond to reading also as scientists, as historians, but that's another topic for another day.

What I am saying then is that whereas requiring students to write new endings to the book they are reading or diaries from the perspective of a character raises lots of problems, it's important for our adverse reaction to that sort of work to not swing us to such an extreme that we do not acknowledge that there are times when the thinking we do as we read has more to do with lingering on an image, feeling an emotion, or crying out to the world then discussing our thoughts, and sometimes this leads us to reach for a pencil. This kind of writing about reading, then, is about using our pencils to celebrate the parts of the story that move us, using our pencil so that we won't forget the feelings and ideas we've had as we read.

Let me state adamantly that I believe it's a disaster if every child has to do this sort of response to literature, in sync, all on the same day. On the other hand, it is beautiful if a person feels she has the *license* to write this way from time to time during the reading workshop (or during the writing workshop, in response

to reading), so that when inspired to do so, she may take a few minutes to jot a scrap of a poem that is stirring in her soul, saving that scrap to work on later when she has more time to develop her writing. Or the child might take a few minutes to write as if she was the author of the book, writing a scene that she thinks is implicit in the book, just because this is the truest way to capture her ideas. And it is right that a reader may respond to reading by picking up his pen and writing that letter of outrage or gratitude to the author.

Of all of these, the one kind of writing that we have found is especially powerful is that in which the reader articulates the effect a book has had by writing about an image that lingers. You know how, long after you've forgotten the title and author, you remember the star pressed into the child's hand, the tiger stalking back and forth in its cage in the woods, or the boy carrying his dead dog through the snow. In literary theory, that's called writing the *residue* of reading. If children want to write creatively in response to reading, you might channel them toward writing in ways that capture the images that last for them. When a reader shares an image that stayed with him and explores why this image imprinted itself on him, this is gorgeous work. When readers write about the lasting images, this gives them a window into their intuitive, deeply felt, sometimes buried emotional responses to the story. When a reader is finishing a book and clearly has been moved by that book, then, you might, in a conference, teach that reader that one way to hold books in our hearts is to write and talk about the images that stay with us as we close the last page.

## Writing During the Reading Workshop Can Provide Grist for Literary Essays

Earlier in this chapter I pointed out that usually teachers don't take time for crafting and developing literary essays within the reading workshop itself. But teachers do sometimes use the reading workshop as a place for students to develop seed ideas that they bring with them to another time of the day, using those seed ideas as grist for their writing mills. (As I write this, I'm aware that some of you will be confused with the boundaries I establish and defend between writing time and reading time. Obviously I know you will organize your teaching as you decide, and this may just be my obsession. But I do urge you to protect your children's time to write regularly and to read regularly.)

In any case, if your children are not only developing ideas but also writing to organize and craft those ideas into coherent, compelling literary essays that can be published and read by others, then you may want to channel students to collect responses to reading in ways that will pay off in their essays.

It can help to point out to readers that many of us collect and grow ideas as we read by literally copying (or quoting) lines or passages that feel important to us and then writing about why these feel important. Often, as we do this writing, we shift between writing about that one part of the text and writing about another part that "goes with" the first, and writing how these parts relate to what the whole text seems to really, really be about (deep down). It can help to use thought prompts that support an interpretive sort of thinking. These are elaborated upon in the final unit in the series, but for now let me say that it can help to use prompts such as, "When I first read this I thought…, but now I am realizing…." or "Others may think this is about…, but I'm coming to believe it is really about…."

When students are reading novels you might guide them by suggesting that it tends to pay off if they write and think about places in the text where they learn something surprising or essential, perhaps about a character in the story, or if they write about images that seem to matter especially in the story or about significant lessons that the character (and the reader) learned.

Your students will already know that when they are thinking about their own responses to a book, it helps to return to the text, paraphrasing sections that illustrate their ideas, and that it is important to unpack those passages, exploring the relationship between that passage and the reader's larger idea.

Once your students have worked on writing literary essays and received instruction on writing literary essays, some of their quick, on-the-run thoughts about reading will inevitably begin to feel like miniature essays. Passionate readers don't have to wait for the unit of study in literary essays to roll around before taking up the pen and writing, "Here's what I'm thinking this book is really, really saying and here's why."

When helping readers do this sort of organized reflection, my colleagues and I have found it helpful to show them that there are several possible ways to frame their thinking. I write about this at some length during an assessment interlude in Unit 4.

A reader can make a claim about the text and show that this claim is true across the text. Poppleton is a good friend in this instance, that one, and in that one. *Skylark* is a novel about how people deal with loss. It shows how Papa deals with loss, how Sarah does, and how Caleb and Anna do.

A second way to frame an essay (or an essay-like entry) is by conveying that the reader-writer has been on a journey of thought and has had a change of thinking. The frame "I used to think…, but now I realize…" is a powerful one. "I used to think this was a book about a family—Pa, Sarah, Anna, and Caleb— but I have come to believe it is a book about a place, the prairie." "I used to think *Number the Stars* was a book about Annemarie, who put herself at risk to help her friend, but I have come to believe this is a book about all the brave people of the Resistance, who put their own lives in jeopardy to save the Jews." There are, of course, various phrases that can support this sort of a journey of thought. Instead of starting one paragraph with, "I used to think…" and the next with, "But now I realize…,' a student might write, "In the beginning I thought…, but now I am coming to see…." or "When I first read this, I thought…, but now, after studying it closely, I realize…."

Finally, students can also use writing to capture the complexity of their ideas, using a sentence frame such as, "My feelings about this story are complicated. On the one hand…, but on the other hand…." Again, there are variations on this. "My ideas about (whatever) are complicated. I think…. But I also think…."

## Final Thoughts About Writing About Reading

Readers who have been invited to convey their ideas in writing about books often develop a passion for writing about literature and a writerly relationship with reading. Inviting youngsters to write about reading can be a wonderful thing. Helping them use writing to set their minds on fire as they read can be beautiful. Showing them ways to post their thinking about books on www.amazon.com and www.barnesandnoble.com and www.goodreads.com can be a powerful thing. Inviting them to post responses to what others have written can make a good thing even better. Showing them the children's authors who publish letters from young readers on their websites can fuel their passion for writing about reading because your children will aspire to be featured on a favorite author's website.

But readers who have been forced to write about their books, and especially to write about books they do not even want to read, tend to dislike reading all the more because of the writing that is nestled within reading. Be careful. When working with writing about reading, you are playing with fire.

# CHAPTER TEN

# Differentiation to Support All Readers

**W**hen Roland Barth, the founder of Harvard's Principal Center and author of many books on school reform, recently spoke to a gathering of principals who lead Teachers College Reading and Writing Project schools, he asked, "Right now, will you think about and jot down the learning that you are doing in your school?" Then he followed the first question with a second question: "Who knows about this learning?"

Roland then pointed out that the one thing that most defines a great school is that this is a place where everyone's learning curve is as steep as it can be. How important it is, then, that the school's leaders not only are people who learn on the job while at school, but also are people who are willing to be public learners. "You need to learn aloud," Barth said. "Others need to know about your questions, your uncertainties, your enduring passion to learn, your brand-new, wobbly steps forward."

## If the Rallying Cry to Differentiate Is Going to Lead to Real and Lasting Reform, Schools Need to Resist Snake Oil

My lifework has been to help schools become places where everyone's learning curve is sky high, and I've found, as Michael Fullan, author of *Change Forces*, has also found, that the problem in most schools is not the absence of innovations or even a resistance to innovations. Instead, one of the great problems is that many schools are characterized by such a constant stream of innovations that people never have time to go from mandates to personal beliefs. Or as Richard Elmore has said, "Local reform initiatives are typically characterized by volatility—with schools jumping nervously from one reform to the next after relatively short periods of time—and superficiality—with schools choosing reforms that have little impact on learning and implementing them in shallow ways." Peter Drucker echoes what these two researchers have found: "The failure to exploit existing innovations is more widespread than the failure to innovate in the first place."

This is not a chapter on the process of school reform but, rather, on differentiation. But for me, the two topics are coming together because in the schools I know best, the new buzzword is *differentiation*, and my greatest fear is not resistance to differentiation, but superficial compliance. What anyone knows who has worked in schools over time is that all too often, the deepest and most poignant goals of all are flown across the educational landscape like the signs carried by those giant blimps that float overhead at football games, trailing banners that rally the people to cheer harder, buy more, come again. The blimps that are flying over public schools these days are carrying the hue and cry of "High Standards!" of "Data-Based Instruction," and, above all, of "Thou Shalt Differentiate!"

I see schools complying in knee-jerk ways that create reams of new paperwork, widespread chaos, increasing cynicism, and anxiety and that either create no substantial changes in the actual life within classrooms or, worse, bring classrooms backward toward methods and systems that have already proven themselves to be destructive for strugglers.

This is the problem: this most recent rallying cry is too important for schools to do as usual, mandating compliance and yet supporting no deep, enduring reforms. The truth is that the three rallying cries that are resounding through our schools today need to actually define the new mission of schools in today's world. This Information Age does require that children develop higher levels of literacy skills than even those that were necessary just a decade ago. And the truth is that a sea change is required in which we, as a teaching profession, are going to actually take responsibility for what our kids know and can do. It is endemic across the profession that we say, "A third of my kids hate to read." without blushing at this self-indictment. We bemoan our kids' lack of pride in their work, their disrespect for each other, their unwillingness to spend time outside school reading—without assuming that all of this is a reflection on our teaching. It's always the kids' fault, and the problem is that if we stop seeing all this as attributes of kids and instead take this on as the results of our teaching, then we don't know what to do. Teaching becomes an extraordinarily tall order. What solutions can we reach for that will allow us to really, truly, bring all our kids to high levels of literacy?

One answer to that question—how can our teaching take on the real work of turning kids around?—is that our work with kids needs to become more precisely personal. There won't ever be one way to reach and touch and help all learners. What's required is a teacher who is willing to listen hard, to watch with care, and to learn through trial and error, through taking cues from kids—and that's differentiation. The combination of precisely personalized teaching and of teachers truly holding ourselves accountable for our kids reaching high standards—that's differentiation.

So yes, we need an unrelenting hold on high standards and we need to keep our eyes on kids' actual work, the true data of what they show us, doing both with the spirit of, "It is my job to bring these learners where they need to go." And then, yes, our teaching does need to be responsive enough, efficient enough, and goal-driven enough that we go to the ends of the earth to teach each child. Actually making sure that schools provide all children with access to the richest possible education is perhaps the most urgent need any of us can address. True differentiation is the great civil rights concern of our time.

But any new buzzword will bring out the gold diggers, and this is no exception. The number of phony panaceas being peddled in the name of differentiation is absurd. We shouldn't be surprised. Look at what people peddle in the name of weight loss. Think of the way that big business has jumped onto that goal. The streets are full of people selling laxatives and gastric bypasses, fish oils and stomach clamps that all promise instant solutions. But for the most part, doesn't it seem that well-educated and thoughtful people know enough to roll our eyes at these shenanigans? Why don't we listen with equal skepticism to the instant solutions that are being peddled in reaction to the recent pressures for schools to provide data-based and differentiated teaching? What keeps a school from realizing that this is not just a mandate with which one needs to comply, that this is a mission. This is about kids, the kids who are lost in the pipeline.

Do you remember, over two decades ago, when little Jessica fell into a pipe in Texas? The nation held its breath while scores of miners worked against the clock, with the very best technology available, hoping against hope to reach her

> *The combination of precisely personalized teaching and of teachers truly holding ourselves accountable for our kids reaching high standards—that's differentiation.*

in time. And when she was finally pulled from that pipe, brought into the light, we wept tears of joy. There are literally millions of children stuck somewhere in the pipes of our schools, not able to reach the sunlight. Differentiation is about nothing less than doing for these children what the nation did for little Jessica.

To address the problem of differentiation, a school system needs to begin by saying no. Doug Reeves often tells the story of a gardener who sees row upon row of beautiful flowers at the nursery and comes home with a wheelbarrow loaded with perennials and annuals, only to see that his garden is already choked with thistles, dandelions, crabgrass, and other weeds. That gardener is not going to have success unless he first pulls the weeds to make space for new plants to grow. In a similar way, every school is crammed full of remnants of failed initiatives, defunct innovations, or old mandates, and a good deal of that paraphernalia are old, failed attempts to differentiate. Just as not every weight-loss solution is a responsible one, not everything peddled under the banner of differentiation will help a school, a teacher, to actually do that work. So a school system or a classroom teacher wanting to truly tackle the transformative, challenging work of differentiating must begin by saying no, to say yes.

> *Just as not every weight-loss solution is a responsible one, not everything peddled under the banner of differentiation will help a school, a teacher, to actually do that work.*

Saying no should be easier because one thing we know for certain is that what has been done in American schools in the name of differentiation has not worked. The 2003 NAEP results (National Center for Education Statistics, 2004) shows a thirty-one point gap between Black and White fourth-grade reading scores, and the Hispanic-White gap is almost identical to the Black-White gap. Currently, only one in ten kindergartners in low-income schools will graduate from college. More of those children will end up in jail. Still, an astonishing number of schools respond to the pressure to differentiate by returning like a boomerang to the practices of yesteryear, when the term became predominant.

It's probably important for an educational leader to understand that the term *differentiation* comes with some baggage. The term first became popular as part of a larger emphasis on the industrial model of education. Schools in the early 1900s were flooded with immigrants and aimed for the efficiency of an assembly line. This led to an education system in which different tracks of students proceeded through ditto sheets and exercises, with frequent short-answer, objective tests signaling that a learner could or could not move on and with external rewards—stars or certificates—making up for the lack of an education that was intrinsically motivating.

The history behind the term may be one part of why the pressure for higher standards and for "results" is, in too many places, leading schools backward to a time when strugglers were cordoned off from others, given a regimen of drill and skill, of dittos and frequent tests, and bribed to do well with external rewards for progress. As pressure for results escalates, as fear of sanctions become even more gripping, too many schools are turning to programs for which, in fact, there are no convincing results.

Returning to a factory model of schooling that was dominant in the industrial age will not work for the utterly different world of today because what's needed today is not for a small elite to receive one sort of education and the larger masses to be given low-level, skill-and-drill work that resembles multiple-choice questions on standardized tests. The very *last* thing that a school system should be doing to bring all kids to high levels of literacy is to return, in a knee-jerk fashion, to the interpretations of differentiation that defined American schools in the 1900s. And in too many instances, that is exactly what is happening.

So yes, it is critically and urgently important to help struggling readers. And it is true that real differentiation—let's call it *personalization*, a word that does not have the historical connotations of *differentiation*—is urgently important. But what is needed is for educators to realize that providing the richest and best education possible to every child is not something that can be outsourced to packaged programs or scripted remedies or any other remedy that may promise to be "scientifically based." The irresponsible weight-loss programs make similar promises, and advertisements in *The Enquirer* regularly cite data that promises miracles. We have to be critical consumers—and critical consumers of our reading instruction resources as much as anything else.

## What Does Research Truly Say Schools Need to Do to Support Differentiation?

There are really only a few proven ways to be sure that we are helping strugglers, and the first and most important is to be sure they are taught by good teachers. The only "quick fix" that's available is to be sure that schools that support strugglers provide teachers with communities of practice that support ongoing professional study, collaboration, and kid-watching—and that keep good teachers in the classroom.

Listen to this data. Bembry (Bembry et al., 1998) has released a study that shows that students in classrooms offering high-quality instruction for three years running received scores on standardized reading tests that are 40 percentile ranks higher than students enrolled in classrooms with lower-quality teachers. That is staggering, and there is a mountain of data that conveys a similar message. The best way to support strugglers is to provide teachers with high-quality professional development and with a culture that supports professionalism and keeps good teachers in the classroom.

The Teachers College Reading and Writing Project has confirmed what studies show. In the high-poverty schools that work with the Project to provide teachers with twenty days of staff development support a year (and remember, these schools often contain 1500+ students), the scores for children who were in third grade three years ago and were in fifth grade last year went up an average of 23 percentile points. Last year, 99% of the New York City schools that work with the Teachers College Reading and Writing Project accomplished AYP.

The professional development that will especially help a school is that in which staff developers actually work in classrooms, demonstrating ways of watching what kids actually do and then inventing new ways to reach kids who struggle, providing (and then later withdrawing) supports so that strugglers are able to be full participants in rigorous learning communities. What's needed is professional development that helps teachers in a school work together as inquirers, taking cues from what kids do and don't do and participating in the cycle of teaching, observing, reflecting on teaching, planning teaching, teaching, observing, and so on.

In a school that cares about differentiation and about supporting all learners, this commitment will be reflected in the design of professional development. For starters, literacy professional development won't leave specialists behind! Staff development won't cordon off the reading specialists and English as a second language teachers and speech therapists and guidance counselors and parent coordinators. Inclusion needs to be a way of life for a school, not just a kind of classroom formation for kids. Then, too, the professional development needs to be situated in the full range of classrooms. The topics, too, need to reflect a focus on differentiation. For example, one critical topic is this: "Okay. I have the data. Now what?"

We also know that it is critically important to provide strugglers with dramatically more time reading high-success books (96% accuracy, fluency, comprehension). If a school is lucky enough to have Reading Recovery teachers or other reading specialists, it's extremely helpful if these experts work alongside classroom teachers to assess readers who are enigmas. Some schools use these experts to meet one-on-one with selected children during the final two weeks of summer, conducting assessments in-depth enough to provide the foundation so that a trusted plan of action can be developed for these youngsters. That way, not a moment of the school year is wasted before these youngsters are brought on course, and there can be an authoritative, comprehensive resource that specialists, intervention teachers, parents, the child, and the classroom teacher all refer to (and add to). I'd suggest that in addition to conducting running records and ideally a miscue analysis, follow-up assessments need to be made. If a child has trouble with fluency, for example, then it's important to check that youngster's knowledge of high-frequency words and her oral language. If it is comprehension that holds a child back on running records, then what is the child's comprehension when the teacher reads aloud the passage? What is the child's comprehension when the child is rereading instead of reading for the first time or is given a more supportive introduction or is reading on a topic on which the child has expertise? To develop a full portrait of a learner, of course, we need to talk with parents, hearing what they have to say. More than once, I've found teachers and principals who assume that a child's frequent tardiness and absenteeism reflects irresponsibility but who then investigate more deeply and discover that, in fact, this youngster is the caregiver for younger siblings or for a sick grandparent. Always, talking to a child's parent or caregiver will be illuminating, and of course the partnership that can be established through these conversations can make it vastly more likely that children have time at home to continue reading.

It is also important to make sure that all the texts children are reading across the entire day are texts they can read with ease. It is easy to check this. Ask a struggler to bring you all the books and other materials he's been reading across the whole day—the math book, the science texts, the social studies materials—and ask the child to read aloud a bit in one text and the next. You probably need not even get involved in comprehension checks, because just by listening to the child's fluency alone you'll probably see that in subject after subject across the day, this learner is being denied a chance to learn. Your strugglers can't afford to spend one minute doing work that teaches them they can't read, that texts make no sense, that reading is a stop-and-go process of hacking away at hard words. Your strugglers can't afford one minute that teaches them to sit passively in front of a text, to expect confusion, or to zone out, and yet kids who are given texts that are vastly too hard for them have no real alternative but than to do these things.

Of course, children who struggle can benefit in extraordinary ways from being able to work in a small group or a one-to-one tutorial with a teacher who has special expertise in supporting strugglers. A word of caution. The truth is that schools are rife with instances in which pull-out support hasn't been helpful. The fact that a learner goes for "extra help" doesn't mean that extra help is actually provided. Here again, there is a huge amount of research that can inform supplemental services. I recommend people start by reading Allington's concise review of the research in his book, *What Really Matters for Struggling Readers*. The entire book will help, but there is also a chapter that targets this topic.

This is what we know. It is a terrible problem when a struggler is pulled from the regular classroom during language arts time to receive extra help in language arts. This is especially dire if the struggler is pulled from the regular classroom sometimes and not all the time. Such interruptions all but guarantee that the struggler will be confused and out of sorts and disoriented when he or she is in the classroom—all feelings he or she is apt to experience anyhow, but they'll be compounded in dramatic ways if the child is taken from the classroom in sporadic, intermittent ways.

We also know it is a problem if the child goes for extra help with reading and doesn't get time to read during that interlude. The irony is that the chances are great that there will be no reading during reading support time! Instead, kids are given flash cards, dittos, games, exercises—anything but what they really need, which is time to read. Then, too, it's less than 50% likely that even when pulled out for extra help, the child will be given a book that is appropriate for him or her.

Finally, we know that when readers who struggle are taught, in general, and especially when they receive extra help, there can't be a one-size-fits-all approach to supporting strugglers. Kids who are successful readers have it all together. They generally are pulling off the combination of things that are necessary for reading to work. This means that successful readers are somewhat similar to each other. Strugglers, on the other hand, are sitting on a three-legged stool and one leg is missing. But every struggler will not be missing the same leg! Some struggle with phonics, unable to decode words. Others struggle with comprehension or with comprehension of expository texts. Others, above all, are inexperienced readers, needing vast amounts more time reading. The important thing is that a child who struggles with phonics needs an entirely different sort of help than a child who struggles with comprehension, so any one-size-fits-all approach to supporting strugglers is, from the start, a problem. It is for this reason that the data strongly suggests that if kids are going to be pulled from a classroom for small-group support, those groups need to be comprised of four or fewer learners and constituted so that these are learners who need similar support. Any plan to support strugglers by working with them in groups of eight or more kids, constituted simply because these are all kids who are failing to thrive, is a setup for disaster.

Many schools prolong the school day for strugglers with before-school, after-school, and during-recess help. It is, of course, wise to support children without taking them out of their regular literacy time, so this is well intentioned. But we must also be careful that we do not take away from children the times when school stands a chance of being a good thing and take from the school's budget all funds that could otherwise be spent provisioning classrooms with rich libraries and providing teachers with professional development and with time to work and study alongside each other. I agree with Allington that before taking away a learner's normal free time, "it's incumbent on schools to ensure that very nearly 100 percent of the school day's instruction is appropriate to each child's needs." Allington goes on to say, "I would argue that creating after-school or summer school programs is professionally unethical unless we are absolutely sure that all children receive optimal instruction all year long during the regular school day. All of us need to focus our primary efforts on ensuring that children have access to high-quality teaching in their classrooms before we consider adding extended-time interventions" (2006).

It could be, after all, that the best way to support a child who struggles to read is to bring art, dance, athletics, drama, and music back to school. Think for a moment of what it is that school asks kids to do, and imagine if we were asked to do the same. Think of something you are very bad at. For me, for example,

fixing my computer is high on that list, as are complicated math problems and disciplining an unruly and contemptuous class full of adolescents. Now imagine that you and I were expected to engage in that work, day in and day out, most of every day. What's worse—imagine we were expected to do this publicly, alongside people who were good at it, and our progress was publicly monitored. Is it really any surprise that strugglers act out? Might one part of the solution be for schools to reconsider maintaining a full-time, constant, laser-like beam on the one thing that strugglers can't do? Isn't it possible that a rich program in the arts could allow some children who struggle in reading to find a reason to come to school, to walk with pride?

My point is really not to argue against summer school or Saturday school—both can be wonderful things—but both are expensive in time, money, and energy. It's important that we first make sure that time in school is regarded as precious and that every minute supports a child's learning. Then we need to remember that the most important thing we can do during summers and school vacation is to simply provision kids with tons and tons of high-interest books that they can read and want to read.

It's not a small thing for a school to look the issue of supporting summer and vacation reading in the eye. Summer reading loss has a more devastating effect on strugglers than most of us could possibly predict. The important thing to understand is that a solution is right at hand. If children are sent home with backpacks full of high-interest books that they can read and want to read, that, in and of itself, can prevent a huge amount of slippage. Otherwise—when children do not have access to books across the summer—it generally takes until November for children's reading levels to be back where they were when school let out in June. For children who are already behind, that slippage is not a detail.

But my bigger point is that the way to turn around a school so that strugglers begin to get traction as learners doesn't require a snake oil solution. You do not need an enormous computer lab with huge programs that flash words at children or get them "uh bah cuh-ing" in unison. You need to realize that the solutions are right there within reach and are rather obvious. But they require work. They require common sense. They require the courage to say no. They require collaboration. They require that we step up to the job at hand, saying, "This is my mission."

# Becoming a Teacher Who Truly Differentiates Requires Each of Us to Outgrow Ourselves

In addition to this, every teacher needs help differentiating in the true sense of the word. And perhaps this begins simply by realizing that some of the most important, intellectually challenging work that any of us will do as teachers is the work of truly learning to reach every learner where he or she is and helping that learner go the distance. I think the first step in truly supporting every child is for each one of us to take ownership of this work. Every teacher needs to take on the mission—not thinking for a moment that our most vulnerable learners can be outsourced to the remedial reading teacher, the English as a second language specialist, or the Reading Recovery teacher. If others are available to help us make sure that every moment for these children is treated as precious indeed, then that is great—but ultimately the classroom teacher needs to know that differentiation is not the work of a school system. It is the work of a classroom teacher. And we need to know that our actions can hurt or they can help.

*…the most important, intellectually challenging work that any of us will do as teachers is the work of truly learning to reach every learner where he or she is and helping that learner go the distance.*

To really take responsibility for providing a classroom in which you differentiate in ways that help your children, it helps to pause and think for a moment about your history as a teacher and to ask yourself, "When in my teaching have I experienced instances when differentiation was deeply important to kids and aligned to my best beliefs about what human beings need to grow?" You can also think, "When in my life has the effort to differentiate zapped energy, distracted teachers and learners, and made people feel victimized or defeated or discouraged?" Or you can think about differentiation in your own life, asking, "When have I, as a learner, received opportunities to learn that felt differentiated and that made a world of difference for me?" You could ask, too, "What would it take to give learning opportunities like these to all children in my classroom and my school?"

I suspect you will come from this recommitting yourself to the important job of making sure that you give everyone in your classroom the access and support necessary to shine. I think, for example, of Paneotis, who was new to his school in fifth grade and whose demeanor perfectly fit the term *curmudgeon*. He hated school, hated everything about it and everyone in his classroom, and certainly he hated the reading workshop. Then his teacher, Kathy Doyle, read *Listen to the Wind*, the picture-book version of *Three Cups of Tea*, a book about Greg Mortensen's efforts to build schools in Afghanistan and Pakistan. Listening to this book, Paneotis recalled something he had heard earlier about Beads for Life and suggested his class could become involved with this program. They could use it as a way to earn money to send to Pennies for Peace, the effort that rallied children to help Mortensen's effort. Kathy didn't know what Beads for Life was, and she was embroiled in a hundred other things at the time, but this was the first bit of initiative Paneotis had shown, and she was not going to let the opportunity slip by. Within three days, she'd found someone who could visit her class to talk about Beads for Life, and soon her children were listening to the story of these beads, made by African villagers from rolled up paper, that could be sold as a way to help the villagers, but also as a way to make money for a cause—in this instance, for Mortenson's program, Pennies for Peace.

Organizing the class to get behind this effort was Paneotis's first step, but three days later, he came to school on a Monday morning with a bracelet that he himself had made from rolled-up paper. He showed it to his teacher, and her jaw dropped. "How? What? Where?" she asked, and out came the story. On Saturday morning, he'd woken up at 5 A.M. to read on the Internet about the process of making these beads. Then he'd fashioned himself a tool out of a large paperclip, and worked for four hours before making a single bead out of rolled-up paper, just as the villagers were doing. Then he proceeded to make beads enough for the entire bracelet.

When the children heard about this, they were floored. Soon a group had signed up to stay in from recess to receiving tutoring from Paneotis, and before long he'd traveled through all the classes of the school, teaching the entire building how to make Beads for Life.

Paneotis was transformed. He went from being an apathetic, disengaged learner to being one of the most vitally engaged leaders in the school. And of course, the power of this is that it was not just Paneotis who was changed, but all who witnessed his transformation were changed as well. Think for a moment about the YouTube clip showing Susan Boyle's singing. Did you see it? Did you see that rather frumpy woman walk on stage, and laugh a bit about her claim that she wanted to be a professional singer? Did you listen as she stood there and sang like a skylark? And did you find yourself rising from your seat along with the crowd in that hall, along with those cynical judges, feeling this unbelievable sense of "Oh my gosh. I was so wrong. She is so drop-dead beautiful?" And did you feel yourself becoming bigger at that moment? I did. Susan Boyle blasted through my old expectations, my crabbed, little stereotypes, my ways of boxing people up, just as Paneotis did for his classmates and his teacher.

In the end, perhaps the secret of differentiation is not that we dole out something different to this one and that one—a ditto here, a drill there. Perhaps differentiation is really all about you and me being willing to become different to meet each learner where he or she is. What a beautiful goal—for each of us to look each learner in the eyes and to convey to that learner that I am willing to become different to help you go the distance.

That's what I have seen good teachers do, time and again. I think about Katie Even, one of the teachers who piloted the final draft of these units of study. Katie teaches an inclusion class of third graders, and she said that what she found really worked for teaching her kids fluency was bathroom songs. One of her book clubs got involved, somehow, in writing little ditties that they then sang together—repeatedly, over and over. To the tune of "Twinkle, Twinkle Little Star" they sang "Boy that diaper's really stinky/Hope I don't get poo-on-my pinky." And oh, their fluency, their phrasing! Oh their joy, their engagement, their sense of solidarity! Who would have thought it? The solution to struggling readers is potty humor.

Of course, that is not really what I am saying. What I am saying is that what's needed for all kids to succeed is for all of us to be willing to engage, to listen, to take cues from kids, and to go the distance. I think of Naomi Shihab Nye, the author of *Habibi* and so many other beautiful books, who once said, "Whenever you love somebody who is different than you, you have to grow a little larger. It's a risky thing—you find your empathy grows. Your heart stretches—it can hold more" (Nye, 2002). That's differentiation.

# CHAPTER ELEVEN

# Standards and Standardized Tests: Smarter, Not More, Test Prep

Variations of the reading workshop that are described in this series (and even variations of the specific units of study) are already in place in thousands of schools. You can see this work in as many as half the schools in New York City, in a great many of the suburban schools on Long Island, in Westchester, and in New Jersey, as well as in schools across the country and indeed across the world. Visit many of Connecticut's highest-performing districts—you'll see the reading workshop. Visit Seattle's schools—you'll see the reading workshop. Visit many KIPP schools, Promise Academy schools, elite private schools, or many of the urban elementary schools in cities across the U.S.—in Boston, Madison, San Francisco, Los Angeles, Chicago, Providence, Portland, Alexandria, Albany, Atlanta, Houston, Durham, San Diego, Washington DC, and the list continues. In all these settings and a great many more, you'll see thriving reading workshops.

People who choose balanced literacy approaches to teaching reading do so because we want students to become avid, reflective, critical readers who comprehend with depth and vigor and who construct richly literate lives for themselves in and out of school. We want kids to carry books with them everywhere, to have favorite authors and series and genres, to turn to reading for adventure and solace, illumination, and information. We also want children to grow up as ethical compassionate citizens who can walk in the shoes of others who are different from themselves and who expect to outgrow their own thinking by taking in and talking back to the ideas of others. We want all this—and, yes, we also want kids to demonstrate that they meet the standards and do well on the standardized tests that have such important consequences.

# The Common Core Standards and *Units of Study* in the Reading Workshop

These units of study aim to be a gold standard for teacher education and curriculum support. They aim to synthesize reading research, state-of-the-art teaching, and the knowledge gained from a community of practice that has long been at the forefront of supporting demonstration sites in the teaching of reading and writing, into the Monday, Tuesday, Wednesday of classroom teaching. So when people ask, "Do the *Units of Study for Teaching Reading* meet the new Common Core Standards?" the answer is that these units aim not to *meet* standards, but to exceed them. These units of study tell the story of a reading curriculum in action, and this curriculum supports deep comprehension and interpretation skills. The young people are never led to believe they are working toward a checklist of skills, toward a list of standards. The goal for them is much more lasting and more significant than any iteration of the standards. And frankly, it is not just young people but also you and I, their teachers, who need goals that are dearer to our hearts than that of some current list of standards. Standards fluctuate and frankly are often not high enough. Many state standards barely teach students to be proficient, let alone to be expert readers. National standards will be rewritten every few years, as different political parties come into power and as educators continue to be held responsible for everything related to the new generation. The wisest course is for all of us to teach toward a horizon of excellence, and we'll find that the standards are easily incorporated into the rigorous teaching and learning that takes place in our classrooms.

Yet the flip side of this is that assessments will always be designed with standards in mind, and none of us can be oblivious to the assessments that do have power over our students' lives (if not our own). A teacher (or if not a teacher, then a superintendent) will need to take the standards to which her community is held accountable, lay the standards alongside the curriculum, and think, "Okay, in what ways *does* this curriculum support these standards? In what ways do we need to add to or revise this curriculum so that we can rest assured that we're covering all our bases?" When you lay these units of study alongside the Common Core Standards, you'll be able to say, "Ah yes, we're teaching that, and that, and that…." Check, check, check.

For the past two decades, I've always kept standards in mind when thinking about curriculum for literacy. That does not mean that standards have been *foremost* in my mind, but they have been part of my consciousness. This is true because I was part of the group of twenty-five or so literacy experts from across the nation who contributed to an earlier effort known as the New Standards Project, led by the National Center of Education and the Economy and the Institute for Learning. Those standards were piloted in New York City, a place that has always taken seriously the challenge of bringing all students to high common standards. The newer Common Core Standards stand on the shoulders of earlier efforts toward national standards like the New Standards Project, as well as reflecting contemporary priorities that come from recognition that if our students are going to compete in the twenty-first-century global economy, they need new levels and kinds of literacy. The other reason that the standards have been part of the consciousness out of which this work has evolved is that the Teachers College Reading and Writing Project (TCRWP) has always worked in large-scale ways with whole cities, whole towns, whole districts. Large-scale comprehensive work requires attentiveness to standards.

There are times when you may find that you need to show how the units of study help students meet standards. When those conversations arise, I encourage you to take a shared stance that your goal as a reading educator is for students to exceed standards. When you need to do so, you should feel confident that you can point to any item on the list of reading standards, and show a series of lessons that teach your children those reading skills. Let's take a look, for instance, at a list of skills that are important in the Common Core Standards, and as you look at these you'll see a match that will not surprise you. Of course we want young people to be able to synthesize, to compare, to interpret. Of course we want them to be familiar with significant literary traditions and genres. Our goal is for these units of study to carry students and teachers across years of study. The Common Core Standards, for example, call for students in grades 3–5 to be able to do the work described here, all of which is also supported in *Units of Study for Teaching Reading*:

- Students in grades 3–5 need to be able to read closely to determine what a text says, grounding an account of their reading in specifics and quotes from the text.
- Students need to be able to determine the main idea(s) or big themes from texts and to talk or write about these, supplying supportive details from the text.
- Students need to be able to relate parts of the text to each other, noting how characters' motivations go with their actions, how the

setting interacts with the plot, how one event in a historical or scientific account causes another. Strong students should be able to do this work in ways that show relationships between several different aspects (as in comparing several characters or showing the relationship between several historical events). Students should be able to show this thinking in writing as well as in talking when called to do so.

- Students should be able to think about (and write about) perspective and point of view in texts.
- Students not only need to solve words (as in pronouncing them), they also need to interpret words and phrases in texts, attending to the author's craft. They need to be aware of the tone of the words and the ways that some authors use metaphor, allusion, tone, and the like to create meaning. When reading nonfiction, readers need to be able to determine the meaning of words in academic texts.
- Students need to be able to analyze the structure of texts, paying attention to ways different texts (or different kinds of texts) are structured differently and to ways in which text features help readers of nonfiction texts search for and think about information.
- Students need to be able to synthesize information from multiple sources (diagrams, pictures, charts, digital sources).
- Students need to be able to read critically, assessing whether the text's claims are warranted, and to compare and contrast information or story elements from different texts.
- Students need to be able to read texts at a level of complexity that matches that put forth by the standards. For grades 2 and 3, the texts mentioned are within the span of level J–S. For grades 4 and 5, the texts mentioned fall within the levels of S–X. Some of the texts cited represent levels of difficulty that are far beyond those generally regarded as on-level.
- Students need to be able to participate in discussions in which they draw on relevant material, build on ideas of previous speakers, ask and answer questions that seek clarification, and build conclusions that incorporate ideas put forth by others as well as their own ideas. When called to do so, they also need to be able to summarize key ideas or claims and supporting details, either orally or on the page.

The Common Core Standards will presumably influence school systems to emphasize the close reading necessary for a reader to be able to summarize a text, to ascertain the main idea(s) of that text, and to talk and write about the text in accountable ways. These standards suggest that it will be important for the curricula to support students to be attentive to the *structure* of texts. These priorities are also found in *Units of Study for Teaching Reading*, where readers are explicitly taught to draw on a sense of story structure to read fictional and nonfiction narratives and where they are taught to extrapolate "boxes and bullets" (or main ideas and supports) from expository texts.

Then, too, these recent standards emphasize thinking across two or more texts to synthesize or compare and contrast information. Almost every unit of study ends with students doing this work. In nonfiction, for example, students synthesize several texts on one subtopic, comparing the different ways the texts present that topic and integrating information from those various texts. The historical fiction unit ends with students thinking and writing across several texts that address the same theme. The standards also call for readers to be attentive to the challenges that specific genres pose and to the way texts are and are not representative of genre characteristics. Genre, of course, is one of the defining features of the units of study, with students studying and reading mystery, fantasy, historical fiction, folktales and fairytales, biographies, and the like.

Of course, the four units of study in this series are not meant as a young person's entire literacy curriculum. You'll draw also on units that are described in less detail within *Constructing Curriculum*, including one on helping readers read with an awareness of the ways in which myths, legends, folktales, and fairytales underpin many contemporary stories. You'll also teach literacy across your curriculum, using social studies, science, and math instruction as additional opportunities to support content area literacy.

## The Case for (and Against) Standards

The debates will rage forever, for and against standards. Some will argue that trying to fit every learner into one-size-fits-all expectations ignores the unique contributions that each individual could bring to a community in favor of homogeneity. Many will argue that until we provide equal opportunities to learn—including equal access to healthy diets, living conditions, and medical services as well as to books, good teachers, preschool education, effective schools—it is

unreasonable to expect teachers to shoulder responsibility for ensuring that all children can reach high standards.

Those arguments against standards have merit, but there is also a way in which they have nothing to do with the counterargument. The effort to establish common standards exists in large part because when educators say, "It is not reasonable to expect this student to succeed like others," this decision compounds all the disadvantages that learner has already encountered. And the "tyranny of low expectations" is a very real tyranny. A learner slaps together a bit of work, and if the teacher has decided this learner is not in the upper tier of the class, the teacher may not look aghast at the child's perfunctory efforts and may fail to say, "No way this is your best—do it again." Instead, the teacher may shrug and think, "What can you expect?" or "I guess this is adequate, *considering*…" and what follows will be a list of reasons why that student can't be held to the same standards as others. The intention behind this sort of thinking is a kind, considerate one—but the result is not kind, because in the end, that learner *will* be held to the same standards as anyone else. Realizing this, most school systems have come to the conclusion that it is not helpful, for example, to give a student who is well behind grade expectations an A, arguing that the grade can be for effort and worrying that a poor grade would fuel the learner's low self-concept.

The standards are part of an urgent effort to push and shove and hoist and pull the entire system of education toward higher expectations. That work is utterly necessary, because right now not enough educators really do have high expectations. A student takes five days to read a sixty-page-long little book, and too few teachers say, "This book should take you a day, not a week. Starting today, you need to really pump up the amount of reading you are doing because this is way out of line." A student records his "thoughts" on Post-its, and they are not thoughts at all but facts that are right there on the page of the book, and it is entirely likely that student will continue for months, even years, without someone saying, "This needs to end. You are recording what is right there in the book. The Post-its are for your thoughts. Why don't you take out the ones that add nothing to what is already in the book and substitute them with Post-its that hold your own thoughts?"

The standards are also an effort for the educational system (and every one of us in it) to assume responsibility for our students' work. This accountability needs to occur at every level. It means that it is problem for a principal to say, "My teachers are the type who come in late and leave early." Instead of passing this off as someone else's responsibility, it would be helpful for the principal to hold

A GUIDE TO THE READING WORKSHOP

herself accountable and think, "I haven't yet found a way to tap into teachers' passions for teaching so that they start being more willing to invest themselves in their teaching." In the same way, the standards are an effort to impress on teachers that it is not okay to say (in the spring of the school year, even), "Half my kids read below grade level" or "My kids can't handle expository nonfiction" and for that teacher not to see this as a commentary on herself. Standards-based, assessment-based teaching instead thinks, "I haven't yet succeeded in helping all my students to… What can I do next to turn this around?" And that stance *is*, I believe, utterly necessary at this juncture in the evolution of America's school systems.

## Standardized Tests and Standards: Are the Tests We Have Now Effective Measurements?

I do not know of a single educator who believes that the tests and the assessment system that we have now are good measures of students' learning or teachers' teaching. I urge people (especially teachers and principals in high-need schools) to read Linda Darling-Hammond's newest book, *The Flat World and Education*, and especially the third chapter of that book, to become more articulate advocates for performance assessments and for better assessments in general. There is a great deal of evidence that whereas almost a decade ago the emphasis on higher standards led to higher levels of achievement for at least some parts of the population, translating those standards into tests that are given in every school year and therefore are more and more apt to be dominated by short-answer questions that assess level-level skills has not been helpful. And there is certainly agreement among many people that the New York state standardized test is not reliable as a measurement for differentiating between strong and truly excellent levels of achievement. The good news is that the Gates Foundation and the U.S. Department of Education realize that higher standards must be accompanied by tests that measure higher levels of thinking and of scholarship, and this suggests an eventual resurgence of performance assessments.

But this *Guide to the Reading Workshop* can't take up the big challenge of talking back to a flawed assessment system. What this book can do, instead, is help teachers and principals who want to teach reading through balanced literacy and, more specifically, through a reading workshop, understand ways to achieve the requisite scores.

## Are There Data To Show that the Reading Workshop Approach Works?

Yes, the data show that this approach works. If you want the evidence, first read Allington's *What Really Matters for Struggling Readers*. That book reviews the extensive research that demonstrates that students benefit from lots of time to read high-interest books of their own choosing, especially if these are books that they can read with 96% accuracy, fluency, and comprehension. Allington's book will suggest you are on the right track if you also provide students with explicit instruction in skills and strategies, with one-to-one assessment-based support for those who struggle, and in general, with teachers who participate in a professional learning culture that values reflection, collaboration, kid-watching, and study.

If you want more data that suggest this specific "program" works, then it may help you to know some of the statistics that show New York City's progress. Eight years ago, New York City's chancellor held a press conference in PS 72, a New York City school that has for years been a stronghold of Teachers College Reading and Writing Project's work, and he announced that the approach to reading in that school was to be the approach to reading across the entire city.

That announcement was made without teachers necessarily having the knowledge to teach reading workshops well, but nevertheless basals were removed from classrooms across the city and teachers were expected to teach using a reading workshop approach. I wrote a very rough, underdeveloped, first-draft version of what, almost ten years later, you now hold in your hands, and we gave 100,000 copies of binders containing these and other rough, early units of study to teachers. We turned the auditoriums at Teachers College into assembly-line shops to collate the binders and rented huge trucks that distributed these free binders across well over half of the elementary schools in the city. We began working with coaches and, to a lesser extent, principals from 500 of New York City's elementary schools and 100 of New York City's middle schools. Meanwhile, other providers—the AUSSIES, America's Choice, the UFT—also helped other New York City schools teach effective balanced literacy reading workshops.

That situation wasn't perfect. New York City is the nation's largest city, with problems that are not easily solved. In New York City, as elsewhere, early work toward higher standards has morphed into a more myopic focus on multiple-choice tests, and it takes heroic efforts for educators in the city to beat back the encroaching curriculum of test prep that results from a system that has become totally oriented to sanctions and rewards around increased scores on standardized tests. Still, despite it all, New York City has done well in contrast to other large cities, and that, in and of itself, is a testimony to the effectiveness of reading workshops, even when implemented in conditions that are challenging. I'm proud of the entire city's progress and concerned that the progress continues; we still have far to go.

It is not easy to segment out a group of New York City schools that are high implementers of this reading workshop. Some of those schools are now tackling areas of the curriculum other than language arts, so they are no longer working with us. But still, it is worth noting that the Teachers College Reading and Writing Project has worked for at least the past three years on-site for fifteen to thirty days in approximately 175 New York City elementary and middle schools (many containing 1200+ students). The tests in New York State have been consistent across those three years.

- Proficiency levels of children in these 175 schools who were third graders at the start of this time and became fifth graders at the end of this time improved from 63% to 79%, a level of proficiency that exceeds the city's average of 75%.

- Some people are specifically interested in our data from high-need schools. In the sixty-eight New York City schools in which 75% or more of the children are eligible for free and reduced-cost lunch and that have been working with my organization to teach reading using the units of study contained in this series, the average score on the state test in 2007 was 649, with 50% of the children passing, and in 2009 was 663, with 73% of the children passing. This means that for schools that have for the last three years taught reading using the units of study described in this series, 23% more children passed the test than did three years ago, suggesting that this approach to teaching reading has been effective in high-poverty schools when measured by standardized test scores.

- Then, too, it is important to look at high-performing schools. Of course, many of the elite private schools and highest-performing suburban schools have always taught reading through literature-based reading workshops. For years, most of the highest-performing schools in New York City have been schools that work with the Teachers College Reading and Writing Project. There are scores of schools that parents regularly fight to have their children attend, and most of these schools are TCRWP schools. The rate at which test scores have increased at those schools will not, of course, be dramatic because their scores were already high and because those schools have each been given a hefty list of NCLB high-need transfer students, but if you were to investigate the method of teaching reading used in most of the high-achieving districts in our region, you'd find it is a variation of the reading workshop. Certainly this is true for suburbs such as Scarsdale, Chappaqua, Great Neck, Roslyn, Westport, Darien, Greenwich, Mamaroneck, and so forth.

Having said this, what research really shows is that there is no magic bullet. Although it is common for schools that have taught reading using the units of study described in this series to find that children's skills increase in notable ways, the payoff on standardized state tests is especially apt to happen when educators are savvy about the test and tweak curriculum so that it sets children up for the specific demands of the test. For example, there are some states in which a unit of study on reading biography or reading expository nonfiction needs to be timed in specific ways because of the state test. In other states, fiction writing (with its opportunities for supporting all sorts of punctuation) pays off. In New York State, it has been important for us to study not only what children are asked to do in their extended responses but also the actual papers that achieve the highest scores.

In schools where youngsters have not been performing as well as they should, a few weeks of efficient, intelligent test preparation, right before the test, can also make an important difference.

## How Can You Provide Strategic Test Preparation?

*Remember that reading tests aim to test reading—and children's text levels and reading rate can't slip because prior to the test, there's no time to read!*

The first thing to remember as you prepare children for state reading tests is that the tests are, in fact, designed as *reading* tests. They are intended to test the level at which a child can read. As I mentioned earlier in this book, you can go to the Project's website and download (at no cost) the assessment tool that the Project has developed and use it across your school, as thousands of other schools do. This tool essentially allows you to conduct running records on children's work with passages of texts ranging from A to Z and then ask a few literal and inferential comprehension questions, and in this way determine the level of text that each child can read with fluency, 96% accuracy, and comprehension. The tool does *not* assess deep, high-level comprehension. Children are reading 250-word passages, not whole novels, so the assessment is far from ideal, but it provides a quick indicator of at least basic proficiency.

The TCRWP has developed Web-based software known as Assessment Pro that allows us to synthesize children's running record data as well as their data on other assessments such as high-frequency words, words per minute, spelling development, and so on with data on children's socio-economic status and their state standardized test scores. We have this data from well over 50,000 children across several years. As mentioned earlier, data have revealed trends that are far clearer than we ever dreamt possible, showing that as the level of text difficulty that children can read increases, so too does the average score they receive on the test. That is, the increase in text level correlates to an increase in tests scores, on average, in a precise pattern that is repeated over and over, in grade after grade.

### As reading levels increase, the increase in scores and in percentages of students who pass creates a precise pattern.

Let's take a magnifying glass and look, for example, at one grade level—fourth grade. If you read the chart above, you will see that of the fourth graders who, in March of fourth grade, could only read a level N book, 51% of these children passed the test and their average score was rock bottom for passing—650. Now follow what happens to children who are reading not level N books but a level up—O books—in March of fourth grade and progress along the chart. You'll see that as the level of text difficulty the child can read increases, the likelihood that the child will pass, and the average scores earned, progress in synchrony with the reading levels.

The important thing is that this pattern is repeated through every time frame, across every grade level (save for eighth grade, when this becomes less clear). This suggests that students need to move up text levels, that is, they need to read more to achieve higher test scores.

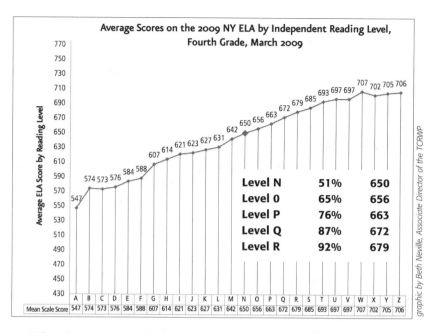

graphic by Beth Neville, Associate Director of the TCRWP

| Level N | 51% | 650 |
| Level O | 65% | 656 |
| Level P | 76% | 663 |
| Level Q | 87% | 672 |
| Level R | 92% | 679 |

What does this mean? It means that the way to help children earn better scores on the state's standardized test is *not* to take them out of books they can read and instead channel them to spend days and weeks working with little passages that resemble the test. Children can progress from one level of text difficulty to another only after reading great volumes of books at the one level—so that's the work that we need to focus on if we want to see a rise in scores.

Having said that, it is important to also keep in mind that standardized assessments test not only the level of text that a child can read but also the child's reading rate—the pace at which she reads with strong comprehension. Children who read at high reading levels with solid reading rates, meaning they read with stamina and fluency, do well. Children who read below grade level or who read so slowly that they take an unusually long time to finish books and texts perform less well on state tests. Thus, it seems that the strongest preparation for state tests is to teach your children to be stronger readers. This reinforces our belief that even if a school's only goal is to raise test scores (how tragic that would be!), it still is not wise for that school to allow test preparation to spill out across the entire year. Every school will want to tweak curriculum so that readers develop the skills they'll need for particular tests (more on this later), but that's an entirely different matter than putting little passages followed by multiple choice questions into kids' hands starting in September!

# Spend Limited Time on Carefully Focused Test Preparation

On the other hand, if your school is under tremendous pressure to increase test scores, you absolutely can help that to happen by devoting some time, three to four weeks, to test preparation. During high season for test prep, you will probably want a forty-minute workshop for reading test prep, in which you help children read short passages and handle multiple choice questions. If you have a writing-about-reading component on the test, you will want to conduct a similar workshop for writing test prep. Meanwhile you need to maintain time for independent reading. The latter will no longer include minilessons and teaching shares but should still provide a five-minute interlude for partnership conversations. During that independent reading time, you will probably spend a bit of your time maintaining children's reading lives and devote most of your time to small-group work to support the test-prep work you will have gotten going during those portions of the day.

Let me first stress that the independent reading time can't be sacrificed simply because the test is around the bend. Children need at least a protected half hour of in-school independent reading, where they continue to read the books they choose, so they maintain their rate and level of reading. (Children who read below grade level need more time than this.) Remember, children slip down several levels during the summer if they do not have access to books they can read. The last thing we want is for children to slip down several levels during a month of frenetic all-consuming test prep that keeps kids working with texts they can't actually read! Be sure to keep your eye on your children's reading logs so that their volume of reading doesn't slip precipitously during this time.

Because your teaching time during the independent reading portion of your day will probably be channeled toward small-group work that supports some test-specific skills (I'll describe this later), during the month before the test, when you begin to turn more of your attention toward test preparation work, you may want to launch children into partnered reading of series books (or some other high-interest genre) so they can read, read, read and talk easily about their reading with each other. Of course, you will also want children to continue

*Children need at least a protected half hour of in-school independent reading, where they continue to read the books they choose, so they maintain their rate and level of reading.*

reading these books at home. Don't be tempted to channel all their independent reading to the home, because research and experience both show that children only read for homework if they are also progressing through the same book in school.

In the sections that follow, I'll share with you some of the ideas that the Teachers College Reading and Writing Project community has developed for supporting test preparation. I do so with a hearty thanks to Kathleen Tolan for doing the lion's share of the thinking and pilot-teaching that informs these suggestions.

## To Teach Students to Read Passages and Handle Multiple Choice Questions, You'll Need to Gather and Make Some Materials Ahead of Time

To prepare for the reading test-prep strand of work, you'll need to spend some time gathering your materials. We recommend beginning by collecting state tests from previous years, remembering that the tests given in earlier grades will be extremely valuable to you. We suggest you then sort the passages by genre and difficulty level (which can simply be grade level) so that a fifth-grade teacher has all the narrative nonfiction passages, for example, that were included during three previous years of tests, with these passages from the third-grade tests across those three years at the start of a test-prep binder that the teacher creates, the narrative nonfiction passages from the fourth-grade test over those three years next, and then those from the fifth-grade test.

Similarly, your binder will include a section of realistic fiction passages. First, you might have two realistic fiction stories from the third-grade test given two years ago, then another realistic fiction passage from last year, then the easiest realistic fiction passages from fourth grade, followed by more difficult fourth-grade passages, and so on.

The logic behind this resource is that we always want to provide scaffolding and then withdraw it, allowing children to continue with increasing independence. One of the easiest ways to scaffold readers is to give them easier passages. Also, we are extremely aware that many test prep materials that are packaged and sold to teachers actually give kids a bum steer, because those materials are often not aligned to the actual standardized test! This is an easier way to be sure that you are not wasting your limited test-prep time with materials that are not in fact aligned to the test.

As you design these packets, keep in mind the specific genre that your children will encounter on their test. For example, on the New York State test, in recent years children have needed to be ready for these genres at these grade levels:

### Grade 3

Feature article (science), Poem, How-to fiction (realistic fiction), Biography, Expository article, Allegory (fable)

### Grade 4

Feature article (science, social studies), Fiction (realistic fiction, historical fiction), Poem, Nonfiction text (excerpt from book), Biography, Allegory (fable, folktale, legend)

### Grade 5

Fiction (realistic fiction, historical fiction), Article (science, history, art), Poem, Biography/Autobiography, Allegory (folktale)

I can include this list only because my colleagues and I follow the New York State website that supports the test. Be sure that someone in your school is keeping an eye on your state's website. When tests are as high stakes as they are, it is amazing to us that many schools devote a huge amount of children's time to test prep and extraordinarily little teacher time to the research that can inform this work. Remember that you need to be as informed as possible. Knowledge is power.

If you need extra materials for extended-day or small groups, you can take a text such as a short story, article, or poem and make a series of test-like questions to go with that passage. Good sources for these texts are *Highlights*, *Cricket*, *Cobblestone*, *Read and Rise*, *Storyworks*, and *Sports Illustrated for Kids*. I also recommend including short texts that your children know extremely well in this packet—say, a typed-up version of Donald Crews's *Shortcuts*—because if children are working in a text with which they are already familiar, then this spotlights the new work that is now required of finessing the multiple choice questions.

In any case, after collecting and leveling the short texts other than those found in previous years' tests, you'll need to write questions for them, making these match the kinds of questions that will be asked on the state test (this, of course, becomes powerful study-group work for teachers). You might put these questions in the same order for each text, so the first question you write for each of these passages is a main idea question, the second is a vocabulary-in-context question, the third is about mood/emotion/tone, the fourth is a genre question, and so on. Then, make the same kinds of questions for different levels of texts—a story at a J/K level, a story at an M/N level, and a story at a P/Q level. This will allow you to track how a child is doing on particular kinds of reading work at each level. It may be that one child can't answer the first question on many passages, and you already know this is a main idea question; that knowledge will help you lead small-group work for this child. On the other hand, it may be that another child can answer main idea questions only until the text is a level N. Then you know that over that level he doesn't need main idea help so much as he needs strategies for reading too-hard texts, such as skimming, summarizing, underlining, jotting, and using pictures and headings. Teach him those as you continue to sharpen his main idea strategies.

You will already have sequenced the texts from easier to harder, and you'll start the readers working with easier texts, helping them nail the genre of test-prep reading and multiple choice questions while first working with texts that are short and brief for them, then showing them how to move up levels of difficulty. You absolutely do not need to creep up levels, working with every text in your binder. But you will use some of your earlier passages with some of your struggling readers so they have more time working with scaffolds. Do not buy into the idea that strugglers need weeks of "practice" holding texts that are totally overwhelming for them. You will absolutely need to teach strugglers some survival skills with impossibly difficult passages, but you'll want most of their time to be with passages they can handle. The last thing these readers need is to spend the three weeks prior to the test working with texts they can't read!

## What Might You Teach Once Children Are Reading Accessible Test Passages?

One of the first things you will need to teach when children read short passages for a test is that they need to expect the texts to go by them quickly and to be extra alert from the very start. If this is a realistic fiction text, for example, children need to realize that they can't plan to get to know the characters and the setting over the course of a day's reading work! Instead, because everything is condensed, children need to anticipate that everything is more important than in book-length texts.

It will help to rev up children's expectations for what they will glean from a text based on the genre of the text. In fictional stories, you may want to teach children that above all they'll be thinking about what challenge the main character faces and how he or she resolves that challenge. Readers can approach a fictional story knowing that immediately they'll learn who the characters are, then they'll learn what the problem is, and by the end of the story they'll glean lessons that the character learned.

On the other hand, if the passage is an *expository nonfiction* text, readers may expect to pay attention to and infer from the structure, headings, and topic sentences. Children will want to be alert for questions about the purpose or main idea of the article. They may be asked to provide evidence to support the author's argument or to differentiate between fact and opinion. It will help for them to learn to pay attention to signal words such as *and, or, but, however, therefore,* and *on the other hand* as they read nonfiction passages.

If the text is a *poem*, readers may expect to pay attention to what the big meaning of the poem could be, what the poem is mostly about, or what it demonstrates or teaches. There may be questions about imagery or the meaning or symbolism of a part or line. They may have to answer a question about figurative language such as personification, simile, or metaphor. In all texts, for all grades, readers consider the author's purpose, asking themselves, "What does the author want to teach us? What does he or she want us to feel?"

You'll probably also want children to practice handling the multiple choice questions. There are several parts to this. On the one hand, you will want to help your students understand the wording of the questions. One way to do this is to use the language of the test away from the reading workshop. If your test often asks, "What is this passage mostly about?" then you'll want to help children become accustomed to that question. You might even make a collage of clothes, perfume, deodorant, and jewelry and ask, "What is this mostly about?" helping children understand that a good answer would be "things you wear." If your test often asks children, "What is just before (or just after)… ?" then you may want to talk about the daily schedule, suggesting children notice what will happen just before lunch or just after reading time. Again, you could ask children to tell you about music class, thinking about the word that "best describes" it.

You will also want to help children learn strategies for handling multiple choice questions. There are a few predictable traps that kids get into. One, of course, is they read the question and then instead of thinking of an answer and searching for that answer among the alternatives, they simply look over the optional answers. They see one statement that is absolutely true, that is clearly mentioned in the passage but that does not answer the question, and they figure because yes, this is in the passage, it must be the right choice. To make it less likely that children get lured from the right answer by distracter options, it helps to teach them to read the question and then to predict what the answer might be (rather than to select it from among possible multiple choice suggestions). Some teachers literally white out the optional answers, asking children to write the answers rather than select among options. Sometimes instead of asking children to write in the answers, teachers ask them to circle the part of the text that provides the answer to a particular question. This, of course, is a way of signaling to children that their answers need to be text-based, not drawn from personal experience, which is a good lesson to teach, although in the end you will want children to recall the text, to think about the text, to answer a question and not to always actually look back on the text. Looking back can slow a child down too much for this to be a workable strategy for all children. However, you will want to teach children how to look back, because there will be times when they need to do this, and the important thing is that they first need to think, "Will this probably be in the beginning of the passage, the middle of it, or at the end of it?" and then to scan just that section of the passage, not the entire thing.

Another predictable challenge when working with multiple choice questions is that children will generate a possible answer to the question and then scan the options and not see their answer among the choices. For example, the question might ask, "How does the character feel?" and the child might think to herself, "Nervous." But then the options contain *apprehensive*, not *nervous*. This problem is not easily resolved during the weeks just before the test, but you can point out to children that they need to be ready to consider synonyms, and you can help children develop a sense for alternate ways to describe a character's traits. You may create word walls with alternate ways of saying "brave" or "nice" or "happy" or "mad" (*upset, frustrated, depressed, morose, enraged*). Some people suggest children sort these words in order of intensity, with *peeved* at one end of the spectrum and *enraged* at another. If children during their independent reading are asked to jot occasional Post-its recording how their character feels, you can help them return to those Post-its to use more precise language. But my larger point is that you will want to help children understand that even after they generate a possible answer to a multiple choice question, they need to be prepared to find a variation of that answer among the list of options.

When you ask children to read passages and answer questions at the end of them, you will still want to think about how your work can go from being more to less scaffolded so that your children are working on increasingly difficult (and increasingly test-like) work over time. So you might decide to use your easiest or most familiar realistic fiction passage, and also start with you reading the passage and the question aloud, and with children being invited to do the work collaboratively with partners. My colleagues and I strongly feel that more of test prep should be done with a partner (more on this as this chapter continues), but for now let me point out that it is much easier to assess what children are thinking and doing if they are externalizing their thinking by sharing it with a partner.

Assessment will be the key work that you need to be doing. Which of these kinds of questions seem to pose no difficulties for most of your children? Which pose many difficulties? Can most of your children grasp how to answer vocabulary-in-context questions, or will that be something for you to explicitly teach? If you have discovered that children need help tackling words in context or ascertaining the main idea, then you'll want to demonstrate how you go about doing this, just as if you were teaching a minilesson, using think-aloud to illustrate the three or four steps you take to do the work.

As the week progresses, you'll lift the scaffolds that you provided early in the week. So children will progress from work with easier fiction texts to work with harder fiction texts, from work in which you read the passage aloud to work in which two readers progress through one text, pause to talk about it, and then tackle the questions together to work in which readers read alone and then compare and contrast and defend their answers, helping each other ascertain which of them was right.

As children do this, encourage them to make as much of their thinking visible as possible—partly because this will encourage them to do that thinking and partly because this will help you to reconstruct their thinking. So when they find a passage in the text that they take special note of as they read, encourage them to underline it. If they see a word they anticipate will be in a vocabulary question, they can circle it. When a child looks back and finds the answer to question 3 in a certain passage, alongside that passage the child can jot a 3. Marking up the text in this way helps teach children to go back to the text and it helps you

or the child to later reconstruct how the child went about getting an answer. As they proceed through their multiple choice questions, you will be glad if they cross off the options they know are wrong and write questions beside answers that leave them unsure.

## Help Children Anticipate the Work They'll Need to Do—the Questions They're Apt to Be Asked—for Each Kind of Text

This work can then be repeated with other genres. Whatever the genre, you'll teach them to use the same strategies of first noticing the kind of text that this is and using their knowledge of that kind of text to help them preview the text, breaking the text into manageable chunks as they read, summarizing a chunk of text on the run as they read it, and then progressing to the next chunk, marking the text as they read it, predicting answers to questions, writing the answer (for a time, but later thinking it), and then matching it to the choices. Gradually, you'll trust that children can just say the answer in their mind and match it to the choice.

It is impossible to emphasize how important it is that all your work be assessment based. Time will be of the essence, and children will not need help on everything. You'll want to learn what causes them difficulty and select with care what you're going to teach. Always be conscious that by the time the test comes, children need to be working without the scaffolds you will have provided early on in the progression of your test prep. You will probably want to teach kids that some of what they did temporarily a few weeks before the test will slow them down too much for them to be able to continue doing this work on the day of the test. Even if children are allowed to jot on the test booklet, for example, you may decide that this slows them down too much. Some children may not be able to look back (only to think back) to the passage to locate answers to questions. Always keep in mind that all children will not use the same strategies to do well on the test.

## Teach Students to Deal with Difficulty

For some of your children, the test will be written at levels that are too hard for them, and these children will require some special coaching. You'll probably want to teach them to keep going and to not get demoralized when the text is too hard. Usually it will help them to skim texts that are very hard for them, to summarize as they read with an eye toward the main idea, to move past hard

words unless there are questions that refer to those words, and to only slow down to dig into hard parts if they need to do so to answer a question. You'll also want to help them deal with unknown and scary words. Because this work will occur on the brink of the test date (because well in advance of the test they'll be working mostly with just-right texts), now is probably not the best time to teach readers to persevere over difficult words or to make a stab at pronouncing them. Instead, for now, teach children to substitute a synonym or best-guess understanding and to keep on reading. Tell them to underline the difficult word too, so when they reach the end of the passage they can go back and tackle that word if necessary. The question they will most likely need to do this for will read something like, "In line 16, what does the word 'X' mean?" Keep in mind that to answer that question children do not need to pronounce the word. Instead, it will be more important for them to be able to produce contextual clue-based synonyms. These sorts of questions can often be figured out by thinking about what's happening not just in that particular sentence, but in that part of the story or article.

As students approach the test, you can also teach them specific multiple choice strategies, such as monitoring time by figuring out how many questions there are and how many minutes they have. Teach them strategies for elimination. For example, you might want to teach them to eliminate the answers that are found in the passage but don't answer the question. Show these children (and all children) how to mark their answer sheet in such a way that they avoid skipping any questions as they go. Teach them to return to questions they were unsure of if they have time at the end, and, most of all, teach them to keep going! This kind of teaching and learning is not invigorating and can only be sustained for a few weeks, so do it intensely but briefly.

## Use Your Read-Aloud Time to Support Children's Work on the Test

Meanwhile, for the two or three weeks before the test, you may want to use your read-aloud time to support children's work on the standardized test. If you decide to do this, you'll first of all read short passages aloud, ones that are similar to those they'll encounter on the test. You'll want to help children join you in thinking about the sort of reading work they should be prepared to do as they take in the passage. Then you can, as you read, prompt them to support their listening and thinking work so they take in texts that unfold swiftly, with their minds alert, ready to answer predictable questions. For example, when you read aloud short fiction, encourage children to get ready to listen by thinking about what they know about how stories go, and about their jobs as readers. They are mostly listening for *character, problem,* and *solution.* You may want to prompt them to listen for clues about the setting and the characters and to give them time, after listening for just a bit of the story, to turn and talk about what they've learned about the characters, their relationships, and the challenges they face. As you get ready to read the end of the story, you may want to prompt them to listen for how people change and how problems are solved, again giving them an opportunity to talk about their observation. Finally, you'll probably coach them to infer possible lessons the story teaches and to talk about the author's possible purposes. The next time you read aloud, you might decrease some of the scaffolds by no longer channeling students to do particular work. Instead you can set children up to talk with partners beforehand, reviewing what they know about how stories go and what they need to pay attention to as they listen. You may still interrupt the story with times for children to turn and talk or to stop and jot, but this time you may leave it up to them to decide what they should probably be thinking about at this point in the story. Finally, your read-aloud could lead children to answer test-like short-answer questions.

Be sure to read aloud some nonfiction. Students should expect that a nonfiction text is going to teach them something. In narrative nonfiction they need to use what they know about stories (paying attention to characters, including the obstacles they face and their achievements) and what they know about nonfiction (looking for the specific idea it teaches and how the story demonstrates the idea). You'll especially want your test-prep read-aloud to include narrative nonfiction because this seems to predominate in a lot of standardized tests. Similarly, reading poetry aloud supports children's work on the multiple choice section of the test. Some of the questions you'll want them to think about are, What is this poem mostly about? What does it teach? What is the big meaning of the poem? Teach them also to notice structure and to recognize and name imagery and figurative language in a poem and to consider their effect.

All in all, we must remember that no matter the state standard or national goal for our teaching, the horizons we lead our students toward are neither nearby nor narrow. We teach for no less than to offer our children ways to understand and make meaning of the world; we offer them skills and strategies for learning and for becoming more powerful. The lessons we teach in the service of test prep can also be lessons in learning that we all can use all we know, every reading and strategizing skill, to tackle tests—and not just tests, but any daunting or distasteful or high-stakes task. With these efforts to grapple with the challenges in front of us, we also move closer to the horizon where we learn and understand the world in deeper ways than ever before.

# CHAPTER TWELVE

# Planning a Year-Long Curriculum for Teaching Reading

In reading, as in writing, children benefit from being part of a buzzing community of practice, where learning occurs sideways, from each other, as well from the hands and mind of a teacher. Children benefit from being immersed, all together, in a whole-class study that leads to lessons being wrapped throughout the classroom in the form of anchor charts and exemplary work, celebrated often and posted everywhere. And children also need to feel, as the year unfolds, that their work in reading has seasons. Always they read, read, read. Always they integrate all the skills of proficient reading to make meaning. Always they think, write, and talk about texts. And, sometimes, the class is turned totally upside-down by a study of character; sometimes, everyone has become a detective, reminiscent of a giant Clue game, with readers piecing together clues from their books, not from a game board, to find "Whodunit, where, and with what?" The challenge to make sure that all kids are learning with us does not mean each child needs to work as an island, doing his or her own thing, untouched by anyone to the right or to the left! It *does* mean that we are always working to support children in the ongoing reading work they are able to do—and almost able to do. It does mean that we are always aiming to teaching children about goals and strategies and skills that they can apply to their reading lives, now and from now on, no matter what the topic and focus at hand.

## Planning Curriculum

In the schools I know best, teachers have some release time toward the end of a school year to meet with colleagues across their grade level (sometimes across two grade levels that decide to work in sync) to plan what we refer to as "a curriculum calendar" of shared units of study. When teachers of grades three and up plan units in *writing*, it is essential that those units do not last longer than a month because usually the units scaffold the children's work on a single piece of writing, and eight-, nine-, and ten-year-old children do not often have the rehearsal and revision skills to work productively for more than a month on a single piece of writing. But in units of study in reading, children are always reading a great many books pertaining to that unit—those working at lower text levels may read three books a week, while more proficient readers read closer to one longer book per week. So there is no special reason why units of study in reading can't last, say, six weeks, as long as the teacher has enough books to sustain such a unit. (That is, a unit on fantasy can't last six weeks if teachers have no way to provision readers who are reading level N/O books with sufficient fantasy books at a level they can read with ease.) Let's imagine, then, that some units last a month and some six weeks, although you may decide differently in your school.

## Unit 1: Building a Reading Life

When teachers meet to plan the sequence of their curriculum in reading, usually there isn't a lot of discussion about the first three units. It almost goes without saying that the first unit needs to launch kids' into their own reading lives, helping them choose just-right books, carry those between home and school, read for longer stretches of time, and work on basic comprehension. The unit needs to be straightforward enough that teachers are freed to conduct running records.

### Building a Reading Life
### Stamina, Fluency, and Engagement

In this, the first unit of the year, we launch the reading workshop. We pull out all stops in an effort to help all our students to become avid readers. We wear a love of reading on our own sleeves, help students fashion their identities as people who care about reading, create a social life that revolves around shared books, and above all we help students develop a sense of agency about their reading lives, taking responsibility for becoming the kinds of readers who not only make sense of books, but let books change their lives. We meanwhile induct children into the structures, routines, and habits of a richly literate reading workshop. Students learn how to choose books that are just right in level and interest, to carry books between home and school, to collect and study data about their reading rates and volume, and they learn to push themselves to read with increasing stamina, fluency, and volume. In reading partnerships, children learn to retell and summarize texts and to share ideas that are grounded in the specifics of their books.

If youngsters have been in reading workshops for years, this unit will need to be spun out a bit differently than if this is children's very first experience in the unit, and in *Constructing Curriculum* you'll see the ways a master teacher taught this to brand-new third graders and the way a master teacher taught it to sixth graders who've been immersed in reading workshop for most of their lives.

## Unit 2: Following Characters into Meaning

It almost goes without saying that by the time Unit Two rolls around, teachers will want to devote that unit to supporting higher-level comprehension skills around fiction reading. One of the most obvious ways to do this is through a unit that the kids will think is a unit on character, but that you'll teach in ways that spotlight whatever higher-level thinking skills you determine your students need. This is a description of this unit, as brought to life in the two volumes of Unit Two. You will probably teach both portions of this unit, one after the other, as a single coherent unit:

### Following Characters into Meaning
### Vol. 1: Envisionment, Prediction, and Inference

It is essential that stories ignite a vital sort of imagination, one that allows readers to live inside the world of the story, to identify with the characters, seeing and sensing situations from inside the characters' minds. This, the first portion of the unit, highlights personal response, envisionment, and empathy to strengthen that connection between readers and characters. In this volume, you'll also learn how to use informal assessment to help you clarify several reading skills progressions—learning what predicting can look like in early stages and then in advanced stages, for example—so that you can lay out learning pathways for readers, helping them to develop more powerful reading skills.

### Following Characters into Meaning
### Vol. 2: Building Theories, Gathering Evidence

Whereas the first portion of this unit, contained in Volume 1, helped children approach their study of character *aesthetically*, walking in the shoes of characters, seeing through the characters' eyes, empathizing, and predicting, in this second volume, the focus of the unit shifts so that now we help readers approach texts *efferently*, pulling back to develop a bird's-eye view of a text, gleaning facts and insights about characters that they then carry away from the text, synthesizing this information into evidence-based theories and talking about these theories with others. Our goal by the end of the unit is for readers to be able to shift between these stances—with aesthetic reading enriching the efferent reading and vice versa—blending together the advantages of being lost in the text with the advantages of being analytical about it.

Although the units described above are foundational, you might decide to abbreviate one and extend the other during a subsequent year. Then again, after teaching these units for a year and learning from the professional development embedded in them, you might decide that some grade levels in your school will author new versions of these important units. In *Constructing Curriculum*, you'll see various ways that teachers have adapted this unit so that it's always fresh and tailored to specific grades, but frankly you could alter the unit simply by bringing a different read-aloud text front and center and by imbuing it with your stories and your kids' stories. That is, although Kathleen Tolan and I have woven *The Tiger Rising* through a character unit, you might be teaching seventh graders and might instead read aloud *Hunger Games*.

## Unit 3: *Navigating Nonfiction*

After teaching a couple of units of study that develop your students' muscles for reading fiction, you will very likely want to shift to a unit of study that supports their abilities to read nonfiction, although at this point your students would also be ready for you to shift into genre-based book club units that we generally teach after four to six weeks of nonfiction work. You'll want to take account of your resources for nonfiction reading. If you have tons and tons of just-right books on a topic within your social studies or science classroom, then you have the choice of bringing down the walls between your reading workshop and your social studies or science unit, inviting students to read on a topic that you are studying. One of the units in *Constructing Curriculum* offers a template for doing this. But most of you will probably decide that a topic-based nonfiction unit could easily be taught in the spring, and for now you'll want to develop your students' muscles for reading nonfiction. This is a description of the way Kathleen Tolan and I decided to angle such a unit.

### Navigating Nonfiction in Expository Text
#### *Vol. 1: Determining Importance and Synthesizing*

In this unit of study, we teach young readers that if they read nonfiction texts with an attentiveness to the underlying structure of those texts, this can help them take in, synthesize, learn from, and respond to large swaths of nonfiction

texts. That is, once readers recognize a text structure, they can use that information to structure their own reading, allowing parts of the text to coalesce into that structure, taking on greater significance, while letting other parts of the text fall away. In Volume 1 of the unit, then, we teach students that most expository nonfiction has a central idea and supporting evidence, and that once readers know this, they can read with an eye for that main idea as well as for supportive specifics, gleaning outlines and summaries that can then become foundational to their thoughts about the texts. This sort of reading helps readers get their minds around the main concepts that an expository text teaches.

### Navigating Nonfiction in Narrative and Hybrid Text
#### *Vol. 2: Using Text Structures to Comprehend*

In Volume 2 of the unit, we teach students to read *narrative* nonfiction with attentiveness to structure, using story grammar to synthesize and determine importance across large stretches of text. Once students recognize that most narrative nonfiction has a central character with goals and struggles, that the texts convey an underlying idea, and that many nonfiction narratives culminate in an achievement or a disaster, we can help them use that information to structure their reading, allowing the events and details of the text to click into that narrative structure and therefore to be memorable.

For the last weeks of the unit, students will use all they have learned about nonfiction reading to pursue research projects in small groups on topics related to their interests. We teach students the strategies that readers use to synthesize information, to take on new vocabulary, and to deepen their thinking through writing. Once students have begun their research, we teach them ways to think critically about their nonfiction texts, examining authors' means and motives. In the end, our goal is to teach readers that each one of them must learn to find a unique angle on a topic, an angle different from that of the authors of the texts they've read. We coach children in ways to read to inform their own purposes, and in the end we structure an opportunity for them to teach others.

## Unit 4: *Tackling Complex Texts*

By this time, you and your colleagues will have lots of options available to you. Most of the teachers we know best decide that their youngsters will profit from shifting toward book clubs (some people refer to these as literature circles) in which children talk not just with a partner but with a small group of readers and progress in sync with those readers through a sequence of related books. Book club units of study can be overtly designed around a cluster of related reading skills—say, inference and interpretation—or they can be designed so that children, at least, think this is a unit about a particular kind of text (mysteries, humor, series books, fantasy, biographies) or around topics (social issue book clubs, freedom fighters). We have found that the most supportive, most scaffolded units for teachers and kids alike are those in which the whole class reads a particular genre, or kind of book, so generally the next unit of study will be book clubs that support kids work within a particular genre.

Of course, it taxes a school's resources if all children grades 3–5 are within one sort of book club unit, so generally teachers will decide on different genres for different grade levels. Most third graders seem to be reading mysteries much of the time, so this unit is a special favorite for that grade level (though its appeal endures across grade levels). It's common, then, for this next unit of study to be mystery book clubs for third graders and historical fiction book clubs for fourth, fifth, and sixth graders. (Fantasy, though, is also a great favorite, and certainly it is a favorite in the middle school grades.)

Although the children will think this is a unit on a genre, *you'll* know that you are in fact teaching the skills of proficient reading. If your children are reading mysteries, you'll probably highlight the skills of close reading, inference, and prediction. This unit is described in *Constructing Curriculum*. If your children are reading historical fiction, you could angle their work to especially develop their muscles in envisionment, in building the world of the story. Mary Ehrenworth and I made a different decision, as you will see in the following overview of the unit we wrote on historical fiction book clubs.

### Tackling Complex Texts: Historical Fiction in Book Clubs
### *Vol. 1: Synthesizing Perspectives*

In this first volume of the unit, we aim to teach readers to read complex texts with deep comprehension. With support from a book club, readers will learn to keep track of multiple plotlines, unfamiliar characters, and shifts in time and place. Historical fiction is uniquely challenging in that it requires readers to synthesize text about the evolving setting with text about the changing characters, who are likely to be vastly different from the readers themselves, and then readers must further synthesize that information with the text of the plot and, usually, with several crucial subplots, all of which often involve unexplained gaps in time and unfamiliar circumstances and consequences. You'll also teach readers how to construct a sense of the setting not just as a physical place but as an

emotional place, and in doing so, you'll help students read with attention to the mood in the text. A town that undergoes war or sudden violence will change rapidly, and readers of historical fiction need to notice ways that changes in setting affect different characters differently. In this unit, we rely on historical fiction to invite readers to work hard to comprehend challenging texts. We aim to help students develop a passion for the genre and for history, and we aim to help them develop the imagination to walk in the shoes of characters—and people—whose lives are different from their own.

### Tackling Complex Texts: Historical Fiction in Book Clubs
### Vol. 2: Interpretation and Critical Reading

The second portion of this unit embarks upon the ambitious, intellectual work of interpretation. First within one text, then across texts, and then between texts and their lives, we teach readers to grow nuanced ideas and to read to be changed. As their books become more complicated, readers learn that those ideas are not just about what's happening but also about concepts. They learn not to recite back ideas a teacher gives them, but instead to develop their own ideas, doing the hard, intellectual work that children need to do to grapple with themes. Readers make their ideas more complex as they consider the perspectives of characters whose voices are absent as well as those whose voices are present in texts, and as they become not only participants in but also students of an era in history. Readers learn, too, to develop literary language for some of the things they are intuitively seeing in their books, coming to recognize and to use allusions, figurative language, and symbolism to convey ideas that are not easily contained in ordinary language. Although this volume begins as a study in deep comprehension of complex texts and specifically of interpretation, it ends by helping readers appreciate the fact that individuals can take action and make choices that change the world.

## Authoring Your Own Units

By this time, you and your colleagues will want to think about all the work you have done in preceding years, asking, "Could some of that be brought into an upcoming unit of study?" Perhaps you taught an author study in a way that worked. Surely you could design a unit of study that invited young people to construct their own author studies.

Perhaps by this time in the year, you want to bring down the walls between your reading workshop, your writing workshop, and your social studies workshop and to show kids the possibilities of a unit that crosses all disciplines on a topic you love. Again, *Constructing Curriculum: Alternate Units of Study* has some help for you in the form of some units and some frameworks for units, as well as a chapter with some rules of thumb and suggestions for writing your own units, but you'll also want to rely on other resources as well.

Then, too, your children may have ideas for a unit, so you and your colleagues may decide to reserve one unit of study to author with your students and to use this as a way to add to your repertoire in future years. Go to it!

# CHAPTER THIRTEEN

# About the *Units of Study* Series

The *Units of Study for Teaching Reading* series brings you a rigorous and compelling reading curriculum, one that has been piloted in thousands of schools over a score of years. The series will allow your teaching to stand on the shoulders of a large thought collaborative. The ideas, methods, and classroom structures that you'll learn in this series have been under development for the past twenty years, by a network of professionals working together in lab-site classrooms, think tanks, graduate courses, funded research projects, summer institutes, reading clubs, and model schools. In all these sites, the Teachers College Reading and Writing Project has researched, developed, field-tested, adapted, collected evidence on, and ultimately refined the literacy instruction that this series now conveys to you. Over the course of those years, this team has brought in and learned from many other reading experts, including Marie Clay, Randy Bomer, Donald Bear, David Booth, Peter Johnston, Pauline Gibbons, Nancy Anderson, Gay Su Pinnell, Dick Allington, Jerry Harste, Kylene Beers, Smokey Daniels, Tony Petrosky, Ellin Keene, Lori Hellman, Stephen Krashen, Tim Rasinski, Steph Harvey, Frank Smith, and others. The series, then, is an ambitious undertaking!

*Units of Study for Teaching Reading* is intended to synthesize a school reform effort, a course of study in the teaching of reading, and a grades 3–5 reading curriculum; together, these three strands can help you bring all your students into a reading workshop characterized by deep levels of investment in reading and clear instruction that moves learners along learning pathways to higher-level comprehension skills. It allows you to learn to teach reading by inviting you to watch master teachers working with real kids and by meanwhile standing alongside you as you watch, helping you see the replicable methods that are being used, the responsive decisions that are being made, and the alternatives we could have considered instead. Meanwhile, you will come to understand a reading curriculum as it unfolds not just in your classroom but also across your district. You'll learn ways to provision whole schools for a reading workshop, to establish a system-wide method for assessing readers' growth and communicating that information to parents, and to plan a spiral curriculum across the years.

This series was not written from the armchair. It stands on the shoulders of the work of the Teachers College Reading and Writing Project. This organization involves sixty staff developers, several reading specialists, two data specialists, four former superintendents, and of course an extraordinary collection of graduate students. The TCRWP also involves a network of dedicated teachers, principals, and superintendents, many of whom have been contributors to the organization for several decades.

The methods for reading instruction contained in these pages have been shared with hundreds of thousands of educators, including those who attend the many institutes that the Teachers College Reading and Writing Project offers every February and throughout every summer. These institutes have been a way to pass the baton to others; those who attend the institutes have, in turn, created classrooms and schools that are beacons of excellence and teaching hubs for their region, and in this and other ways, word has spread. Over the years, more and more teachers and principals have found that the reading workshop, like its sister structure, the writing workshop, can give children unbelievable power as readers, thinkers, researchers, and citizens. Being part of this work has given teachers new energy and joy, reminding us of why we chose this field in the first place. Demand for support in the teaching of reading has skyrocketed. This *Units of Study for Teaching Reading* series is part of our effort to provide that support.

> *Over the years, more and more teachers and principals have found that the reading workshop, like its sister structure, the writing workshop, can give children unbelievable power as readers, thinkers, researchers, and citizens. Being part of this work has given teachers new energy and joy…*

## The Series Can Help You Teach in Ways that Are Differentiated

*Units of Study for Teaching Reading* starts by helping you put the bottom-line essentials of a research-based reading program in place and then helps you become a diagnostic professional who teaches in data-based ways. One of the premises of this book is that teachers can and must collect data that is as close to reading as possible—data about the number of minutes and pages that children are reading, about the levels of text difficulty in which children can be successful, and about children's abilities to do whatever skills of proficient reading you decide to highlight. The series goes further and helps you support and track your children's evolving abilities to predict, envision, synthesize, find the main idea, and interpret. Too often reading skills are thought of as something that readers can do or cannot do; this series suggests, instead, that we need to construct learning pathways so that we teach skills by moving kids along trajectories that we, meanwhile, are constructing and refining as we teach.

In each unit of study, you will learn a rich repertoire of ways to provide focused, explicit instruction for a handful of skills and strategies of proficient reading. Within one unit, for example, you'll learn that you can rally all your students to read expository texts, paying attention to the main ideas of those texts, creating little mental outlines as they read. The crucial work will be for you to teach in ways that support all children doing this work within their zones of proximal development. For children who are reading the most accessible texts, those main ideas will be apt to be spotlighted in headings and topic sentences. For children reading more complex texts, the main ideas may be embedded in paragraphs; for those working with the most demanding expository texts, the main idea will be implicit, with the texts often containing a wealth of detail from which readers must learn to draw their own conclusions. Like any other essential reading skill, determining the main idea is not something readers learn to do once and for all. Instead, this skill, like every reading skill, develops along a pathway. This means that an entire community of readers can be invited to work toward a particular reading skill. No reader will ever stop working to determine the main idea, synthesize, read critically, and the rest. It's just that the texts in which readers do this work and the nature of the work itself will become increasingly complex, and the scaffolds you provide will vary.

To help you support diverse learners as each one works in his or her way toward shared goals, the series will show you how to collect data you value and to work together with colleagues to provide data-based instruction in which you scaffold your learners so each works in his or her zone of proximal development. You will also learn ways to assess children to understand a specific child's characteristic ways of working with texts and to use the structures of the reading workshop to create individualized ways of supporting readers in the particular skills they need.

# The Series Is Designed Not Only as Curriculum but Also as Professional Development

*Units of Study for Teaching Reading* has been designed as a form of virtual staff development, with the demonstrations, information, and coaching folded into the support that can help you work with your children. The materials are carefully constructed so they provide you as well as your children with an intimate and intense course of study.

The series brings you some of the work that the organization I lead, the Teachers College Reading and Writing Project, has been doing for three decades as we support professional learning communities in districts ranging from rural towns in Arkansas and Maine to the buzzing metropolises of Seattle, Chicago, and New York City. We work also in large, systemic ways in nations such as Jordan and Israel, in rural schools in Mexico and the Caribbean, in international schools across the world, and in charter schools including Geoffrey Canada's Promise Academies in Harlem. From our deep engagement with an enormous variety of schools, we have learned not only about teaching reading, but also about teaching teachers and about the complex work of supporting school reform. Those insights on teacher education are implicit in this series.

## We Invite You to Observe Us Teaching a Class of Kids Across the Year

Of course, one of the most beautiful ways for any of us to learn to teach is to watch a teacher-mentor at work within a classroom of ever-so-real kids. *Units of Study for Teaching Reading* invites you into our classroom, giving you the opportunity to join me and coauthors Kathleen Tolan and Mary Ehrenworth (and also our contributing authors and teacher-colleagues) as we teach a class of young people. You'll come to know the young people whose quirks and passions and struggles provide much of the poignancy in these books. You'll watch us go to the ends of the earth to lure, push, support, celebrate, and inform our strugglers—Gabe, Rosa, Tyrell, and others. You'll see us also draw chairs alongside readers who can read anything in the blink of an eye, and you'll join us in realizing that these readers pose their own sorts of challenges. One young reader makes such a compelling case against Post-its that we're totally stumped, another *can* read but chooses not to, and yet another sees so many symbols and

metaphors in any passage of any book that it's all we can do to resist breaking into peals of laughter at her earnest efforts to approximate T. S. Eliot. You'll watch boys in this class catch us by surprise by defying gender stereotypes, throwing themselves into an intensely intellectual and deeply emotional engagement with reading. That is, our kids will be your kids, posing all the challenges that all of us face day in and day out as we teach.

Teachers who have relied on *Units of Study for Primary Writing* and *Units of Study for Teaching Writing, Grades 3–5* will find that this new reading series is even more grounded in classrooms than the writing series, containing five times as much video footage and revolving around a single, lasting community of kids. That was a special priority for me. I am convinced that too often reading curriculum comes to teachers in a way that is divorced from kids, without their voices, passions, and idiosyncrasies. I do not think we can learn to teach from a generic curriculum that has cleansed itself of the boisterous, intimate, complicated work of classroom teaching.

As you watch us work with this class (it is actually a composite class gleaned from five classrooms, representing very different contexts and grade levels), you'll see us mix inspiration, classroom management, demonstration, intervention, on-the-run assessments, one-to-one coaching, and small-group work into a curriculum for teaching reading—a mix that gives a classroom full of kids the education of a lifetime. And you'll see us learn from the kids with whom we are teaching—over and over, day in and day out.

## You'll Be Able to Observe Minilessons and Learn the Infrastructure, Methods, and Content Necessary to Create Your Own Minilessons

In so many ways, teaching is a lonely profession. Most of us work as Lone Rangers day in and day out, month after month, and only rarely get the chance to watch another teacher in action. How can we possibly become masters of our profession if we are not given opportunities to watch what others do? And of course, the truth is that we need to watch not just one day, not just one flash in the pan; our work is long-haul work, and what counts is how it accumulates, across the duration.

We hope readers of the *Units of Study* series will find that these books can do the work that literature has always done: bring you, the reader, inside a world, allowing you to experience that world as if you were a member of it. As we read

C. S. Lewis's *Narnia* series, we join with Lucy, Susan, Peter, and Edmund, pushing our way through the coats in the wardrobe, and suddenly finding there are no more furry coats in front of us, and that instead we are standing, looking at a glen of snow-covered trees. In a similar fashion, we hope you will find yourselves sitting on the edge of the carpeted meeting area, waiting for me to lean toward you from my chair at the front of the meeting area, and to say, "Readers, today I want to teach you that…."

Within this series, the teaching that you participate in has been set onto the page in ways that can be transferable to your classroom, if you wish. Because I've written the story of my teaching (and sometimes of Kathleen and Mary's teaching) with enough detail that you'll be able to picture the fine grain of it—imagining the specifics of how we gather kids into the meeting area, for example, and how we sometimes voice over their quiet reading to lift the level of it—you'll be able to participate vicariously in this teaching. I share the actual words of minilessons—some 150 of which are included in detail and dozens more in less detail—that you can experience, borrow, tweak, adapt, combine, dissect, discard, and outgrow as you wish. Most important, I always step back to draw from the specific examples the transferable techniques and insights that underlie the teaching you will observe. In this way, you can see theory and practice work in synchrony. But the analyses are sidelined, and the kids are front and center. They can't be put on hold, because the teaching unfolds in real time, with tomorrow just around the bend.

## You'll Observe Small-Group Work, One-to-One Conferring and Assessments, and Learn the Replicable Principles Underlying These Workshop Components

Of course, teaching reading involves a great deal more than minilessons! We invite you to watch our conferences, our small-group work of all sorts, our read-alouds, our book promotions, our assessments—the works! Always, these will be unpacked so that you can learn transferable principles. As Kathleen or Mary or I lead a small-group strategy lesson you'll listen in. Before, during, and after that bit of teaching, I'll pause to reveal the simple, step-by-step methods that informed what might otherwise seem like an idiosyncratic interaction. Those teachable moments can be created and, yes, re-created.

The small-group work, one-to-one conferring, interactive read-aloud work, and use of formative assessments that you will witness are included not just because they actually happened in the classroom we bring to you. Instead, the coauthors and I have made a point to use this series to bring our newest, state-of-the-art thinking on each of these topics to you. Typically, someone who cares terribly about one component of teaching reading writes a whole book on just that one component. This is all well and good, except that for those of us who live day in and day out in classrooms, the hardest part is putting the components together into a seamless whole. We chose another route. Instead of writing a book on using formative assessments to inform units of study in reading, or on expanding our images of possibility for small-group work, or on how a teacher can avoid feeling empty-handed when conferring with readers who are reading books we don't know, or on a year-long sequence of work to support writing about reading, we have treated these topics, and many others, as threads within the tapestry of this series. The art of teaching involves weaving best practices together, because an effective reading program must have enough coherence, simplicity, and flexibility to allow us to teach, expecting the unexpected.

## You'll Find Explicit Instruction in Methods for Teaching Reading Well

I am convinced that teachers as well as kids benefit from explicit instruction, including instruction in research and theory as well as in methods of teaching. Embedded into the series, then, are mini-lectures and seminars on topics as diverse as ways to support fluency in proficient as well as in struggling readers and on ways to teach readers to think about the perspective from which a story is told and to imagine perspectives that are not revealed in a story. For example, we hope you'll find yourself feeling as if you've received admission tickets to a conference day on ways to link specific levels of text difficulty (M and N and O and P and so forth) into broader bands of text difficulty (K–M, N–Q, R–T) so that you can crystallize an understanding of the challenges readers encounter at different bands of text difficulty and make this knowledge portable and useful.

But the explicit teaching that you will receive is not just about the *content* of your reading instruction. There are a handful of *methods* for teaching reading (and writing) that you will use repeatedly, and those, too, are explicitly taught to you. Just as it is important to demythologize the skills of proficient *reading* so these become accessible to everyone, so, too, it is important to demythologize the skills of proficient *teaching*, sharing the trade secrets. It is past time to debunk the idea that powerful teaching is based on some inborn talent that some have and others don't. All of us have some talents that can be harvested in the service of teaching, and all of us have areas in which we'll need to become stronger to teach as well as we possibly can. The good news is that teaching is a profession, and as such, it can be taught and learned.

The books will also accompany you, as a teacher, into your own classroom, providing scaffolding that will allow you to teach in ways that are patterned after the methods and content in these units. The books do not provide a script for your teaching, but they can shore up your teaching, providing you with the scaffolding necessary to teach in state-of-the-art ways, and then the books will function as a live-in coach for your teaching.

One of the distinguishing features about this series and indeed about the whole line of Heinemann's *first*hand resources is the way in which these weld theory and practice. Too often, practical, nuts-and-bolts instruction is divorced from theory on the one hand, and from real-life classrooms on the other hand. *Units of Study for Teaching Reading* and its two sister series in teaching writing instead weave theory and practice together in a new way. The books show state-of-the-art teaching, convey the logic and information upon which that teaching is based, and pull the curtain back from this teaching to reveal the principles that informed the teaching decisions, the alternatives that could have been considered instead, and the transferable methods that underlie this powerful instruction. The books also aim to give you opportunities to teach and to learn teaching while receiving strong scaffolding, on-the-job encouragement, and guidance.

## You'll Find, We Hope, Inspiration and Energy for Teaching and Children

We've written *Units of Study for Reading* to be inspirational. As more and more is asked of teachers, and more and more pressures are placed on those of us in this profession, it's important to remember that great teaching is the result of people digging deep inside ourselves to draw on the internal reserves of talent, energy, imagination, and love that we sometimes didn't even know were in us. No effort to lift the level of reading instruction will ever work if it does so by bypassing teachers—and this includes our personal lives, our relationships to literacy and each other, our reasons for choosing this profession in the first place, our dreams for kids, and above all our desires to fashion our own lives and to work with a sense of personal agency and professional judgment.

This is the opposite of a generic script for an impersonal sort of teaching. It is, instead, the intensely intimate story of my teaching—of our teaching. You'll hear about my new flat-coat retriever puppy, Emma, about my indomitable mother who has taught me so much about the need to protect a person's power and agency even when that person struggles, and you'll hear about my memories of reading *Exodus* when I was an impressionable adolescent and yearning for a cause worth living for. Like all good stories, the story of my teaching, of our teaching, has a universal message. We've written in ways that we hope will touch you, will remind you of your own stories, will inspire you to listen to your own children, and will encourage you to author your own teaching.

Although the coauthors and I have worked hard to make this a curriculum for you as well as for your children, the part that involves you requires *you*. In the end, the professional development is in your hands. The most important contribution the series can make is that it can help you and your colleagues fashion a community of practice, one in which your language and methods and, indeed, the journey of your teaching, is shared. It's heady, intellectual, joyous work. Welcome aboard.

## The Series Is Designed to Support a Coherent Approach to Teaching Reading Across a School, and to Create a Community of Practice

Earlier, I cited a recent study by Bembry and others that shows that if a youngster has access to a strong teacher for three consecutive years, then that child's scores on standardized reading tests will be as much as 40% higher than the scores of students who meanwhile have not had that access to strong teachers. That is staggering data, yet those are the results we should be aiming toward.

I am convinced, though, that the children in this study and others like it benefit not just from the lucky break of landing in the classrooms of good teachers for three years in a row. Those "lucky breaks" happen in schools that are communities of practice, in schools that make teachers strong. These will be schools in which a spiral curriculum is planned, with one grade level standing on the shoulders of another. The teachers in such a school will meet across the grades to talk and think about how a unit of study in character will be different in first, second, third, and fourth grade. When will the emphasis on secondary characters move front and center, instead of being something for more proficient readers? At what grade levels will teachers tend to emphasize that sometimes characters play a symbolic role in a story? These will be schools that think carefully about special support services, making sure that a child's work with a reading specialist is aligned to and not disruptive of the classroom work. This will be a school where there is a book room full of multiple copies of books for book clubs and guided reading and inquiry groups. This will be a school with a systemic approach to assessment, where teachers at the end of one year make book baggies full of just-right books for each child, so that for the first two weeks of the new year, each child is reading books selected at the end of the preceding year.

The days of classroom teaching being a solo endeavor are long gone. It is critical that across a school, teachers take up shared methods of teaching, because this means that when one teacher has special finesse with that method, others can use a prep to watch that teacher at work, learning from her. It means, too, that one teacher can head across the country to study from an expert, with everyone in the school waiting for the goods when that teacher returns, arms full of new information.

It is especially important for schools to become communities of practice because methods of teaching are also methods of learning. If every year, every teacher needs to induct kids into whole new ways of acting in a classroom, into whole new cultures and expectations, then kids spend half their time trying to adapt to the whims of each new classroom. How much better for a school to decide upon some shared methods, and to think about how, over time, children's roles will become more proactive, more complex, and more responsible!

I was just in Portland, Oregon, and a principal from outside the city said to me, "What your writing series has done is that it has brought my whole staff into a shared conversation. Our school has become a community of practice. We started out working 'by the book' and now we're dancing on the edges, looping in some other work we also love, addressing some issues unique to our setting, but, because of the units, we're doing this together, in a cohesive community of practice. I can't wait for your new series to do that same work for us in reading." I can't imagine a more important compliment.

For those who use this series, bringing it with you into the classroom each day and putting it at the center of professional conversations in your school, the books can be transformative. Whether you are a new teacher or you are a master teacher who has been heralded by your region as the best of the best, I am passing the baton of all we've learned to you, inviting you to not only join but to also contribute to a community of practice. I do hope that if you and your colleagues start by working "by the book," you progress from that point, like the principal from Portland said of her staff, and "dance on the edges, looping in what you know and love" that is not here.

In the end, the books are designed to put themselves out of a job. They will bring not only your students but also you and your colleagues on a learning journey; as you use this scaffold to support stellar teaching, you will also kick it aside, using the principles embedded in the books to author your own mini-lessons, small-group work, and conferences in response to what you see your children needing. Send the ideas you author to our website so we can share them with the larger community of practice.

# The Components and Structure of the *Units of Study* Series

This series supports a spiral curriculum in which four especially essential units of study adaptable for grades 3–5 are written in great detail, and ten other units are written in less detail. This allows you to progress from teaching that is heavily scaffolded to that which is less scaffolded, a progression that is not unlike the one you will offer your students. It also allows you and your colleagues to make decisions about how your teaching will progress as readers develop, with different alternate units being brought to life in third grade, fourth grade, and fifth grade, but with readers across all grades participating in the same core studies.

## Sessions

Each unit contains seventeen to twenty-one sessions. A session represents a day, although sometimes teachers will take the content of one session and distribute it across two days. The components of each session are described below. The units are always divided into parts, or bends in the road, and in each part of the unit, the work that readers do is a bit different. In the nonfiction unit, for example, readers read expository nonfiction during the first part and narrative nonfiction during the next part. It is possible for teachers to teach the first part of a unit and to save the latter part for another year.

Each session contains the same component pieces. That is, each begins with a one- to two-page prelude and a "Getting Ready" section that helps you gather

resources and your wits so that you are ready for the day. On the CD-ROM, resources are provided so that you need to do a minimal amount of behind-the-scenes work to prepare for teaching. Each session contains a minilesson that lasts approximately ten minutes and that adheres to the same architecture. There are examples of the work that students did during this session in the *Units of Study* book and on the accompanying CD-ROM. The session then provides you with detailed help in the conferring and small-group work you are likely to do that day, a possible mid-workshop teaching point, and a possible share. Many, but not all, sessions are followed by an interlude designed to help you use data to inform instruction.

### Prelude

To teach well, our teaching needs to come from deep beliefs about what learners need and about what matters in life, in school, and in the process of becoming powerful readers. The prelude for each session attempts to answer the question of why, out of all the world, this bit of teaching is so important that it merits the attention of all these learners. Of course, as part of this, the prelude situates one day's minilesson and workshop within the research and scholarship on that topic. The prelude is also a place for me to talk directly with teachers—call it a daily keynote address. I think that too often, words of inspiration are reserved for the large statewide conferences or the thick teaching volumes, and really, the inspiration that we need most is that which helps us take a big breath before the upcoming school day, reminding ourselves of the majesty and significance of the work we are attempting to do.

### Getting Ready

You can think of this portion of a session as the string tied around your finger, reminding you of all the little (and sometimes big) things you need to orchestrate so that once a day's reading workshop begins, once you take your place at the front of the meeting and say, "Readers, can I have your eyes and your attention," you won't have to say "Oops" and make your way through the sea of increasingly restless kids to the place where you left that all-important book, Post-it, or chart. The required materials are kept at a minimum, and when possible the CD-ROM contains charts, rubrics, and short texts that you need, but there is no way around the fact that to teach reading, you need lots and lots and lots of high-interest books at levels that your children can read.

### Minilesson

Listen in while I teach children a ten-minute minilesson. You'll hear the actual language I use and hear some of what children say in response, too. It will be as if you're the visitor, participating from the margins of the class, watching how I convene children to the meeting area, doing so in a sequential way that teaches them what is expected and then holds them accountable to those expectations. Each reading minilesson will follow the same architecture, an architecture that also underlies writing minilessons, that relies the basic principles of effective teaching: Connection, Teaching, Active Involvement, and, finally, Link.

### Italicized Coaching Commentary

As teacher-educators, my colleagues and I often teach in front of teachers. We do this not to show one special minilesson, but instead to extrapolate generalizable principles from specific instances. As you read the minilessons and indeed most of the teaching contained in these books, I'll be at your side, ready to coach you to see why my coauthors and I have taught the way we have and to see the aspects of today's teaching that are transferable to other days. I'll help you see, too, the other choices we could have made, the assessment we'd be doing as we teach and the ways we'll use data to inform our continued teaching.

### Conferring and Small-Group Work

Someone once said that we never step in the same river twice, and it is certainly true that when conferring and leading small-group work, children always catch us by surprise. Still, we need to plan to be ready for the unplanned. Certainly any experienced teacher who has taught particular strategies before knows in advance some of the challenges kids will encounter and some of the likely ways in which she's apt to respond to those challenges. This section accomplishes three goals:

- *This section will help you plan for your conferences.* On the one hand, the session on conferring and small-group work helps you to anticipate the ways in which you will differentiate your teaching in response to the very different readers in your classroom. Often this section is organized to show you how you might help students who are novice and those who are more proficient at the particular strategy you have taught that day. By showing you how you can differentiate your teaching of a host of different skills and

strategies, this section develops your abilities to teach responsively and to use data on the run to inform your teaching.

- *This section will help you widen your repertoire of ways to work with small groups.* These sections combine to function as a book on the topic of teaching reading through conferences and small-group work. Many teachers feel a bit at sea when we pull a chair alongside a reader, ask how's it going, and hear, "Fine. It's okay." What are we to say, to do, that can ascertain where the learner is in a journey toward skill development and that can help that learner develop skills that are just beyond his or her reach? You'll learn a repertoire of ways of leading small-group work. Those of us who teach reading as our lifework will want more than one way of thinking about the sorts of teaching we can do while working with a small group of readers. You'll see guided reading sessions, but more than this, you'll see expert teachers drawing from a wide repertoire of different ways for supporting young readers.

- *Finally, these sections will convey to you a wealth of content for your teaching.* During minilessons we invite readers to tackle important work, but much of our teaching happens in small groups and in conferences. By listening in on these, you'll learn scores of other possible minilessons and in general develop more expertise on whatever topic the minilesson addresses.

### Mid-Workshop Teaching Point

It is inevitable that in the midst of a reading workshop, you'll want to interrupt the hum of the workshop to teach the entire class. Often this teaching helps translate the minilesson into practice or helps readers go a step beyond whatever they learned in the minilesson. Sometimes this teaching encourages readers to write in response to reading. During units of study that channel readers to spend some of the class time working with a book club of others who are reading shared books, the mid-workshop teaching point functions as almost a minilesson for book clubs.

### Teaching Share

Often our best teaching is that which we do in response to kids' work. The teaching shares allow us to address the problems kids have encountered, to cite particular examples of work that set the standard or pave the way for others, and to help kids integrate what they have done with what they learned earlier.

## Anchor Charts

You will want to be sure that your teaching cumulates and lasts and that you encourage youngsters to draw on the full repertoire of all they have learned. One way to do this is to create anchor charts that are developed incrementally as your teaching proceeds and that provide an enduring reminder of all that youngsters have learned and can draw upon. The books themselves contain one version of every chart, but in the many photographs that show classrooms in the midst of these units of study, you'll see countless ways in which teachers and classes have made their own charts that are variations on those in the books. These are included on the CD-ROM, not as charts you will want to download and post— because your charts need to grow bit by bit on the heels of your teaching—but as mentor texts.

## Assessment Sections

Each unit contains several assessment sections and, on the CD-ROM, informal assessment instruments, plus charts, rubrics, or lists that reflect ways in which we have analyzed data gleaned from these informal assessments. The assessment sections are deliberately interspersed into the unit, echoing the way assessment will be integrated into your instruction. You will see ways to create informal assessments and to mine them for insights that can inform your instruction and ways to be sure that your teaching is supporting students so they will do well on high-stakes tests.

## Letters to Parents and Other Caregivers

You will want to communicate with parents and other caregivers so they understand a bit about your teaching. On the CD-ROM, you'll find letters to parents describing each of the four units contained within these books, in addition to letters that you might send home to inform parents about their son's or daughter's assessment data.

## Bibliographies of Children's Literature

Each unit contains a book list, on the CD-ROM, of several hundred carefully chosen books, leveled and clustered into groupings that will be helpful for you. That is, the book lists for the historical fiction unit include books at a variety of levels, grouped by historical era. The book list for expository nonfiction specializes in books on high-interest topics, many of which are structured to help readers learn to ascertain the main idea and supporting information as they read. The expository books are clustered according to heavily scaffolded structures and more lightly scaffolded structures. There are a dozen topics around which the nonfiction books coalesce. All or most of the books on these lists are available through Booksource, in their Units of Study libraries.

## The DVDs: Inside Views of Workshop Teaching and Workshop Classrooms

This series is supported by two companion DVDs that present views into reading workshops in a wide variety of school settings and with all kinds of teachers and children. These DVDs are meant to introduce the concepts of the reading workshop, help us create a vision for what is possible in the teaching of reading, and also to convey how both master teachers and less experienced teachers bring the reading workshop's structures and rituals to life with children. For each unit of study you can observe how my colleagues and I initiate minilessons, teach reading strategies, conduct conferences, and guide small-group instruction. The DVDs are ones that can be used as a resource for introducing a reading workshop, or later in a teachers' professional development they can be used as a resource for studying—and discussing, visualizing, and practicing particular facets of reading workshop teaching.

My hope is that now—with this book and the *Units of Study* books we've written for you, filled with all our wisest methods and brightest teaching—now, you'll decide to step into teaching alongside us for a time, bringing to the teaching your own wisdom and experience, your own knowledge of what is best for children. Together we can grow beyond even this, the very best teaching we've yet imagined for our children.

Afflerbach, P., P. D. Pearson, and S. Paris. 2008. "Clarifying Differences Between Reading Skills and Reading Strategies." Newark, DE: *The Reading Teacher*, 61(5)

Allen, Debbie and Kadir Nelson (illustrator). 2000. *Dancing in the Wings*. New York: Penguin.

Allington, R. L. 2006. *What Really Matters for Struggling Readers: Designing Research-Based Programs*, 2nd ed. Boston: Allyn & Bacon.

Allington, R. L. "Response to Intervention: How to Make It Work." Speech, Teachers College Reading and Writing Project Principals as Curricular Leaders Conference, New York, NY, October 8, 2008.

Allington, R. L., and P. Johnston. 2002. "What do we know about exemplary fourth-grade teachers and their classrooms?" In C. Roller (Ed.), *Learning to Teach Reading: Setting the Research Agenda* (pp. 150–165). Newark, DE: International Reading Association.

Applegate, K. A. 2007. *Home of the Brave*. New York: Holtzbrinck

Asher, Sandy. 1999. *But That's Another Story*. New York: Walker Books.

Babbitt, Natalie. 1975. *Tuck Everlasting*. New York: Holtzbrinck Publishers, LLC.

Baylor, Byrd. 1974. *Everybody Needs a Rock*. New York: Simon & Schuster.

Bembry, K., H. Jordan, E. Gomez, M. Anderson, and R. Mendro. 1998. "Policy implications of long-term teacher effects on student achievement." Paper presented at the Annual Meeting of the American Educational Research Association, San Diego, CA, April 13–17.

Betts, E. A. 1946. *Foundations of Reading Instruction*. New York: American Book Company.

Blackwood, Gary. 1999. "Who Waxed Mad Max?" In S. Asher, *But That's Another Story*. New York: Walker Books.

Bomer, R. 1995. *Time for Meaning: Crafting Literate Lives in Middle and High School*. Portsmouth, NH: Heinemann.

Burnett, Frances Hodgson. 1987 (1911). *The Secret Garden*. New York: Penguin.

Burton, Virginia Lee. 1939. *Mike Mulligan and His Steam Shovel*. New York: Houghton Mifflin.

Calkins, L. et al. 2006. *Units of Study for Teaching Writing, Grades 3–5*. Portsmouth, NH: Heinemann.

Calkins, L. et al. 2003. *Units of Study for Primary Writing*. Portsmouth, NH: Heinemann.

Calkins, Lucy. 2001. *The Art of Teaching Reading*. Boston: Allyn & Bacon Educational Publishers.

Calkins, L. 1994. *The Art of Teaching Writing*. Portsmouth, NH: Heinemann.

Chall, J., and S. Conard. 1991. *Should Textbooks Challenge Students?: The Case for Easier or Harder Textbooks*. New York: Teachers College Press.

Clay, M. 2001. *Change Over Time in Children's Literacy Development*. Portsmouth, NH: Heinemann.

Clay, M. 2000. *Running Records for Classroom Teachers*. Portsmouth, NH: Heinemann.

Clay, M. 1987. "Learning to be learning disabled." *New Zealand Journal of Educational Studies*. NZJES 22.2 155–73. Wellington: New Zealand Council for Educational Research. Available at http://www.nzcer.org.nz/pdfs/9500.pdf.

Collins, Suzanne. 2008. *The Hunger Games*. New York: Scholastic.

Covey, Stephen. 2004 (rev). *The 7 Habits of Highly Effective People*. New York: Free Press.

Creech, Sharon. 2003. *Love That Dog*. New York: HarperCollins.

Crews, Donald. 1996. *Shortcut*. New York: William Morrow.

Curtis, Christopher Paul. 1999. *Bud, Not Buddy*. New York: Random House

Dahl, K., and P. Freppon. 1995. "A comparison of inner-city children's interpretation of reading and writing instruction in the early grades in skills-based and whole language classrooms." *Reading Research Quarterly*, 30(1), 5–74.

Darling-Hammond, L. 2010. *The Flat World and Education*. New York: Teachers College Press.

Darling-Hammond, L., B. Barron, P. D. Pearson, and A. Schoenfeld. 2008. *Powerful Learning: What We Know About Teaching for Understanding*. San Francisco: Jossey-Bass.

Darling-Hammond, L., and G. Sykes. 2003. "Wanted: A National Teacher Supply Policy for Education: the Right Way to Meet the 'Highly Qualified Teacher' Challenge." *Education Policy Analysis Archives*, vol. 11.

DiCamillo, Kate. 2001. *The Tiger Rising*. Somerville, MA: Candlewick.

Dillard, Annie. 1989. *The Writing Life*. New York: HarperCollins.

Drucker, Peter. 1985. *Innovation and Entrepreneurship: Practices and Principles*. New York: Harper Paperbacks.

Duke, N. K., and D. Pearson. (2002). "Effective practices for developing reading comprehension." In A. E. Farstrup & S. J. Samuels, eds. *What Research Has to Say About Reading Instruction*, 3rd ed. pp. 205–242. Newark, DE: International Reading Association.

Duncan, A. "Teacher Preparation: Reforming the Uncertain Profession." Speech, Phyllis L. Kossoff Lecture, at Teachers College, Columbia University, New York.

Elmore, R., P. Peterson, and S. McCarthy. 1996. *Restructuring in the Classroom: Teaching, Learning and School Organization*. San Francisco: Jossey-Bass

Estes, Eleanor, and Louis Slobodkin (illustrator). 1944. *The Hundred Dresses*. Orlando: Harcourt.

Fletcher, Ralph. 1980. *Fig Pudding*. Boston: Houghton Mifflin.

Flor Ada, Alma. 1993. *My Name Is Maria Isabel*. New York: Simon & Schuster.

Foertsch, Mary. 1992. *Reading In and Out of School: Factors Influencing the Literacy Achievement of American Studies in Grades 4, 8, and 12 in 1988 and 1990*. National Report Card, NAEP.

Fountas, Irene, and Gay Su Pinnell. 2006. *Leveled Books, K–8: Matching Texts to Readers for Effective Teaching*. Portsmouth, NH: Heinemann.

Fullan, M., P. Hill, and C. Crévola. 2006. *Breakthrough*. Thousand Oaks, CA: Corwin.

Fullan, M. 1993. *Change Forces: Probing the Depths of Educational Reform*. New York: Routledge.

Gardiner, John Reynolds. 1980. *Stone Fox*. New York: HarperCollins.

Gardner, Howard. 1983. *Frames of Mind*. New York: Basic Books.

Gardner, J. 1991. *The Art of Fiction: Notes on Craft for Young Writers*. New York: Vintage.

Gilligan, C. 1993. *In a Different Voice: Psychological Theory and Women's Development*. Cambridge, MA: Harvard University.

Gipson, Fred. 1956. *Old Yeller*. New York: HarperCollins.

Gladwell, M. 2005. *Blink: The Power of Thinking Without Thinking*. New York: Little, Brown and Company.

Guthrie, J., and N. Humenick. 2004. "Motivating students to read: evidence for classroom practices that increase reading motivation and achievement." In P. McCardle and V. Chhabra, eds. *The Voice of Evidence in Reading Research* (pp. 329–354). Baltimore: Brookes Publishing.

Hansen, Joyce. 1999. "New Day Dawning." In S. Asher, *But That's Another Story*. New York: Walker Books.

Harvey, Stephanie, and Anne Goudvis. 2005. *The Comprehension Toolkit*. Portsmouth, NH: Heinemann.

Hattie, J. 2008. *Visible Learning: A Synthesis of over 800 Meta-Analyses Relating to Achievement*. London: T & F Books.

Hesse, Karen. 1992. *Letters from Rifka*. New York: Macmillan.

Howe, James, and Melissa Sweet (illustrator). The *Pinky and Rex* series. New York: Simon & Schuster.

Johnston, P. 2004. *Choice Words: How Our Language Affects Children's Learning*. Portland, ME: Stenhouse.

Jukes, I., and T. McCain. 2002. "Living on the Future Edge." InfoSavvy Group and Cyster.

Kafka, F. Letter to Oskar Pollak. 27 January 1904.

Krashen, S. D. 2004. *The Power of Reading: Insights from the Research*, 2nd edition. Portsmouth, NH: Heinemann.

Lowry, Lois. 1993. *The Giver*. New York: Random House.

Lowry, Lois. 1989. *Number the Stars*. New York: Random House.

MacLachlan, Patricia. 1994. *Skylark*. New York: HarperCollins.

MacLachlan, Patricia. 1985. *Sarah, Plain and Tall*. New York: HarperCollins.

Marshall, James. 1972–1988. The *George and Martha* series. New York: Houghton Mifflin.

Merton, R. 1968. "The Matthew Effect in Science." *Science* 159 (3810): 56–63.

Mochizuki, Ken, and Dom Lee (illustrator). 1993. *Baseball Saved Us*. New York: Lee & Low Books.

Mortenson, G., and D. Relin. 2007. *Three Cups of Tea*. New York: Penguin.

Mortenson, G. 2009. *Stones into Schools*. New York: Penguin.

Mortenson, G., and S. Roth (illustrator). 2009. *Listen to the Wind*. New York: Penguin.

National Endowment for the Arts. 2007. *To Read or Not to Read*. Washington, DC.

No Child Left Behind Act of 2001, Pub. L. No. 107-110, 115 Stat. 1425.

Nye, N.S. 2002. Transcript of "Naomi Shihab Nye: A Bill Moyers Interview." Public Broadcasting System.

Paterson, Katherine, and Jane Clark Brown. 1991. *The Smallest Cow in the World*. New York: HarperCollins.

Paterson, Katherine. 1987. *The Great Gilly Hopkins*. New York: HarperCollins.

Paterson, Katherine. 1977. *Bridge to Terabithia*. New York: HarperCollins.

Paulsen, Gary. 1987. *Hatchet*. New York: Simon & Schuster.

Paulsen, Gary. 1993. *The River*. New York: Random House.

Pearson, P. D., and M. Gallagher. 1983. "The instruction of reading comprehension." *Contemporary Educational Psychology* 8: 317–344.

Peterson, R. 1992. *Life in a Crowded Place: Making a Learning Community*. Portsmouth, NH: Heinemann.

Pressley, M., A. Roehrig, L. Raphael, S. Dolezal, C. Bohn, L. Mohan, et al. 2003. "Teaching processes in elementary and secondary education." In W. M. Reynolds & G. E. Miller, eds., *Handbook of Psychology, Volume 7: Educational Psychology* (pp. 153–175). New York: John Wiley.

Rawls, Wilson. 1961. *Where the Red Fern Grows*. New York: Random House.

Rivkin, Steven G., Eric A. Hanushek, John F. Kain. "Teachers, Schools, and Academic Achievement." *Econometrica* 73 (No. 2): 417–458.

Rebell, M., and J. Wolff. 2008. *Moving Every Child Ahead: From NCLB Hype to Meaningful Educational Opportunity*. New York: Teachers College Press.

Rylant, Cynthia, and Mark Teague (illustrator). 1997. *Poppleton*. New York: Scholastic.

Rylant, Cynthia. 1992. *Missing May*. New York: Orchard Books.

Sarason, Seymour. 1996. *Revisiting "The Culture of the School and the Problem of Change."* New York: Teachers College Press.

Silverstein, Shel. 1974. "Invitation." In *Where the Sidewalk Ends*. New York: HarperCollins.

Smith, Doris Buchanan. 1973. *A Taste of Blackberries*. New York: HarperCollins.

Swanson, H., M. Hoskyn, and C. Lee. 1999. *Interventions for students with learning disabilities: a meta-analysis of treatment outcomes*. New York: Guilford Press.

Taylor, B., P. D. Pearson, D. Peterson, and M. Rodriguez. 2003. "Reading growth in high poverty classrooms: The influence of teaching practices that encourage cognitive engagement in literary learning." *Elementary School Journal*, 104: 3–28.

Taylor, Mildred. 1976. *Roll of Thunder, Hear My Cry*. New York: Penguin.

U.S. Department of Education. 2009. *NAEP Reading Report Card for the Nation*.

Vygotsky, L. 1978. "Interaction between learning and development." In *Mind in Society* (trans. M. Cole.) pp. 79–91. Cambridge, MA: Harvard University Press.

White, E. B. 1952. *Charlotte's Web*. New York: HarperCollins.

Whitman, Walt. 2006. "Song of Myself" from *Leaves of Grass*. New York: Simon & Schuster.

Wiles, Deborah, and Jerome Lagarrigue (illustrator). 2001. *Freedom Summer*. New York: Simon & Schuster.

Wood, D., J. Bruner, and G. Ross. 1976. "The role of tutoring in problem solving." *Journal of Child Psychology and Psychiatry*, 17: 89–100.